Michael G. Elasmar
An Introduction to Self-Report Measurement

Michael G. Elasmar

An Introduction to Self-Report Measurement

Concepts, Principles and Expectations

DE GRUYTER

ISBN 978-3-11-159085-1
e-ISBN (PDF) 978-3-11-159099-8
e-ISBN (EPUB) 978-3-11-159107-0

Library of Congress Control Number: 2025931497

Bibliographic information published by the Deutsche Nationalbibliothek
The Deutsche Nationalbibliothek lists this publication in the Deutsche Nationalbibliografie;
detailed bibliographic data are available on the internet at http://dnb.dnb.de.

© 2025 Walter de Gruyter GmbH, Berlin/Boston, Genthiner Straße 13, 10785 Berlin
Cover image: Jorm Sangsorn/iStock/Getty Images Plus
Typesetting: Integra Software Services Pvt. Ltd.

www.degruyter.com
Questions about General Product Safety Regulation:
productsafety@degruyterbrill.com

This book is dedicated to Kathleen, Geo and Joey

Contents

Preface —— 1

Chapter 1
An intuitive need to measure the invisible for understanding thoughts, feelings and behaviors —— 5

Chapter 2
Measuring the invisible: Practical uses and function within the method of science —— 18

Chapter 3
From observing behaviors to conceptualizing self-report measurement and developing a measurement mindset —— 25

Chapter 4
What can a researcher do to meet the self-report measurement assumptions? —— 56

Chapter 5
Principles and expectations: Statement content and placement —— 60

Chapter 6
Principles and expectations: Response category characteristics —— 77

Chapter 7
Principles and expectations: Motivation to self-report —— 96

Chapter 8
Principles and expectations: Respondent abilities —— 128

Chapter 9
A roadmap for quantifying the errors stemming from violations of the principles of self-report measurement: The Red Flags Approach (RFA) —— 152

Chapter 10
Implications for extracting self-report measurement from social media text content - What role can Artificial Intelligence (AI) play? —— 178

Chapter 11
A recap and some notes on the relevance of self-report measurement in the age of Artificial Intelligence (AI) —— 208

List of figures —— 211

List of tables —— 213

Index —— 215

Preface
An introduction to self-report measurement: Concepts, principles and expectations

Why write a book on self-report measurement?

As I write this paragraph, I am in my 32nd year as a university professor. Throughout these decades, I have been using self-report measurement in my own academic work. In 1997, I also created a graduate program concentration at Boston University that focuses on self-report measurement and have taught most of its classes since the start. One of the first things I noticed when I created this concentration was the absence of a comprehensive book that provides an intuitive explanation of what self-report measurement entails, the assumptions we make when using self-report measurement, and offers practical implications for those who are new to the field and are attempting to integrate self-report measurement into their projects. This was very surprising to me given the multitude of fields within academia, government and industry that utilize self-report measurement on a regular basis. The existing books often assume preexisting and homogeneous basic knowledge among their readers regarding what self-report measurement entails. As a result, they often present technical information about specialty areas within the science of self-report measurement without introducing the basics. Over the years, I've learned first-hand that such pre-existing basic knowledge varies greatly, even among seasoned researchers, and cannot be assumed to exist at all among beginners.

Back when I was in graduate school, one of my most used measurement resources was a book by Jean Converse and Stanley Presser (Converse & Presser, 1986). In it, the authors devote a section summarizing the results of studies that provide guidance to researchers on what to do and what not to do for self-report measures to be effective. Often times, I wished that the section in Converse and Presser's book (Converse & Presser, 1986) would be expanded to include more applied guidance. My wish came true when I came upon Howard Schuman and Stanley Presser's book titled "Questions and Answers in Attitude Surveys" (Schuman & Presser, 1996).

The need for practical guidance about specific aspects of self-report measurement is tangibly felt over the years by looking at the posts published on the listserv of the American Association for Public Opinion Research (AAPORnet). Numerous researchers from a variety of disciplines and industries frequently ask for advice. Typical questions include: How many response categories should I use? Why is the client asking me to use more than a single question about a same variable? Should I worry if some respondents are finishing more quickly than others? The advice provided by other AAPORnet users in response to these types of questions typically varies and depends on the training of the person giving the advice, the discipline they specialize in, and the research traditions of the organization to which they belong.

When faced with these types of questions in my work and classroom, I looked for published resources. I found books that approach self-report measurement theory from a mathematical perspective (e.g., Allen & Yen, 2001), books that focus on specific aspects of self-report measurement (e.g., Spector, 1992; DeVellis, 2012), books that provide advice on how to ask questions in surveys (e.g., Bradburn, Sudman & Wansick, 2004), and books that provide a psychological analysis of what takes place when we set out to measure someone's thoughts (Sudman, Bradburn & Schwarz, 1996; Tourangeau, Rips & Rasinksi, 2000).

All the books mentioned in the preceding paragraphs provide valuable information and were consulted when writing this book, however, none encompasses all three related aspects of self-report measurement:
1. A basic explanation of what self-report measurement is for beginners
2. Principles of sound self-report measurement practice based on science
3. A road map for quantifying the errors associated with self-report measurement

This book represents my integration of various knowledge pieces I gathered over the years, and my first-hand experience using self-report measurement over three and a half decades.

While a lot of effort went into this book, the principles, expectations and observations I set forth are certainly not comprehensive or absolute. I hope that a new generation of researchers will be inspired by this endeavor and improve upon this book.

Who will likely read this book?

This book is intended for anyone who uses self-report measurement through surveys, experiments, and/or attempts to extract opinions from social media text. Even seasoned researchers might find its content to be relevant as I attempt to bring a different and simplified perspective on this topic in comparison to how it is typically presented. The explanations provided and information compiled are as relevant to academics as they are to industry practitioners. I have tried to write in a language that is understandable regardless of training. The only two chapters that assume a pre-existing level of technical knowledge are Chapters 9 and 10. Perhaps readers who don't already have this technical knowledge will be encouraged to obtain it after realizing the possibilities that such knowledge will provide them. In addition to those who would typically use self-report measurement in surveys and experiments, Chapter 10 of this book builds a bridge between self-report measurement as used in the social sciences and the opinion-extraction approach within computer science. Chapter 10 proposes a methodology which integrates AI into the processes that can be used to transform social media text content into self-report measures to capture the building blocks of shared thought-processes.

Acknowledgements

Over the years, more than two dozen graduate students participated in locating relevant literature, categorizing sources, and systematically extracting and organizing information for Chapters 5, 6, 7 and 8. This wasn't an easy project as the material gathering spanned multiple disciplines and numerous fields of inquiry. I am grateful to the graduate students who participated in this project over the years. I have done my best to recall everyone, and I apologize in advance if I am missing names. In the final stage of writing this book, Aakshi Sinha helped ensure that the book met the publisher's guidelines, formatted the manuscript and copy-edited my writing. Yueling Feng helped me extract and organize the data and run the R analyses for Chapter 10. Katherine Michel pinpointed flow issues in my writing, and Michaela Muto helped me integrate and streamline the extensive literature reviews for Chapters 5, 6, 7 and 8.

Although some graduate students collected relevant articles prior to 2011, it was in that year that systematic work toward this book started. Here is an alphabetical list of the names of graduate students who assisted me since 2011 (I am using the names they held when they were working on the book):

Emily Allen; Amy Barrett; Sanya Farooqi; Yueling Feng; Karoline Frano; Rori Gallagher; Alicia Hong; Miao Huajuan; Meredith Knight; Minzhi Lu; Nicola Meyer; Katherine Michel; Michaela Muto; Lauren Peyton; Jenna Radin; Aakshi Sinha; Alex Siracusa; Allison Sommer; Shira Stothoff; Lauren Taylor; Yvonne Tran; Christy Wood; and Suya Xiong.

I also am grateful to my wife Kathleen Sim Elasmar for using her artistic talent and creating the pencil drawings in Chapters 3 and 10.

A few words about my mindset about self-report measurement

I am deeply grateful to my mentor, the late John E. Hunter of Michigan State University, who sparked my interest in the science of self-report measurement. His methods for conceptualizing and quantifying the error associated with self-report measurement have had a lasting impact on my thinking. While I credit him for shaping my perspective on self-report measurement, I take full responsibility for how I interpret and apply his teachings and any criticism my interpretations may invite.

So, what is self-report measurement? Hopefully, by reading this book you will find out.

References

Allen, M. J., & Yen, W. M. (2001). Introduction to Measurement Theory: Waveland Press.
Bradburn, N. M., Sudman, S., & Wansink, B. (2004). Asking Questions: The Definitive Guide to Questionnaire Design – For Market Research, Political Polls, and Social and Health Questionnaires: Wiley.
Converse, J., M., & Presser, S. (1986). Survey Questions: Handcrafting the Standardized Questionnaire: SAGE Publications.
DeVellis, R. F. (2012). Scale Development: Theory and Applications: SAGE Publications.
Schuman, H., & Presser, S. (1996). Questions and Answers in Attitude Surveys: Experiments on Question Form, Wording, and Context: SAGE Publications.
Spector, P. E. (1992). Summated Rating Scale Construction: An Introduction: SAGE Publications.
Sudman, S., Bradburn, N. M., & Schwarz, N. (1996). Thinking About Answers: The Application of Cognitive Processes to Survey Methodology: Wiley.
Tourangeau, R., Rips, L. J., & Rasinski, K. (2000). The Psychology of Survey Response: Cambridge University Press.

Chapter 1
An intuitive need to measure the invisible for understanding thoughts, feelings and behaviors

Objectives of Chapter 1: This chapter is designed to introduce the reader to some key concepts, including the notion of measuring the invisible as used in the context of this book. In addition, this chapter will introduce indicators, errors, and the universals of intuitive measurement for less visible human-related characteristics. These key concepts will be further developed in subsequent chapters and are important components of the measurement mindset that the reader should develop after reading this book. This mindset is equally important to both academics and industry practitioners who are involved in the measurement of human thoughts, knowledge, feelings, intentions, behaviors and/or associated characteristics.

An intuitive tendency to use our senses to make inferences about others *unintentionally*

Let me start by stating that we as humans routinely make inferences about invisible aspects of other humans, every time we receive information about them. This is the case whether we sought such information, or it came to us without intentionally seeking it. These invisible aspects are usually related to what other humans think, how they feel, what motivates them to behave in specific ways, what they care about, and other similar aspects. The following story is used to demonstrate this idea by making you conscious about the process of making inferences about other humans. In the story below, we will be reading about an individual as part of reading the news. As you are reading this story, try to follow along, and, as I provide you with the facts of this story, pause a moment to keep track of what is crossing your mind.

The story is about a police arrest that took place on a major highway in Massachusetts. The story line goes as follows:
1. Police officer driving in a cruiser spots a handwritten paper license plate on a BMW on the highway.

    What is crossing your mind? Maybe the driver just bought the car? Maybe the driver lost the license plate and created their own temporary plate while on their way to the registry of motor vehicles?
2. Police officer pulls the BMW over to the side of the road and asks for the male driver's license, registration and proof of insurance. The driver lives in Massachusetts but cannot produce a registration for the car and the car is not insured.

    What is crossing your mind now? If the car is not registered or insured, maybe the driver just bought it and has not had a chance to register it and insure

it yet. But wait, the driver had a handwritten license plate affixed onto the car, so maybe something illegal is happening here.
3. Police officer asks driver to step outside the car and searches the car. Police officer finds a handgun and ammunition. The handgun is not registered – the driver is not licensed to carry a firearm and/or ammunition in Massachusetts.

What is crossing your mind now? Something illegal is happening here. Maybe the driver is a gang member, maybe he was about to carry out a crime?

Notice how, as the story evolved, your brain couldn't help but make inferences based on the facts presented to it. Each fact was used by your brain as a sign for something hidden about the driver. You inferred what was hidden by using your senses and reading the facts. And as your brain was given more facts, it adjusted its inference of what the driver is hiding. By the end of the story, you had multiple signs of something illegal about the driver. The most basic inference is the person driving the car does not seem to believe that they need to follow the laws of the state where they reside, and they could get away with not following the laws. If you reached this conclusion or a similar one, you did so due to multiple signs given to you in the news story. Each sign was used by the brain as an indicator of something your senses never saw directly. You weren't there when the car was pulled over, you did not see the car or driver, yet your brain reached a conclusion about the driver's mindset. And the reason it did so is that your brain was given multiple indicators about the driver and all these indicators pointed to a common inference: the driver is someone who does not believe the laws of the state in which they reside apply to him, and he feels he can get away with not following the laws.

The example above demonstrates the intuitive tendency of the brain to use indicators that can be observed by our senses to reach conclusions about aspects that cannot be observed by our senses. Those aspects that cannot be observed are invisible. Notice in this context, you did not seek these indicators or prompt them in a way to see the invisible. You were simply reading through existing information, noted the indicators from the facts stated in the existing information, and then made an inference about an invisible characteristic of the person at the center of the news story based on these indicators. The notion of using indicators to try to see the invisible will be with us throughout this book and will be a critical pillar for measuring and understanding human thoughts, feelings and intentions.

In general, observations about the world that surrounds us can be formal or informal. Informal observations do not use specific tools and do not quantify what is being observed whereas formal observations do. The example given in the news story embodies informal observations made by reading a news story. Another example of informal observation is when you might look at two cars and notice one is larger than the other. If you were to use a measuring tape to determine the size of each car in inches or centimeters you would be turning your informal observation about the relative size of the cars into a quantified formal observation. Often, what begins as informal observations can be turned into formal observations through measurement. In a general sense, the term measurement in this book refers to the act of systematically and formally observing some aspect of the world that surrounds us. According to Nunnaly (1978) "[m]easurement consists of rules for assigning numbers to objects in such a way to represent quantities of attributes" (p. 3). Attributes are characteristics that are deemed important to observe to understand a specific situation or solve a particular problem. This book falls within this general understanding of the subject of measurement but will be confined to the attributes related to measuring human thoughts, knowledge, feelings, intentions, behaviors and/or associated characteristics. It addresses one specific aspect of this endeavor which is self-report measurement along with its challenges and its particulars. But before dealing with the specific aspect of measurement this book is about, it is useful to begin, as I did above, by asking whether we, as humans, engage in intuitive measurement to make sense of the world that surrounds us, including our interactions with other humans (see Campbell, 1952 for an in-depth philosophical discussion of this idea).

From the process that led to making inferences about the driver in the news story example, we've already seen how we all have an intuitive tendency to make inferences about the invisible by relying on indicators we can observe with our senses. In the example of the news story, I did not set out to create an environment that allows me to see indicators pertaining to the person driving the car. The news story simply provided me with information I used as indicators of the driver's likely mindset. So, the derivation of indicators from the news story falls under informal and unprompted observation and seems to be a definite intuitive human ability.

What about formal measurement? Does formal measurement also have its roots in intuitive and informal human abilities? The answer is a resounding "yes!" and I will illustrate so in this first section (see Campbell, 1952 for an affirmation that the methods of science have their origin in intuitive thinking). I ask you to keep an open mind as you follow the example below and I demonstrate the progression from informal measurement to formal measurement and the challenges anyone faces when attempting to capture variables important to them. The term "variable" is used here to refer to concepts that change in value across humans and might include age, gender, hair color, attitude toward music, brand loyalty or any other human characteristic involving a behavior, a thought, a feeling, an intention, etc. These aspects not only vary across humans but also vary in the degree to which they are visible to the observer. For example, I would be able to directly see with my own eyes someone's hair color whereas I would not be able to directly see with my own eyes whether someone is selfish. Yet, the most intriguing variables about humans are those that we cannot directly see: the invisible.

The intuitive need to measure the invisible *intentionally*

Let's pretend for a moment you are single and interested in a relationship with another person. Let's also pretend it is important to you that the other person with whom you are considering a relationship is not selfish. Being selfish, in this context, is the human attribute you decided to intentionally observe. You decided to observe it because this attribute is important to you. How can you observe whether a person is selfish? After all, you can't look at someone and based on their appearance determine if they are selfish. Maybe you can look at how they behave?

The need to define what you need to measure

Before you go about observing any information about anyone you need to be clear in your own mind on what it is that you're trying to observe. In this example, you need to determine what makes a person selfish according to your understanding of this concept. Your definition would need to specify what the person needs to say, or how a person should behave for you to reach the conclusion that they are selfish. And the reason for this is you can't even begin to observe something you haven't defined. Let's say you spend time thinking about this issue and you conclude that a person who tends to take for themselves more than they give to others is a selfish person. Now that it is clearer in your mind what it is you need to observe, how would you then go about figuring out if the person with whom you are considering a relationship is selfish?

The need to see the invisible

You could, for example, keep track of their behaviors within contexts that allow them to exhibit whether they are selfish. In this example, you are deliberately creating a context in which you are prompting your date to engage in certain behaviors. Your goal is to observe their behavior to determine if their behavior indicates whether they are selfish.

One such context could be during a date that involves sharing a dessert. You could ask them to share the dessert and watch whether they split it unevenly and take the larger portion for themselves. If they do so, then this would be one indicator they are selfish. Or would it? A single indicator would surely not be sufficient since it is possible that they took the larger portion of the desert not because they are selfish but because they were hungry or took a smaller portion not because they are not selfish but because they are watching their calories, or they took either a smaller or larger portion by pure coincidence. In either one of the preceding possibilities, the single indicator you used would not have captured what you set out to capture but you wouldn't know it.

Making errors when observing the invisible

It is important to stop for a moment here and consider the two types of mistakes that are possible when using indicators. The term "error" is used to indicate the possibility of using an indicator that does not really serve the purposes for which you are using it: if you thought observing the size of the cake portion your date takes is an indicator of selfishness when, in reality, it is an indicator of diet consciousness, then you would be making an error in judging whether your date is selfish. If you thought observing the size of the cake portion your date takes is an indicator of selfishness, when in reality, your date cut a smaller or larger portion by pure coincidence, then you also would be making an error when judging whether your date is selfish. Both errors are not desirable to make, as what you would have observed through the indicator is not what you set out to observe and, as a result, the errors would prevent you from determining if your date is truly selfish. It turns out that both errors are possible in the context of measurement and have been given specific labels by researchers to differentiate them. The first of the two errors is known as a systematic error and the second is known as a random error. The differences between the two errors will be clarified in a later section of this chapter and also discussed in Chapter 3.

The need for multiple indicators

Since using a single indicator to observe any invisible concept might result in misleading information, you decide that you need to observe instances of multiple behaviors using multiple indicators to obtain multiple bits of information all of which are seen in contexts that allow your date to exhibit a selfish behavior. Other contexts might include: you go to a bowling parlor and allow your date to play when it is your turn to play and see whether they reciprocate; you decide to share a soda can with your date and observe whether they pour more times in their cup from the same can than they pour into your cup; you have dinner at a restaurant on multiple occasions and observe whether or not, after paying for dinner yourself on one occasion, your date makes a genuine offer to pay for subsequent dinners. Each one of these instances during which you observe your date's behavior is an indicator of being selfish based on how you defined this idea or concept. What these four indicators have in common is they all potentially allow you to observe whether your date exhibits a behavior of taking more for themselves than they are giving you. By keeping track of these behavioral indicators and depending on the consistency of the behaviors that you are observing, you can draw a conclusion about whether the person whom you are dating is selfish. The more indicators you have that overlap with the definition of the concept you're trying to capture, and the more consistent they are, the more likely it is that they point to a pattern of behavior, and the more confident you will be in your conclusion. The indicators you used are observable manifestations of the invisible concept you are interested in capturing.

From intentional observations to a formal representation of the measurement process

The simple example above demonstrates that informal observations of the invisible are intuitive, and illustrates very important relationships between the concept you'd like to measure and the indicators you are using to capture the concept. The concept in this example is "being selfish" which you defined as a person who tends to take for themselves more than they give to others. The indicators were all observed during your dating interactions, and they were:

> "When we were sharing a cake, did they cut for themselves a larger piece of a cake than they gave me?
> When we went bowling, did they fail to reciprocate after I invited them to play when it was my turn?
> When we were sharing a soda, did they pour more times in their cup than they poured into mine?
> When we went out to have dinner at a restaurant, did they fail to make a genuine effort to pay for dinner after I had paid for previous dinners?"
> If you answered "yes" silently in your head to all four indicators, then you will likely conclude the person you are dating is most probably selfish.

If we were to formalize the intuitive logic used in this example into a diagram, what would this diagram show? Figure 1.1 illustrates the intuitive relationships that exist between the concept you wanted to capture and its indicators. (For those of you familiar with measurement modeling or the Classical Test Theory – see Spearman, 1904; Gulliksen, 1950; Lord & Novick, 1968; Nunnally, 1978 – you will find the diagram to be familiar as it is based on the conceptualization that Classical Test Theory puts forth). The diagram is read from top to bottom. Here is a recap of what this diagram illustrates: You wanted to capture whether your date is selfish. You used four indicators of being selfish. Why did you use these indicators? You did so because you assume that whether a person is selfish will be seen through each of the actions that the indicators capture. In other words, the invisible notion of being selfish that is present in the individual's mind will affect specific choices of behaviors that directly emanate from it. In the diagram, this is represented by the arrows going from the invisible concept you wanted to capture "Selfish" to each of the four visible indicators you used. Why did you decide to use more than one indicator? Because the behavior captured by a single indicator might be occurring by coincidence or for a different reason than you thought it would take place (the notions of systematic and random errors noted earlier). This is true for each indicator. So, each indicator has a potential level of error associated with it. But altogether as a set, if they point to a consistent pattern of behavior that is in line with the definition of the concept you are trying to capture, the set of indicators would give you confidence that what you are observing is the closest thing to the invisible concept you set out to capture. The notion that each indicator, on its own, is not perfect is partially illustrated in the diagram by the arrows going from the error to each indicator and partially from the arrows going from the invisible concept to each indicator. Each indicator might have a level of error associated with it since each indicator is not perfect. The arrows coming from on top represent the potential for systematic error and the arrows coming from the bottom represent the potential for random error.

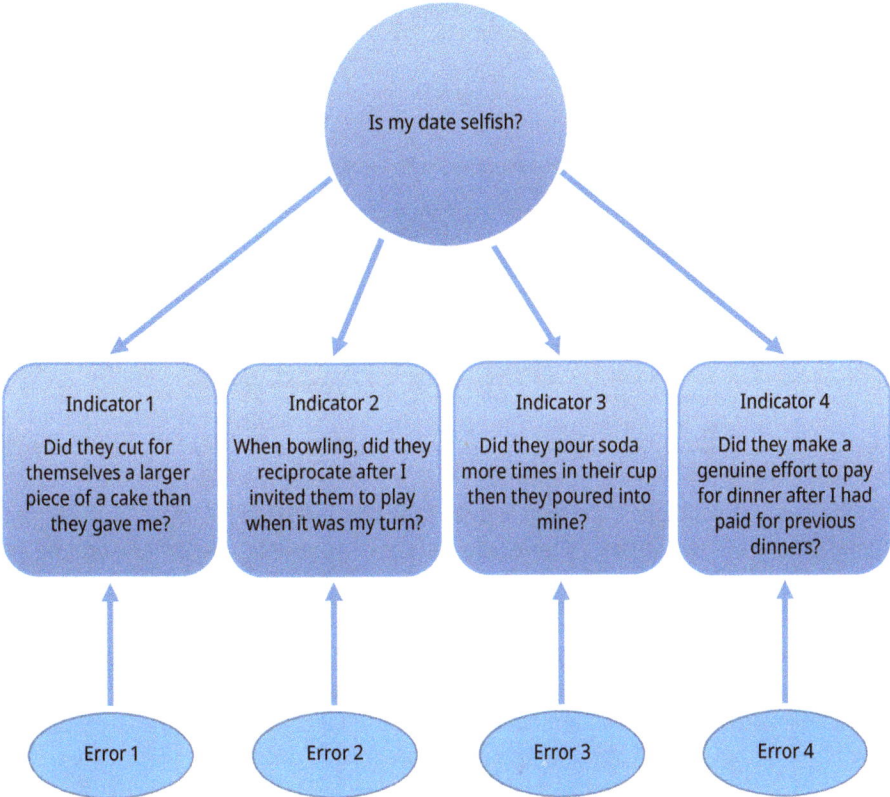

Figure 1.1: A formal representation of an intuitive measurement process. Source: Author.

Making the intuitive process of measuring the invisible a bit more formal

What if you wanted to systematically externalize the observations about your date's behaviors that you stored in your head? How would you do so? You could, for example, write down whether you observed them behave in a manner consistent with what each indicator is asking you to observe. For example, you could write a "yes" or "no" after observing your date's behavior on each of the indicators you used:

"When we were sharing a cake, did they cut for themselves a larger piece of a cake than they gave me?" yes or no;
"When we went bowling, did they reciprocate after I invited them to play when it was my turn?" yes or no;
"When we were sharing a soda, did they pour more times in their cup when they poured into mine?" yes or no;
"When we went out to have dinner at a restaurant, did they make a genuine effort to pay for dinner after I had paid for previous dinners?" yes or no.

If you do so, you would end up with a set of "yes" and "no" answers. For example, if you dated four people you might end up with a grid like the one in Table 1.1.

Table 1.1: Yes and No answers on the four selfishness indicators that you observed.

Name	Indicator 1	Indicator 2	Indicator 3	Indicator 4
Alex	Yes	Yes	Yes	Yes
Chris	Yes	Yes	No	Yes
Pat	Yes	Yes	Yes	No
Joey	No	Yes	Yes	No

As mentioned earlier, if you get a set of four "yes" answers, then you are likely to conclude your date is most probably selfish. If you get a set of four "no" answers, then you are likely to conclude your date is most probably not selfish. And while these two preceding scenarios point to a systematic pattern in your date's behaviors, you might also get a mix of "yes" or "no" on the indicators. A mixed set of "yes" or "no" would, of course, make your conclusion about whether your date is selfish less certain and, depending on the frequency pattern of "yes" and "no", perhaps even very uncertain. In Table 1.1 the patterns suggest Alex is more selfish than the others, with Joey being the least selfish. The fact that you are now systematically writing down and externalizing your observations about your date begins a more formal process of measurement.

Scaling up and formalizing observations

Let's say that you are using a dating app and, as a result, you dated 25 people over a period of one year and would like to systematically compare all of them on whether they are selfish and the purpose of doing so is to choose the one who is the least selfish for a long-term relationship. You would repeat the same observations you made regarding the first person you dated using the same indicators for all your dates. For each person you are dating there would be a set of four "yes" or "no" answers on the indicators. Now you have lots of observations about 25 people. To streamline your ability to see what you captured and allow more objective comparisons across the persons you are dating, you decide to assign a numerical code to each indicator as follows: If a person gets a "yes" on an indicator you transform this observation to numeral "1" and if they get a "no" on an indicator you transform this observation to a "0". Doing so would allow you to add across your indicators to arrive at a total "selfishness" score between 0 and 4 for each person that you are dating, with the higher the score a person gets indicating a higher level of selfishness. This selfishness score is an externalization and formalization of what you observed about each of your dates by using the indicators that you chose. A sample of what this numerical conversion would look like for four people that you dated is presented in Table 1.2.

Table 1.2: Numerically coding the four indicators for four individuals that you dated.

Name	Indicator 1	Indicator 2	Indicator 3	Indicator 4	Score
Alex	1	1	1	1	4
Chris	1	1	0	1	3
Pat	1	1	1	0	3
Joey	0	1	1	0	2

The advantage of arriving at a selfishness score is that you can now sort the persons you are dating from "low" to "high" in terms of how selfish they are with a "0" being not selfish and "4" being highly selfish. Doing so would allow you to analyze the persons you are dating as a group, figure out which of your dates are similar to one another based on their selfishness score and which ones are different from one another. If you are able to capture more information about the persons you are dating, such as their age, level of education, where they went to school, etc., and formalize these concepts by assigning numerals to them, you can then conduct data analyses focused on whether older dates are more (or less) selfish or whether more educated dates are more (or less) selfish, and so on.

By transforming your observations into numerals and scaling your observations to the many people being observed, you will undoubtedly need to store your observations in a computer program. By doing so, you are creating a data file. And you can then use this data file to conduct all sorts of analyses.

If you followed the examples above and they make sense to you, then you have understood the essence of what this book means when using the term "measurement of the invisible" in the context of observing human characteristics.

Takeaways from the example of intuitive measurement

The ideas introduced in the simple example above will be with us throughout this book and these are summarized in Table 1.3 and labeled as the universals of intuitive measurement for less visible human-related concepts:

Table 1.3: Universals of Intuitive Measurement for Less Visible Human-related Concepts.

a.	That a concept that needs to be captured must be justified as important, relative to other concepts, to solve a specific problem;
b.	That a concept that needs to be captured first needs to be defined.
c.	That a single indicator is not sufficient to capture a concept that is not readily visible;
d.	That multiple indicators are best when capturing a concept that is not readily visible;
e.	That when using multiple indicators, all indicators must be consistent with the definition of the concept that a researcher is trying to capture;
f.	That when using multiple indicators, there are two sources of influence that affect how well the set of indicators will allow the person making the observations to be confident that the observations made through the indicators reflect the concept that the person needs to measure: 1. the influence of the invisible concept onto each indicator (the potential for systematic error) and 2. the influence of things other than the invisible concept onto each indicator (the potential for random error).

Behavioral measurement versus self-report measurement

The simple example given earlier illustrates a basic instance of behavioral measurement. Behavioral measures are instances when a researcher can systematically observe the behavior of individuals who are important to a research project. It is critical that individuals who are being measured behaviorally are not aware they are being measured, and thus behave more naturally. When this happens, behavioral measures are powerful because they are more likely to reflect how a person naturally reacts in each context. Behavioral measures, when used correctly, can tell a researcher what individuals do, and when behaviors are indicators of an individual characteristic, such as selfishness, they can also serve as a source of information about the characteristic being measured.

Behaviors on their own, however, are unable to reveal the thought-process (interrelations among beliefs, attitudes, emotions, etc.) that resulted in the behavior being observed. For example, knowing a person buys and consumes soda, votes for a candidate, eats lots of candy, or frequently uses Facebook does not tell us, on its own, why they do what they do. Why do we need to understand the reason individuals do what they do or the thought-process that led them to their behaviors? Researchers need to understand the thought-process to know what drives behavior. This is certainly true of researchers who are trying to instill a change in behaviors in the context of health, such as encouraging people to eat more fruits and vegetables, in the context of politics, such as persuading people to vote for a specific candidate, or in the context of technology use, such as increasing the use of a specific social media network, etc.

The impact of errors on your ability to differentiate among your dates on selfishness

When considering using indicators to observe an invisible characteristic, it is important that each indicator is consistent with the definition of the invisible characteristic that you are trying to observe. Let's go back to your dating goal of finding out whether a person with whom you are considering a relationship is selfish. Suppose that you discussed your plan of using indicators to measure selfishness with a friend, and they suggested you keep track of whether the person you are dating smells good as an additional key indicator of selfishness. You truly dislike body odor smells, so you thought, that's easy to track. You assigned the following codes to it: "0" smells good, "1" smells bad. Your selfishness scores for your dates ended up as those in Table 1.4.

Table 1.4: Numerically coding the four indicators for four individuals you dated with five indicators.

Name	Indicator 1	Indicator 2	Indicator 3	Indicator 4	Indicator 5	Score
Alex	1	1	1	1	0	4
Chris	1	1	0	1	0	3
Pat	1	1	1	0	1	4
Joey	0	1	1	0	1	3

Based on the scores provided in Table 1.4, Alex and Pat are now the most selfish, with Chris and Joey becoming comparable and slightly lower in terms of selfishness. While these scores are quantitative and allow you to differentiate the selfishness level of those with whom you are considering having a relationship, any decision that you make based on these scores would be misguided. Why? Because even though they are quantitative, and as such seem legitimate, the fifth indicator, "whether an individual smells good" is not consistent with the definition of selfishness that you had adopted at the onset of your effort. You might recall you had defined being selfish as someone "taking to themselves more than they give others." While smelling good or bad might be important to you, it is not an indicator of selfishness based on how you defined selfishness. So, including how your date smells in the scoring of selfishness would simply be adding a systematic error to the scores and making them useless in giving you a glimpse into the invisible "selfishness" predisposition that exists inside the mind of your dates. This example illustrates how crucially important it is to adopt a clear definition for an invisible concept you wish to observe and ensure that every indicator you use to observe this invisible concept be consistent with the definition you adopted. The unfortunate consequence of not doing so simply means the scores that you derive would be totally useless, and any decision you make based on these scores would be totally misguided. This critical point is addressed in point "e" of Table 1.3 provided earlier.

Can you capture a concept without having behavioral indicators for it?

Going back to the simple example about dating, if you can't observe your date's behaviors that indicate whether they are selfish, how else would you be able to obtain information about whether your date is selfish? How about asking them? Wait a minute, is it even reasonable to ask? By asking them, you would be relying on their willingness to tell you, their self-awareness regarding aspects of who they are, and their truthfulness in telling you something about who they are. By considering asking them, you have entered the world of self-report measurement. Self-report measurement is an instance when researchers rely on individuals to reveal information about themselves. Can you safely assume that they are willing to answer the questions you are asking, self-aware enough to be able to provide an objective assessment about themselves and uninhibited enough to tell you the truth? You might be thinking, maybe or maybe not, or it depends. Either way, by asking them, you are also making them aware they are being evaluated or measured. And that might make them hesitant to tell you the truth assuming they are self-aware and objective enough to evaluate aspects of themselves.

I am certain at this point you are asking yourself whether self-report measurement is even reasonable to use. Can you count on your date to reveal the truth about who they are? Are there certain questions you can ask your date, about which they are more self-aware and for which their responses will be more truthful than their responses to other concepts you'd also like to capture? For example, can you ask them where they went to high school or whether they watch Netflix or whether they are satisfied with the speed of their Internet connection? If you do, will their response be more truthful relative to their response regarding whether they are selfish? You might be thinking that asking them where they went to high school must surely be more reasonable than asking them whether they are selfish. And this intuitive reaction would be correct for the simple reason that although both "where they went to high school" and "whether they are selfish" are both invisible to you, the latter is more invisible. The idea that there is a continuum for the invisibility of concepts involving human characteristics will be further developed in Chapter 3. The more invisible a concept is, the more challenging will be the process of capturing it. Are there certain ways and techniques to ask your question that can affect how willing and forthcoming your date will be when responding? By the end of Chapter 8 of this book, you will realize that there is a solid foundation of knowledge about such issues that researchers can use when developing self-report measures.

The simple examples provided earlier, aside from illustrating the notion of intuitive measurement and the move from informal observations to more formal measurement, also show the dilemma every researcher faces when using self-report measures to capture variables important to them. While at first look, it is common to see self-report measures as straightforward questions that a researcher can ask, the reality is far more complicated than it first appears.

References

Campbell, N. (1952). *What is Science?* New York, NY: Dover.
Gulliksen, H. (1950). *Theory of Mental Tests.* New York: Wiley.
Lord, F.M. & Novick, M.R. (1968). *Statistical Theory of Mental Test Scores.* Reading, MA: Addison-Wesley.
Nunnally, J.C. (1978). *Psychometric Theory.* New York, NY: McGraw-Hill.
Spearman, C. (1904). "General intelligence," objectively determined and measured. *American Journal of Psychology, 15,* 201–293.

Chapter 2
Measuring the invisible: Practical uses and function within the method of science

Objectives of Chapter 2: This chapter contextualizes the idea of measuring the invisible within the framework of the method of science and its practical functions outside of building theory. Readers might already be familiar with the many stages involved in the method of science. Here, I pinpoint the placement of measurement among these stages. The objective is to remind the reader that measurement of the invisible is part of a more extensive process and has practical uses for both academic and industry researchers.

Measuring the invisible is key to decision-making

Chapter 1 of this book introduced the notion of using indicators to measure invisible concepts important to you. It turns out the line of thinking presented in the previous chapter is for more than evaluating potential partners for a relationship. The same ideas about measurement are also relevant in various academic fields of specialty that involve understanding human characteristics and a wide variety of industries that require an understanding of consumers, technology users, patients, voters, and the like.

The information that measurement reveals is critical for decision-making. When it comes to decisions that depend on being able to predict human behaviors in various fields of study and different industries, every decision-maker faces uncertainty about the outcome of their decision. For example, uncertainty exists for a hospital administrator deciding whether a change in billing policy will affect the likelihood that patients choose to be treated at their hospital in the future; uncertainty also prevails for a public health researcher deciding whether the predictions and explanations of the Theory of Planned Behavior (TPB) help them understand why teenagers vape; and uncertainty is also a significant concern for a vice president for marketing at a theme park deciding whether offering specific stay-and-play packages to visitors will increase their likelihood to visit the particular theme park. To reduce uncertainty, most decision-makers ask that relevant information about the humans at the center of their focus be collected and analyzed. In the case of the hospital executive, such information might consist of patient satisfaction and patient loyalty to a hospital; in the case of the public health researcher, such information might consist of the conditions that either encourage or inhibit vaping among teenagers; in the case of the marketing VP, such information might include what theme park visitors find to be interesting park attractions and reasonable costs for accommodations. The outcome of collecting and analyzing such information is used as knowledge or insights by the decision-makers to reduce the uncertainty associated with their decisions. Information collection and analysis in situations like the ones described above are most often carried out by following the method of science (for a simple overview of the method of science see Andersen and Hepburn, 2015).

The role of measurement in the method of science

A brief look at the process followed by the method of science to locate the measurement task

The typical steps involved in a research process that follows the method of science are listed in Table 2.1. This is the exact listing I have been using for the last three decades in the research methods classes I teach, and it provides a big picture of all the steps needed in each research project that uses the method of science. The steps or step portions associated with this book's subject matter are highlighted in bold.

Table 2.1: Typical 12 Steps of a Research Process following the Method of Science.

Step 1	Consider and diagnose the problem
Step 2	Identify the research question that the project will answer
Step 3	Do the background search
Step 4	Identify the variables
Step 5	Identify the research design
Step 6	**Develop the measures**
Step 7	Select a sample (if applicable)
Step 8	Collect the data
Step 9	**Prepare the data for analysis**
Step 10	Analyze the data
Step 11	Write the report
Step 12	Prepare and deliver the research presentation

While it is not within the scope of this book to focus on the specifics of the method of science or expand upon every step listed in Table 2.1, the purpose of providing these steps is to locate the role of "measurement" within the research process since "self-report measurement" is the focus of this book. Here is a summary of what happens at every step, as listed in Table 2.1.

Step 1: Consider and diagnose the problem: Here, the researchers consider the problem at hand to determine it is indeed the problem that needs to be focused on relative to related problems and to articulate the objective. Typically, academic problems pertain to testing theories to explain and predict phenomena. For example, an academic researcher might wonder what steps must be taken to discourage teenagers from vaping. Typically, industry problems pertain to achieving a business objective or solving a problem encountered by managers. For example, Disney theme park executives might want to know how to increase the number of people who want to visit Disneyland.

Step 2: Identify the research question: Here the researchers articulate the overarching question that will be answered at the end of a research project, and once answered, will yield the type of information that will help solve the problem identified in Step 1. A study's research question is not a question to be asked to participants. It is a question that a project aims to answer when it is completed. For example, concerning the vaping problem identified earlier, the research question could be: What factors influence a young person's likelihood to vape? For industry contexts, identifying a research question entails the translation of the decision-maker's objective into aspects of humans that need to be explained by a researcher to generate information about these humans that would help the decision-maker reach their objective. For example, in the case of Disney's objective stated earlier, the research question could be: What factors influence people's interest in visiting theme parks?

Step 3: Do the background search: Here the researchers conduct what is most often referred to as a "literature review." This step is critical to one of the main characteristics of the method of science, which is that science builds knowledge based on related science over time. As such, this step entails gathering prior studies others have conducted about the same problem that researchers are working on or a closely related problem for the researchers to learn from the findings of these studies. New studies are built on the findings of prior related studies. In the case of the study on vaping, the literature review would need to focus on prior investigations that have explored what drives young people's vaping behavior. In the case of Disney, the literature review would need to identify prior investigations that have uncovered what drives people to visit theme parks.

Step 4: Identify the variables: A variable within the context of this book is a characteristic related to humans or products or services used by humans. This characteristic changes in value across humans or products or services. For example, age would be a human characteristic that changes in value across humans since not all humans are born on the same day. Privacy concern is a variable since humans will vary in terms of how concerned they are about their privacy. Here, the researchers list the variables that are important to capture for their project based on what they learned by doing the literature review. This step is critical as it establishes which variables to prioritize from among the many possibly relevant variables that might have crossed the researchers' minds. Sources of variables include the results of prior studies as extracted through the literature review, established theoretical frameworks relevant to the research question of the study, the business decision-maker in cases where the study involves a business problem, and ideas from the research team. The variables are essentially the components of the problem that a study following the method of science is designed to solve. These variables will be captured and analyzed in later steps.

Step 5: Identify the research design: Here, the researchers determine the general approach they will adopt for the research project. Most common research designs in studies that involve decision-making about human behavior are surveys or experiments, and there are excellent sources to learn more about these methods (Groves et al., 2009; Fowler, 2008; Ruel et al., 2015; Marsden, 2010; Wolf et al., 2016; Nardi, 2018).

Step 6: Develop the measures: Here, the researchers need to figure out how to capture each of the variables identified in Step 4 and then code them into numerals. Numerals are symbols that might or might not have a quantitative meaning (e.g., 1, 2, 3, 4, 5, etc.) as their meaning is determined by what they conceptually represent. For example, a "2" is quantitative if it means the number of times someone has visited a theme park, whereas a "2" does not have a quantitative meaning if it is used to describe "Universal Studios" in a question that asks which theme park a respondent has visited in the past.

Step 7: Select a sample (if applicable): Here, the researchers need to figure out whom they need to study, how many participants will take part in their study, how these participants will be selected, and the source from which these participants will be drawn. Whom a researcher needs to study is known as the population of a study. Population in the research context is not confined to the people living in a specific geographic area. The term "population" in research denotes the elements relevant to a study's research question. The population examples correspond to the research questions given earlier: For identifying the factors that influence a young person's likelihood to vape, a relevant population would be all high school students in the United States. To identify the factors that influence people's interest in visiting theme parks, a relevant population would be all people who have expressed an interest in theme parks or all people who have visited a website that provides information about theme parks.

It is usually not feasible to study the entire population relevant to a specific research question which is why researchers study a subset of that population known as a "sample." They study samples and infer what they observe in the population relevant to their research question. The process of selecting a sample from a population is known as sampling, and there is an entire body of science dedicated to this topic (see Kalton, 1983; Arnab, 2017; Chaudhuri, 2014; Lohr, 2009). When studying small populations, sampling is not necessary as the researchers can study everyone. For most projects, however, the populations of relevant participants would be too large to be able to study, and sampling is necessary. There are many issues to overcome when sampling, and there are also excellent resources about sampling that the reader might want to consult (see Kalton, 1983; Arnab, 2017; Chaudhuri, 2014; Lohr, 2009).

Step 8: Collect the data: Here, the researchers administer the measures they prepared in Step 6 to the sample or group of individuals they've carefully selected in Step 7. The study participants' reactions to the measures used by the researchers are typically captured and stored as numerals in a data file.

Step 9: Prepare the data for analysis: Here, the researchers make sure the data they captured is correctly coded, clean, and in a suitable form for analysis. Among the activities researchers need to undertake at this step is to check to see whether they successfully captured what they set out to capture. Chapter 9 in this book provides a road map for researchers to be able to objectively determine whether they captured what they intended to capture and how well they were able to do so.

Step 10: Analyze the data: Here, the researchers use appropriate statistical analysis techniques to describe the variables they captured, test interrelationships among these variables, test hypotheses they had made, look at group differences, test specific theoretical models, etc. This step involves the tools and techniques provided by the entire field of applied statistics (see Wrench et al., 2018; Heerings et al., 2017; Chambers & Skinner, 2003; Weisberg et al., 1996).

Step 11: Write the research report: Here, the researcher chronicles everything they have done from the start of the research project until its end and focuses on what they learned concerning the research question they had identified in Step 2. The format of such reports differs between academic projects and industry projects. Academic projects follow a relatively uniform research journal article organization (see Rubin et al., 2012; Mligo, 2012; Mligo, 2016). Industry projects are less uniform and vary from one company to another. Academic researchers typically end their reports with conclusions about the phenomenon they are studying, the relationships uncovered among the variables they capture, and the implications for theory-building within their field of study. Effective industry researchers focus on the patterns of variation that they uncovered and the relationships among the variables that they captured to derive actionable recommendations about the problem that had prompted the need for the research project. Effective reports use elements of storytelling to organize the information and communicate the takeaways in a manner to which intended readers can relate.

Step 12: Prepare and deliver the research presentation: Here, the researchers communicate, most often orally, what they have done and found. For academic researchers, presentations are done in the context of academic research conferences, and such talks are typically technical as the audiences to which they are presenting generally are other researchers. For industry researchers, presentations are delivered to higher-ups within an organization and/or clients. Compared to academic presentations, industry presentations are much more visually appealing, consisting of intricate graphics that help the audience visualize what the researcher has uncovered in a manner that does not require the audience members to be trained in research. This is because the audiences of their presentations typically consist of strategists, creative talent and decision-makers rather than other researchers.

The process of research and the notion of error

Steps present in Table 2.1, if not done perfectly, can introduce a large amount of error into a research project. It is a fact that nothing is ever perfect. However, the more errors are introduced and allowed to accumulate, the less likely the researchers will be able to solve the problem that prompted them to carry out the research project. To be able to solve the problem they set out to solve, researchers need to be obsessed with eliminating as much error as possible when executing each step depicted in Table 2.1. At the end of a research project, the amount of information obtained relative to the amount of error introduced in the process of carrying out the project will determine whether the problem researchers set out to unravel will be solved. The more significant the ratio of information relative to error, the more likely it is that the problem will be solved. This notion of error will appear again, starting with Chapter 3, where we begin exploring the idea of measuring the invisible within the context of self-report measurement.

References

Andersen, H. and Hepburn B. (2015). *Scientific Method*. Retrieved from https://stanford.library.sydney.edu.au/archives/sum2019/entries/scientific-method/
Arnab, R. (2017). *Survey sampling: Theory and applications.* Cambridge, MA: Academic Press.
Chambers, R.L. & Skinner, C.J. (2003). *Analysis of Survey Data*. Hoboken, NJ: Wiley.
Chaudhuri, A. (2014). *Modern survey sampling*. London, UK: Chapman & Hall.
Fowler Jr., F.J. (2008). *Survey research method* (4th ed.). Beverly Hills, CA: Sage Publications, Inc.
Groves, R.M., Fowler, F.J., Couper, M.P., Lepkowski, J.M., Singer, E., & Tourangeau, R. (2009). *Survey Methodology* (2nd ed.). Hoboken, NJ: Wiley.
Heerings, S.G., West, B.T., & Berglund, P.A. (2017) *Applied Survey Analysis* (2nd ed.). London, UK: Chapman and Hall.
Kalton, G. (1983). *An introduction to survey sampling*. Beverly Hills, CA: Sage Publications, Inc.
Lohr, S.L. (2009). *Samping: Design and analysis* (2nd ed.). London, UK: Cengage Learning.
Marsden, P.V. (2010). *Handbook of survey research* (2nd ed., J.D. Wright, Ed.). Bingley, UK: Emerald Publishing.
Mligo, E.S. (2016). *Introduction to research methods and report writing*. Searcy, AR: Resource Publications.
Mligo, E.S. (2012). *Writing Academic Papers*. Searcy, AR: Resource Publications.
Nardi, P.M. (2018). *Doing survey research: A guide to qualitative methods* (4th ed.). Oxfordshire, UK: Routledge Press.
Rubin, R.B., Rubin, A.M., Haridakis, P.M. & Piele, L.J. (latest edition). Communication Research: Strategies and Sources. Belmont, CA: Wadsworth.
Ruel, E., Wagner III, W.E., & Gillespie, B.J. (2015). *The practice of survey research: Theory and applications* (1st ed.). Beverly Hills, CA: Sage Publications, Inc.

Weisberg, H.F., Krosnick, J.A., & Bowen, B.D. (1996). *An introduction to survey research, polling, and data analysis* (3rd ed.). Beverly Hills, CA: SAGE Publications, Inc.

Wolf, C., Joye, D., Smith, T.W., & Fu, Y. (2016). *The SAGE handbook of survey methodology.* Beverly Hills, CA: Sage Publications, Inc.

Wrench, J.S., Thomas-Maddox, C., Richmond, V.P., & McCroskey, J.C. (2018). *Quantitative research methods for communication.* New York, NY: Oxford University Press.

Chapter 3
From observing behaviors to conceptualizing self-report measurement and developing a measurement mindset

Objectives of Chapter 3: This chapter is designed to help the reader transition from the notion of measuring the invisible through behavioral observations to measuring the invisible through self-report measurement techniques. It also broadens the idea of self-reporting to include statements shared through social media posts, a topic that will be further explored in Chapter 10. Key concepts introduced in Chapter 1 are further developed here by adding the challenges of relying on individuals to provide the researcher with information about themselves. This chapter provides the assumptions needed for self-report measures to yield useful information, and helps the reader visualize the notion of self-report measurement. This visualization is used as a framework for understanding the idea of measurement error and its validity and reliability components. This chapter also highlights the importance of precision when capturing variation. Finally, this chapter outlines a mindset for self-report measurement to yield helpful information. This mindset is equally relevant to academic and industry researchers interested in capturing thoughts, knowledge, feelings, intentions and related human characteristics.

What is self-report measurement?

In this book, self-report measurement is when researchers rely on individuals to reveal information about themselves (see Lavrakas, 2008). This information might include their demographic characteristics, opinions, knowledge, thoughts, feelings, intentions, and behaviors. It would be very helpful if you could begin thinking about these invisible concepts as building blocks of a thought-process. The objective of using self-report measures is to capture these building blocks to later analyze their interrelationships using statistical tools. By examining the relationships among the captured building blocks, a researcher can gain insights into the shared thought-processes of specific groups of humans associated with particular topics (for more details about thought-processes, please see the explanation in Chapter 10). However, before researchers can use statistical tools to understand the relationships among the building blocks of a shared thought-process, they first need to capture the variation of each of its building blocks. When a researcher tries to capture the variation of these building blocks by relying on humans to provide information about themselves, it is called self-report measurement.

What is *not* self-report measurement?

As is the case in every other aspect of life, it is not whether you do something but how well you do it that affects the outcome. This thought applies equally to bread-making, housebuilding, music-playing, and self-report measuring. Unfortunately, despite a widespread need for it across disciplines within academia and industry, self-report measurement does not typically receive the attention and respect it deserves, and the complexity of its practice is frequently misunderstood and confused with something else. Below are a few examples of situations repeatedly encountered over the years. They illustrate what does not qualify as the type of self-report measurement discussed in this book.

Just give it to the interns. Done!

For over three decades, I've asked students taking my introductory class in research methodology whether they've had an internship. Among those who have had an internship, I asked them to raise their hands if their employer asked them to develop a questionnaire as part of their internship. I am always astounded by how many hands are raised. Essentially, what I characterize in this book as one of the most critical tasks of any research project aimed at capturing information from humans is often relegated to an intern with no prior training in this technique. As will become evident in the explanations provided in this book, having an intern sit down and write a bunch of questions to use in a survey will not yield information that can be counted on for decision-making.

Simply turn the objective into a question, and we're done!

A common error I've encountered in various settings, some of which involve highly intellectual research project planners, is confusing the decision maker's objective with the self-report measurement task. For example, let's say the head of a medical group would like to know how to get more hospital patients to read the materials that their group prepared to facilitate preventative care. This objective needs to be attained at the end of the study. Often, this objective is turned into a wrongly conceived self-report measure, where, for example, patients are asked: "What do we need to do to encourage you to read our materials about preventative care?" Through the explanations provided in this book, it will become clear that simply turning the objective one wishes to achieve into a survey question will not yield any useful information.

Simply turn the research question into a survey question, and we're done!

This error usually occurs with early-career academic researchers who have received little training in self-report measurement and are under pressure to use self-report measures to get published. These researchers are generally very aware of the need to capture variables and can articulate this need as an overarching research question for their study. For example, a researcher has identified their study's research question: What factors influence a consumer's decision to use a health-tracking smartphone app? The error I have seen is simply turning the research question into a survey question to be administered to a sample of respondents. For example, "what influences you to use this health-tracking smartphone app?" As explained in this book, doing so would not yield the type of information that will answer the question the researchers are trying to answer at the end of their study.

Just ask what you need to find out, and we're done!

This error is common among well-intended researchers who wrongly assume that respondents can provide information about the abstract concepts they wish to capture. For example, a researcher is interested in differentiating among people who compulsively shop. Compulsive shopping is undoubtedly a very worthy concept to capture, and if researchers adopt the correct measurement approach, they will be able to capture it. The mistake that I've seen made among some researchers is confusing the concept itself with the measurement of that concept by asking respondents to answer: Are you a compulsive shopper? As will become evident in this book, doing so, or doing something along this line of thinking, will result in useless information for the researchers.

Let's figure out what would be some interesting questions to ask. Done!

This is one of the most common errors I've repeatedly encountered when consulting with industry and academic clients. It confuses two stages of the research process: identifying the information that is deemed necessary for a given project and capturing this information. As explained in this book, doing so is not self-report measurement, will certainly not yield useful information, and will certainly not help solve the problem that prompted a need for a research project in the first place.

What is the traditional context of self-report measurement?

The most common context in which self-report measurement exists is within what has traditionally been labeled as a "Questionnaire," or "Poll." Is it about asking questions? From the perspective of what a study participant sees, they see a question, a questionnaire, or a poll. For examples, please see Pew Research Center surveys: https://www.pewresearch.org/our-methods/u-s-surveys/, and the University of Chicago surveys: https://gss.norc.org/get-documentation/questionnaires.

However, the reality is that it's not about the questions but about the information sought and collected. The questions are tools to obtain information about specific aspects of the individual that are deemed essential to capture and later describe and predict as part of a given research project.

A new context for self-report measurement

What about information individuals reveal about themselves on social media, for example, in Tweets or Facebook posts? Isn't that a form of self-report? Self-disclosures on social media are potentially expressions in the same way that a person answering a question given to them as part of a survey is also making an expression (see Ignatow & Mihalcea, 2018). The difference is that in a survey or experiment, a study participant is asked by a researcher to express their thoughts or feelings, whereas, in the context of social media posts, the user does so without being asked. Of course, surveys are sometimes found on social media, but the social media text expressions I am referring to are those that are communicated without being prompted. Starting in 2014, I have been trying to find a way to transform self-disclosed expressions present in Tweets into self-report measures (see Elasmar, 2019). As part of my efforts to do so, I have come to label self-disclosed expressions on social media as "unsolicited self-report" since, in this context, a researcher does not actively ask individuals to self-disclose. Using this label for these types of self-disclosed expressions helps differentiate them from the traditional information obtained when a researcher asks questions, which I label "solicited self-report." Currently, "unsolicited self-report" expressions are most often analyzed within the specialty of "opinion-extraction" in big data. And the field of "opinion-extraction" has mostly been led by researchers in the field of computer science (see Yang & Cardie, 2012–2014). In Chapter 10 of this book, I address how to shift and refocus current efforts in the field of "opinion-extraction," with assistance from Artificial Intelligence (AI) tools, to better enable the emergence of a sound science. Table 3.1 compares the two types of self-report I refer to in the paragraph above.

Table 3.1: A comparison of solicited and unsolicited self-report along key characteristics.

	Unsolicited Self-Report	Solicited Self-Report
Candor of expression	Very candid on all topics	Less candid on sensitive topics
Ease of availability	Very easily available	Increasingly difficult to obtain
Cost of data	Very cheap	Expensive
Freshness of information	Up to the minute	Not up to the minute
Size of data set	Very large	Limited in size by time and budget
Identification of the concept being captured	Cannot be identified before analysis	Is identified before the analysis
Level of measurement	Limited variation: typically limited to 3 gradations	It can be designed to vary along 5 to 7 gradations
Ability to differentiate among thought-process components (e.g., beliefs, attitudes, intentions, etc.)	Not yet fully developed	Well established science
Methods for assessing measurement validity	Not yet fully developed	Well established science
Method for assessing measurement reliability	Not yet fully developed	Well established science
Data Integrity	Highly susceptible to intentional distortions	Less susceptible to intentional distortions
Generalizability of findings	Currently not possible	Possible depending on the context
Understanding of expression by researcher	Expression requires interpretation by the researcher	Expression crafted by the researcher – interpretation not needed
Unit of analysis	The whole posted content (e.g., tweet, product review, etc.) is typically not linked to individuals	The individual reacting to a specific expression

Is self-report measurement still needed in the era of big data?

As I write these words, technologically, we find ourselves obsessed with our smartphones that, aside from allowing us to easily communicate, keep track of everything we do through them, everything we post on social media, and all the places we go while carrying them. In a sense, a smartphone is an instrument for capturing human behaviors. And these behaviors are progressively being analyzed. Given the enormous amount of information generated by human activities that can now be tracked, the storage of this information has come to be called "Big Data" (see Buskirk, 2020). The field of data analytics applied to big data now provides detailed insights into consumer behaviors as captured by various devices and apps, and these predictions can be very precise. The new norm is to disrupt long-established traditions within industry and government. So, it is fair to ask: Is self-report measurement still relevant?

While data analytics and big data mining might be accurate in telling us, for example, what individuals who purchase a specific product on Amazon might also likely buy, "solicited self-report measurement" is still the only approach that enables us to explain why these individuals buy what they buy. More generally, "solicited self-report" measurement, when used correctly, is still uniquely capable of telling us why people behave the way they do. When it comes to understanding thought-processes that result in, for example, voter intentions or consumer purchases, self-report measures are still heavily used and relied upon for making predictions and strategic decisions. When used correctly, "solicited self-report" measures can result in the type of data that leads to accurate predictions. This is true across a wide array of fields. This is true even now despite the advances in technology and development of cutting-edge algorithms that mine big data (see Chapter 10).

The cartoons in Figures 3.1 and 3.2 illustrate the difference between seeing a behavior and understanding a thought-process.

Figure 3.1: A vivid illustration of behavior versus thoughts. Source: Elasmar, 2024.

In the cartoon in Figure 3.1, if you solely look at behaviors, you will only see everyone looking intently at the same tree. By looking at their behavior alone, you might conclude that they all have the same motivations and are like one another in that they seem interested in the tree. You wouldn't see what drives them to look at the tree or what their mind sees when looking at this tree. Only by looking at their invisible thoughts, which you normally can't see and are represented by thought bubbles in Figure 3.2, will you realize there is a lot that you are missing. Your conclusion based on their behavior alone is insufficient and incorrect.

Figure 3.2: A vivid illustration of behavior versus thoughts. Source: Elasmar, 2024.

While the field of big data is excellent at analyzing behaviors, it is possible that, in the future, it can also effectively describe collective thought-processes about specific behaviors. However, many technical obstacles still need to be overcome before we get there, and I outline some of them in Chapter 10 of this book. So, for the foreseeable future, understanding the mindset of voters, citizens, consumers of media, consumers of products, consumers of services, app users, video game players, medical patients, or humans in general is still only possible through the correct application of "solicited self-report" measurement.

The quest to capture invisible human thoughts, feelings, and related concepts

Self-report measurement is most often used to capture human characteristics that are frequently called "concepts," and these concepts are expected to vary across individuals (e.g., age, beliefs about science, political ideology, usage frequency of Instagram, satisfaction with a doctor's visit, etc.). Concepts vary across humans, so they are often called "variables," and the two terms are used interchangeably. As was noted in Chapter 2, variables are the components of the problem that a specific research project sets out to solve using the method of science. The term "construct" describes a concept to which a researcher has assigned a particular meaning by giving it a specific definition. The word "construct" might remind you of construction or the act of building something. For example, "impulse buying," a concept that varies across humans, becomes a construct when it is defined as "a consumer's tendency to buy spontaneously, unreflectively, immediately, and kinetically" (Rook and Fisher, 1995, p. 306). The definition builds a specific meaning for the concept. The purpose of conducting "a poll" or developing a "questionnaire" for surveys or experiments is to capture specific concepts and constructs relevant to a particular research project. Participant reactions to the measures are captured by the researchers, turned into numerals, and stored in a data file that will be subjected to statistical analysis to describe patterns of responses, test relationships among variables, conduct segmentation analyses, test mathematical models, etc.

Not only do concepts and constructs vary across individuals, but they also vary from relatively simple concepts (e.g., age, hair color, location, occupation, etc.) that might be quite visible or easily observed to more complex concepts (e.g., beliefs about science, extraversion, satisfaction with a product or service, etc.) that are very invisible. It is important to note that in the context of self-report measurement, a complex concept (e.g., environmental consciousness) is not only invisible to the researcher but is also likely to be invisible to the respondent. Complex concepts require a high level of self-awareness that cannot be simply assumed to exist homogeneously across study participants. Complex variables are also known as latent variables, which suggests these are not readily visible.

Figure 3.3: A continuum of concept complexity and invisibility. Source: Author.

Capturing the invisible and the Golden Assumption (GA) of self-report measurement

All analyses conducted on data extracted through self-report measurement, no matter how simple or mathematically intricate, depend on the assumption that the data collected truly reflects the invisible characteristics of the humans being studied – their invisible true thoughts, true feelings, true knowledge, true intentions and/or true behaviors. In many ways, this notion can certainly be labeled the Golden Assumption (GA) of self-report measurement. Without it, all data collected through self-reporting will be useless. The reality is that it is possible to collect information through self-report measurement that does not fully meet this Golden Assumption (GA). It is useful to consider what study participants need to go through when reacting to self-report measures mentally. Tourangeau, Rips, and Rasinski (2000) illustrate the complexity of this process through their "Components of the Response Process" (p. 8) as follows:

Comprehension	Attend to questions and instructions Represent logical form of question Identify question focus (information sought) Link key terms to relevant concepts
Retrieval	Generate retrieval strategy and cues Retrieve specific generic memories Fill in missing details
Judgement	Assess completeness and relevance of memories Draw inferences based on accessibility Integrate material retrieved Make estimate based on partial retrieval
Response	Map judgment onto response category Edit response (Tourangeau, Rips & Rasinski, 2000, p. 8)

Any malfunction in the response process identified by Tourangeau, Rips, and Rasinski (2000) will contribute to the possibility that the information collected will not truly reflect the characteristics of the study participants the researcher set out to capture. And it is unreasonable to assume that all respondents will engage in this mental processing flawlessly when reacting to a question. The good news is there is plenty of science-derived information that can help researchers maximize the chances this assumption is upheld and inform them on how to preempt measurement problems along with techniques researchers can use to evaluate whether the Golden Assumption (GA) was met in their projects. These topics will be covered in Chapters 5 through 9 of this book.

Can the process of self-report measurement be visualized?

It is important to visualize what we aim to do when we set out to use self-report measures to capture a concept or a construct. Doing so helps us appreciate the challenges we need to overcome for the measurement task to be successfully completed. A prelude to visualizing the process of measurement was given in Chapter 1 as part of the simple example about needing to measure selfishness of dating partners. The focus in that example was on capturing and externalizing the invisible. The earliest efforts to capture invisible human characteristics have been traced to China as far back as 2200 BC (DuBois, 1970). In Europe, the idea of capturing the invisible can be traced back to the time of Galileo who, himself, had stated many centuries ago: "we must measure what is measurable and make measurable what cannot be measured." These early concepts of capturing invisible human characteristics were later transformed into more conceptual and systematic approaches by Spearman, 1904, Gulliksen, 1950, and Lord and Novick, 1968.

In the case of self-report measurement, we often set out to measure what Galileo denotes as "what cannot be measured" or what is invisible. Our aim is to make the invisible tangible in the form of data. While this sounds very abstract, Figure 3.4 illustrates the process using a simple example involving self-report measurement.

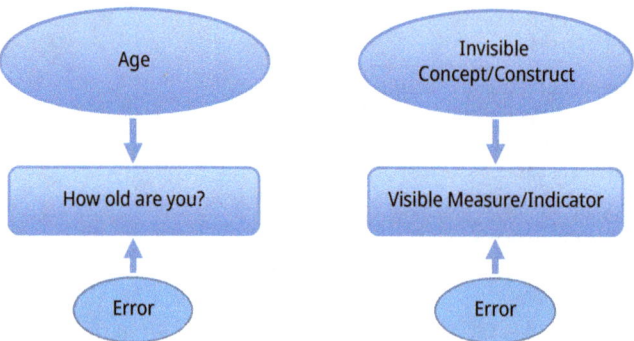

Figure 3.4: An Invisible to Visible Framework (ITVF) for conceptualizing self-report measurement. Source: Author.

For those of you already familiar with measurement modeling, you will notice that in Figure 3.4 (and in Figure 1.1) I am using the layout of traditional measurement models that are based on Classical Test Theory (see Spearman, 1904; Gulliksen, 1950; Lord & Novick, 1968; Nunnally, 1978). I am labeling the diagram in Figure 3.3 an Invisible to Visible Framework (ITVF) because this label is much more descriptive of what the diagram is showing and therefore much more intuitive to comprehend than using the standard label "measurement model" (see Maruyama, 1998). The figure is read from top to bottom. At the top of the diagram is a concept that a researcher wishes to capture. In this example, the concept "Age" is relatively simple and is defined as the amount of time in years since a person was born. The "Age" of a respondent is invisible to the researcher until the researcher asks the respondent "How old are you?" This question becomes the measure or indicator of a respondent's age. When a respondent reacts to this question by answering it, they are externalizing an invisible concept. The researcher hopes that what a respondent externalizes is a true reflection of the invisible concept. In the case of age, the hope is when a respondent says they are 40 years old, they are really 40 years old. It is reasonable to assume that, in the case of age, a respondent is willing, aware and able to disclose a true reflection of this invisible concept. However, this process is not perfect. Even with simple concepts such as age, there could be study participants who are not willing to disclose the true reflection of the invisible for an array of reasons. In the case of age, some participants, for example, might provide a fictitious age because they don't trust the researcher and wonder whether the researcher might misuse this information for stealing their identities. For whatever reason, there is always going to be some participants who don't react to a self-report measure by reflecting the true nature of the invisible concept in response to the measure. Sometimes this happens intentionally, at other times this happens unintentionally when a respondent is simply not self-aware enough regarding specific less visible aspects of themselves. Regardless of the reasons, the very fact that the possibility exists that some respondents' answers will not reflect the true nature of the invisible concepts or constructs that a researcher wishes to capture introduces the notion of "errors due to measurement."

What are "errors due to measurement" and can they be visualized?

In the context of this book, error is a measurement-centered obstacle that comes between the researcher and the truth they seek to capture about concepts important for their research projects (see McNabb, 2014). Whereas the term "measurement error" has traditionally been used in the literature to specifically refer to random errors that affect how a respondent reacts to self-report measures (see Nunnally, 1978), I am using the term "errors due to measurement" (EDM) which encompasses random and systematic errors as explained below since they are both potentially devastating to a research project.

In Figure 3.4, the arrows are pointing in specific directions on purpose. The arrows represent influence and the direction from which the arrow is pointing reveals the source of influence. Under ideal conditions, a reaction to a measure is only influenced by the invisible concept that this measure is designed to capture. In the example in Figure 3.4, ideally the only influence on a respondent's reaction to the question that asks how old they are is the true age of the respondent as it exists within their own brain. Any other influence onto a respondent's reaction to this measure is "error" and should be very weak. Therefore, under ideal conditions, in Figure 3.4, the arrow coming from on top should be very strong and the arrow coming from the bottom should be very weak. If this happens, then the measure would be a true reflection of the invisible and, if this pattern is repeated across all study participants, then the externalization of these concepts and the storage of these externalizations in the form of a data file would be suitable for subsequent statistical analysis. If this is not the case, then depending on the strength of the influence of error (e.g., having weak arrows coming from on top and strong arrows coming from the bottom), the data would not be suitable for statistical analysis. The term "errors due to measurement" (EDM) is the combined effect of systematic errors as represented by the arrows coming from on top and random errors as represented by the arrows coming from the bottom in Figure 3.4. If the arrows coming from on top are weak and the arrows coming from the bottom are strong then we have a high level of "errors to due to measurement" (EDM) and the data collected through self-report measures would not be suitable for statistical analysis. In simple terms, if you don't know for sure what you measured and the measures you used are not consistent, then you can't move forward and analyze your data.

Multiple self-report indicators for measuring invisible concepts

For the sake of illustration, let's say a researcher is working on a problem that involves explaining and predicting why individuals differ in terms of how frequently they purchase products online. As part of the literature review, they conducted in preparation for their study, the researchers identified "impulse buying" as a potential explanation. They hypothesize that individuals who rank high on impulse buying tend to make more online purchases. This simple hypothesized relationship would be an example of a simple thought-process the researcher is trying to test. Before they can test the relationship between these two variables, they need to measure each. As part of this effort, they set out to capture "impulse buying," a predisposition that varies in intensity across people. It is a complex concept, a latent variable, and is certainly not visible. How would they go about capturing this invisible concept?

It is helpful to reproduce the universals of intuitive measurement for invisible concepts (initially presented in Table 1.3 of Chapter 1) to determine the best approach for capturing this concept:

a. In terms of the first requirement listed in the table, here the concept of "impulse buying" was identified through the literature review conducted by the researchers, so it is justified in that it was found to be important in the findings of prior studies conducted to investigate the question of why people shop online.

b. But what is "impulse buying" you might ask? And you certainly would be correct in asking this question. While there is a natural tendency for all of us to assume an understanding of a word or label used to refer to a concept, it was pointed out in

Chapter 1 it is imperative that we clarify the concepts we wish to capture by defining them. In this case, we borrow the definition of "impulse buying" as stated by Rook and Fisher (1995): a "tendency to buy spontaneously, unreflectively, immediately and kinetically" (p. 306). By defining it, this concept becomes a construct.

Table 3.2: Universals of intuitive measurement for more invisible human-related concepts.

a.	That a concept that needs to be captured must be justified as important, relative to other concepts, to solve a specific problem;
b.	That a concept that needs to be captured first needs to be defined;
c.	That a single indicator is not sufficient to capture a concept that is not readily visible;
d.	That multiple indicators are best when capturing a concept that is not readily visible;
e.	That when using multiple indicators, all indicators must be consistent with the definition of the concept that a researcher is trying to capture;
f.	That when using multiple indicators, there are two sources of influence that affect how well the set of indicators will allow the person making the observations to be confident that the observations made through the indicators reflect the concept that the person needs to measure: 1. the influence of the invisible concept onto each indicator (the potential for systematic error) and 2. the influence of things other than the invisible concept onto each indicator (the potential for random error).

c. Following the guidance provided in Table 3.2, since this concept is more invisible, a single indicator will not be sufficient in capturing this concept.

d. So, we will need to find multiple indicators that are consistent with the definition provided above. And these need to be self-report indicators. We notice that Rook and Fisher (1995) used a set of multiple indicators that ask participants the extent to which they agree or disagree on a 5-point scale to a set of statements starting with "strongly disagree" and ending with "strongly agree." We decide to use these indicators. The following were among them:

> "I see it I buy it" describes me
> I often buy things spontaneously
> I often buy things without thinking
> "Just do it" describes the way I buy things

Using the Invisible to Visible framework (ITVF), we can try to visualize the relationships between the invisible construct of impulse buying and its visible indicators in Figure 3.5.

e. According to the guidance provided in Table 3.2, the indicators must reflect the meaning conveyed in the definition of the construct they were designed to capture. In its most basic form, this is a qualitative assessment that is purely linguistic in nature (see face and content validity later in this chapter). It is done by asking how much of

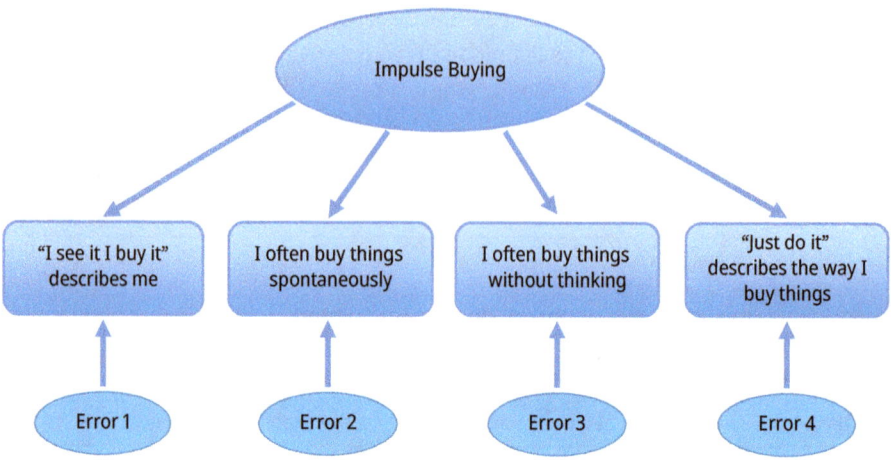

Figure 3.5: The Invisible to Visible Framework used for impulse buying. Source: Author.

an overlap there is between the meaning conveyed by a given indicator and the meaning conveyed by the definition of the construct that this indicator is designed to capture. The more meaning-overlap between them, the more likely the indicator is reflecting the invisible construct and is mostly influenced by it. The less meaning-overlap, the less likely this indicator is reflecting the invisible construct. We evaluate the meaning of each of the four indicators and find that they reasonably overlap in meaning with the definition of "impulse buying."

f. In Figure 3.5, for the indicators of impulse buying to capture the concept they were designed to capture, the influence of a person's impulse buying level on their reaction to every indicator must be much stronger than the influence of other invisible concepts on these indicators. If the arrows coming from impulse buying onto each of the indicators are weak, then we have systematic error. Visually, the arrows coming from on top in Figure 3.5 need to be strong and the arrows coming from the bottom need to be weak. We can try to guess the strength of the influence coming from on top through the qualitative assessment of meaning-overlap between the wording used in an indicator and the definition of the construct this indicator was designed to capture. However, this guessing, while a good starting point, is not very objective and is tainted by our own interpretation of the meaning contained in the measures. We are guessing how the respondents would interpret each measure, but we don't know for sure a respondent's interpretation of the meaning present in a measure would be like our own. Further, when it comes to the arrows coming from the bottom, by simply doing a qualitative assessment, we would have no idea if there were reasons, besides the invisible construct, that are influencing the respondents' reactions to the measures. But we need to know this, don't we? Without this knowledge, we will have no idea if we have random error. Both systematic and random error will prevent you from capturing what you set out to capture and are thus undesirable. If you are wondering if there are objective means to evaluate the relationships between indicators and concepts, the answer is "yes," and these will be described in Chapter 9 of this book. For the current portion of this book, the main objective is understanding the obstacles that need to be overcome when using self-report measurement.

When asking someone to self-report, what are we assuming about them and about the measures developed by the researcher?

The Golden Assumption (GA) of self-report measurement noted earlier consisted of making sure a respondent's reaction to the self-report measures we administer truly reflect the invisible concept we aim to capture. While this idea is noble and serves as a general objective everyone using self-report measures should try to achieve, it is a little vague and, as such, hard to evaluate. Can this general objective be broken down into more manageable assumptions that can potentially be objectively checked? Tables 3.3 and 3.4 present lists of assumptions about respondents and measures for self-report measurement to yield useful information.

Table 3.3: Assumptions made about respondents for self-report measures to achieve their purpose.

When reacting to a measure or answering a question, the respondent	
Assumption A	Is willing to disclose information about themselves
Assumption B	Is truthful and not deliberately lying
Assumption C	Interprets each measure/question the way the researcher intended and in the exact same way that others who are also being measured are interpreting them
Assumption D	Can correctly recall needed information from memory to react to each measure/question
Assumption E	Can easily move from one measure/question to another
Assumption F	Is self-aware
Assumption G	Is reacting to a measure without being influenced by any aspect of the measure itself other than the content that directly overlaps with the invisible concept that needs to be captured.

Table 3.3 presents a list of assumptions about the measures themselves.

In addition to assumptions made about respondents, and listed in Table 3.3, there are assumptions that are made about the researchers that go beyond the basic qualities of being genuine, unbiased, well intended, and honest. The assumptions to which I refer below are specifically related to a researcher's development of self-report measures. If not upheld, these assumptions will also contribute to errors in measurement.

Table 3.4 presents the assumptions that are made about the measures developed by the researchers.

Table 3.4: Assumptions made about the measures for self-report measures to achieve their intended purpose.

Each measure developed by the researcher should...	
Assumption H	Fully captures the concept or an aspect of the concept that it is intended to capture
Assumption I	Precisely captures the aspect of the concept that it is intended to capture
Assumption J	Captures a single concept and no other
Assumption K	Is consistent in its capturing of the concept that it was designed to capture

The more the assumptions in Tables 3.3 and 3.4 are upheld, the less will be the errors due to measurement (EDM). And the more we reduce the errors due to measurement the more likely we will be to uphold the Golden Assumption (GA), and the more suitable the data we captured will be for statistical analysis. For those of you already familiar with the concepts of measurement validity and reliability, you will notice that the assumptions listed in Tables 3.3 and 3.4 are derived from the definitions of "validity" and "reliability" within the context of measurement.

What are measurement validity and reliability, and do I need both?

Validity in the context of measurement is the extent to which the tool you are using to measure a specific characteristic fully and accurately captures what it was designed to capture and "nothing else" (Heaton, 1975, p. 159; see also Frey, 2018). Validity focuses on the systematic errors due to measurement. Reliability is defined as the consistency or stability of a measure (see Frey, 2018). Reliability focuses on random errors due to measurement. How are these two characteristics of measures different from one another?

I will attempt to explain the difference between the general notions of measurement validity and reliability by using a familiar context most readers can relate to and understand easily. These general notions will later be transferred and applied to self-report measurement.

Validity versus reliability of measurement in general, what's the difference?

All of us have used a bathroom scale at one time or another in our lives to determine our body weight. Let's say I have a mechanical bathroom scale in front of me to determine my body weight, and I do the following:

Episode 1: I get on the bathroom scale, and it tells me I weigh 200 pounds. I get off and get on it again, and it tells me that I weigh 210 pounds. I get off and get on it again, and it tells me that I weigh 195 pounds. Given that reliability is a measure's consistency, how consistent is this scale? It is not consistent at all. Therefore, this is not a reliable measure of my body weight.

Episode 2: I get a different bathroom scale and get on it. It tells me that I weigh 200 pounds. I get off and get on it again, and it tells me that I weigh 200 pounds. I get off and get on it again, and it tells me that I weigh 200 pounds. How consistent is this scale? It is very consistent, and so it is reliable! But wait a minute, is 200 pounds my weight? This latter question embodies validity. Even though this bathroom scale is reliable, it could be that 200 pounds is my true weight, or it might not be my true weight. I wouldn't know for sure. Simply because I am getting the same weight reading every time, I get on this bathroom scale does not establish that the number I am obtaining is my true weight. I could be lighter or heavier than 200 pounds. Reliability does not tell me whether the reading I am getting is my actual weight, validity does. You might ask yourself, why wouldn't I trust the weight reading from a bathroom scale? The answer lies in the imperfect nature of measuring instruments. It could be that the spring in the bathroom scale has rusted and is underweighting or the scale is not starting at zero even though it shows a zero reading before you step on it. Anything is possible and you wouldn't know for sure unless you had an objective way of assessing its validity.

Let's say you were trying to capture body weight to differentiate among individuals and were using a weight scale that was consistent. Still, you did not know if the readings from this scale are a true reflection of the body weights you intend to measure. Would you use these weight readings to differentiate among the individuals you measured? Of course not, because if you did, you wouldn't know exactly what you are analyzing. For the weight numbers to be useful, you need to first be sure that the weight scale you are using reflects the true body weights of the individuals being measured, and you also need to make sure this weight scale is consistent in capturing these body weights. Validity, therefore, needs to be established before reliability. Both validity and reliability are necessary for the measures you are using to yield the type of data suitable for statistical analysis.

Validity and reliability in self-report measurement

The notions of validity and reliability as illustrated in the general example above can be directly transferred and applied to the context of self-report measurement. In the example about the weight scale, the reading that you got by stepping onto the mechanical scale was your indicator of your body weight. In the case of capturing impulse buying, study participants are given a response scale that allows them to react to the four measures by expressing their level of agreement or disagreement with each. In this case, the scale ranges from strongly disagree to strongly agree along five levels of agreement: Strongly Disagree, Disagree, Neither Disagree nor Agree, Agree, and Strongly Agree. From among the measures developed by Rook and Fisher (1995) the four I chose to use were:

> "I see it, I buy it" describes me
> I often buy things spontaneously
> I often buy things without thinking
> "Just do it" describes the way I buy things

A participant reacts to each measure by choosing among the five levels of agreement ranging from strongly disagree to strongly agree. After data is collected, the researcher will then convert the participant reactions into numerals.

> An example of such conversion is:
> Strongly Disagree=1
> Disagree=2
> Neither Disagree nor Agree=3
> Agree=4
> Strong Agree=5

You can expect differences in study participants' reactions to each of the four indicators designed to capture the same construct. These could be due to a real differentiation among study participants' levels of impulsive buying. However, these differences in reaction could also be due to a systematic error attributed to the characteristics of an indicator and how it is interpreted by each participant relative to what a researcher meant by it. For example, a researcher might have meant to capture the kinetic aspect of impulse buying by using the indicator "I see it I buy it describes me" whereas the respondents might interpret it as frequency of buying and react to this indicator accordingly. In this case, the researcher might think that they captured "impulse buying" when they captured "buying frequency," a totally different construct. The extent to which an indicator is systematically interpreted in the exact same way as the researcher intended addresses the notion of indicator quality. In a way, all four indicators of impulse buying are likely to differ to a certain extent from each other in terms of quality, but you wouldn't know it by simply looking at how an individual reacted to them.

Although you can't be sure which of the four indicators reflects true impulse buying, having multiple indicators offers a new possibility: if you can somehow (1) determine what these indicators reflect in common and distinguish that from what is peculiar to each indicator, and (2) separate what you find from what is reflected in common by other sets of indicators designed to capture other constructs, then you might determine whether the multiple indicators designed to measure a construct seem to be measuring the same invisible construct. In this example, what these self-report indicators have in common would be your best estimate of an individual's impulse buying tendency. What is peculiar to each indicator would be the error. The more a specific indicator reflects what all indicators have in common, the stronger the arrow coming from the invisible construct to that indicator, and the more this indicator reflects a valid reading. The more valid an indicator is, the higher it would be evaluated in quality. The less a particular indicator reflects what all indicators have in common, the weaker is the arrow coming from the invisible construct to that indicator, the less this indicator is valid and the lower it would be evaluated in terms of quality. Validity is not absolute and as such, researchers attempt to find out the degree to which their measures are valid to be confident they captured what they set out to capture.

Don't you wish a quantitative analytic tool existed to conduct the sort of analysis that would yield what is common in a set of indicators and what is unique in each indicator? With such a tool, you could objectively differentiate among the four indicators of impulse buying in terms of their quality. You would also be able to discard an indicator of lower quality relative to others and keep only the indicators of comparable quality. Using such a tool would allow you to use the higher quality indicators remaining to compute the best available estimate of the relative impulse buying score for each participant in your study. These scores will allow you to differentiate among individuals based on their impulse shopping scores. The good news is that quantitative analytic tools for doing what the above paragraphs describe do exist and, when used correctly, are very helpful in separating valid measures from those that are problematic and arriving at valid best estimates for the constructs meant to be measured (more on this in Chapter 9 of this book).

The preceding very roughly explains the logic of using a technique known as "factor analysis" in the context of testing the internal structure of a set of multiple indicators and addresses several aspects of construct validity (see Nunnally, 1978; Pedhazur & Pedhazur Shmelkin, 1991; Jin, Kim & Kim, 2020).

Just as is the case in every aspect of human life, scientists cannot agree on whether there are many types of self-report measurement validity (see Nunnally, 1978) or whether what some refer to as validity types are, in fact, different aspects of construct validity (see Pedhauser & Pedhauser Schmelkin, 1991). I tend to agree with Pedhauser & Pedhauser Schmelkin (1991) that our primary goal is to establish construct validity, and what some scientists call validity types (face validity, etc.) are, in fact, facets of construct validity. Table 3.5 lists common ways of conceiving validity in self-report measurement.

Table 3.5: Facets of validity in self-report measurement.

Label	Definition	Type of Assessment
Construct Validity	The extent to which a measure captures what it is supposed to capture fully and captures nothing else	Derived by looking at the assessment from the facets listed below
Face Validity	An informal examination of the wording used in a measure to determine if these words, taken altogether, semantically reflect the meaning of the definition of the construct that this measure is designed to capture. We look for an overlap of meaning between a measure and the definition of the construct it aims to capture. We also look for an overlap in meaning across two or more measures designed to capture the same construct	Qualitative
Content Validity	A formal examination of scores derived from self-report measures is used to determine if the relationships among these scores show that all measures used to capture the same construct reflect a single and common meaning (as shown in Chapter 9). If we have quantitative evidence that all the measures designed to capture a single construct are capturing the same invisible variable and no other variable, then we have evidence of content validity.	Qualitative and Quantitative
Convergent Validity	Do the scores, stemming from the measures we use to capture a specific construct, correlate with scores of established measures already shown to capture this same construct or scores of constructs that are known to be related to this construct? If yes, then we establish convergent validity.	Quantitative
Discriminant Validity	Do the scores, stemming from the measures we use to capture a specific construct, correlate with scores of other measures that are known to be –unrelated –to this construct? If no, then we establish discriminant validity.	Quantitative

It might not surprise the reader that the labels for validity and their interpretations vary quite a bit across the social sciences. Table 3.5 lists what I consider a very interpretable set that helps the reader understand what needs to be established before we can say that our measures captured the construct(s) we set out to capture and nothing else. Among the four listed facets of construct validity (face, content, convergency, and discriminant), face and content validity are the most accessible to academic and industry researchers who use existing self-report measures as part of their research project. Existing self-report measures can be found in published studies about the same topic as your research project or in compilations of measures used in specific content areas (e.g., Marketing Scales Handbook; Measures of Personality and Social Psychological Attitudes; Measuring Health: A Guide to Rating Scales and Questionnaires, and others). Regardless of whether the measures you use are adopted from those previously used by others and whether they were validated by previous researchers, you need to establish their face and content validity in your study before determining whether you can use them in your own data analyses or hypothesis testing. In addition to face and content validity, convergent and discriminant validity are typically tested by academic researchers aiming to introduce a new set of measures for an existing construct or proposing a new construct along with a new set of measures.

Some of the existing tools for assessing content validity will be demonstrated in Chapter 9 of this book. It is important to reiterate that measurement of validity is study-dependent, which means a set of measures found to be valid in one study might not be as valid in another. That is why it is critical to evaluate face and content validity in each study regardless of how a set of measures performed in previous studies.

What about the reliability of self-report measures?

For self-report measures, reliability is conceptually achieved if a study participant provides the same answer to the same question if asked the question on two separate occasions (see Carmines & Zeller, 1979). The problem with this conceptualization of reliability is that, at a practical level, there are many reasons why it is more applicable to a mechanical device designed to capture a specific characteristic, such as a bathroom scale capturing weight than it is to a human reacting to a question/measure. Human respondents might not answer the same question the same way twice for reasons unrelated to whether the measure is reliable. For example, a respondent might change their mind due to the passage of time between the two instances in which they were asked the same question. Or a respondent might answer the question differently the second time because they are puzzled by being asked the same question twice. These sorts of problems with the conceptualization of reliability resulted in the emergence of internal consistency reliability (See Carmines & Zeller, 1979; Pedhazur & Pedhazur Schmelkin, 1991; Salkind, 2010) in the context of self-report measurement. Internal consistency reliability involves asking multiple questions or measures that all overlap with the definition of the concept one wishes to measure and, after first confirming the validity of these measures, looking at the consistency in the reactions to these measures within respondents.

For example, in the case of impulse buying, let's say the following two indicators were confirmed to be valid through the course of using relevant quantitative techniques (these techniques are demonstrated in Chapter 9 of this book):

"I see it, I buy it" describes me
I often buy things spontaneously

Reliability would be achieved if Johnny's score on the first indicator is consistent with his score on the second indicator and if this consistency is observed within (not across) all other study participants. Consistency in this example is Johnny's tendency to agree or strongly agree on both indicators or disagree or strongly disagree on both indicators. Inconsistency would occur if Johnny agreed in his reaction to the first indicator but disagreed with the second one. The more inconsistent the patterns of responses are within the reactions of more study participants, the less reliable would be the measures in capturing what they set out to capture. It is important to note that perfect consistency is seldom achieved. Reliability quantifies relative consistency and is the outcome of random error. For example, a respondent might not be paying the same attention when reacting to one indicator as when reacting to another. The technique for quantifying internal consistency reliability will be demonstrated in Chapter 9 of this book. Just as was the case for validity, reliability is also study-dependent, which means a set of measures found to be reliable in one study might not be as reliable in another study. That is why it is critical to evaluate reliability in each study regardless of how a set of measures performed in previous studies.

The order of testing validity and reliability

For self-report measures to be useful, they must be both valid and reliable. There is a specific sequence in the way I list them. Validity must be established first so that reliability can then be tested. It is not possible to reverse the sequence for two reasons:
1. It would be illogical and useless to find out how reliable specific measures are if we are not sure what these measures are capturing, and
2. The algorithm used for quantifying internal consistency reliability assumes that all measures being subjected to reliability testing have already been proven to be valid and, as a result, the algorithm provides a mathematical weight for each additional measure used to capture the same concept (see the formula in Carmines and Zeller, 1979). The algorithm would result in a totally erroneous reliability coefficient if the measures subjected to testing are invalid. In other words, a researcher needs to make sure a measure captures what the researcher set out to capture before testing it for reliability.

With pre-planning, a researcher can quantify validity and reliability and objectively evaluate errors due to measurement (EDM).

Can I conceptually visualize validity and reliability?

Conveniently, the Invisible to Visible Framework (ITVF) shown in Figures 3.4 and 3.5 already subsumes validity and reliability, and Figure 3.6 labels their location within this model.

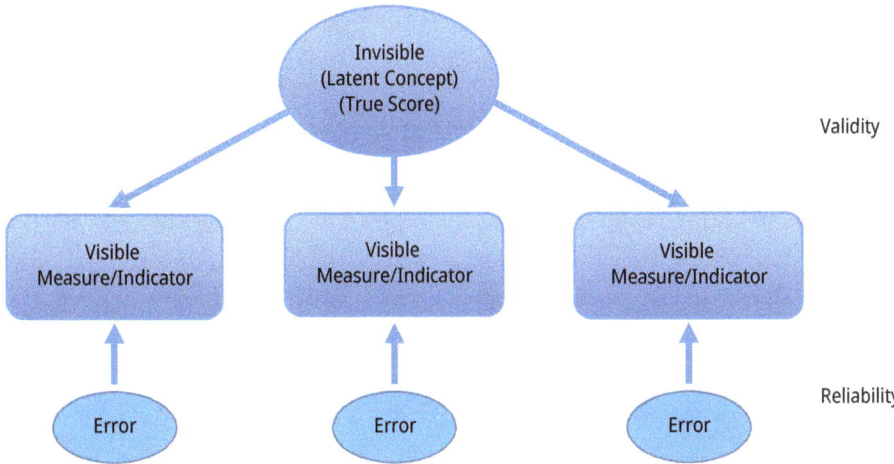

Figure 3.6: The location of validity and reliability in the Visible to Invisible Framework. Source: Author.

In Figure 3.6, the arrow from the top represents validity, and the arrow from the bottom represents reliability. Validity is ideally established if the "invisible construct" is the only influence on the "visible measures/indicators" – low systematic error. Reliability is ideally established if all potential sources of influence other than the "invisible construct" have no influence on the visible – low random error. The relative influence of the arrows coming from the top and the relative influence of the arrows coming from the bottom determine the errors due to measurement. The more valid and more reliable the measures are, the fewer are the errors due to measurement (EDM).

What about the precision with which we capture the variation of these concepts?

In addition to the validity and reliability of the concepts we're trying to capture, we also need to pay attention to the precision with which we capture the variation of these concepts. The level of precision not only will determine how well a researcher will be able to differentiate among individuals along the variables they capture, but also which algorithms they will be able to use and which relationships they will be able to test for these variables. Historically, precision has been discussed within the context of the level of measurement. Scientists tell us there are four levels of measurement across all the sciences. They are known as the nominal, ordinal, interval, and ratio levels (Stevens, 1946). They deal with what a numeral means to the researcher in the context of each of these levels of measurement. A numeral is a symbol (e.g., 1, 2, 3, 4, etc.) that is sometimes quantitative (e.g., a number) and sometimes not quantitative (e.g., represents a response category and nothing else).

Table 3.6 provides a brief description of the characteristics of each of these levels

Table 3.6: The Four Levels of Measurement.

Name	Characteristics	Suitability
Nominal	A numeral represents a category of the variable. No natural zero. No mathematical relationships among numerals.	Demographics that cannot be counted: gender, occupation, ethnicity, and similar concepts that can only be categorical
Ordinal	A numeral represents a rank of a category. The intervals among these categories are not equal. No natural zero. Basic mathematical relationships exist among numerals: 1<2<3, but not how much lower or higher.	Most social science concepts that can be measured at this level can also be measured at the interval level, which provides the researcher with more precision.
Interval	A numeral represents a category. The categories are rank ordered. The interval among the categories is equal or closer to equal than in the ordinal level. No natural zero. More complex mathematical relationships exist among the categories: 1<2<3, and how much lower and higher.	The perfect example here is temperature. However, the following types of social science concepts are closer to the interval level than to the ordinal level. They are typically captured with response scales: Beliefs, attitudes, intentions, and similarly less visible concepts. Also, behaviors that cannot reasonably be counted.
Ratio	The numeral is a number that represents a count. There is a natural zero. Most complex mathematical relationships exist among these numerals.	Behaviors that can reasonably be counted.

Table 3.6 shows the characteristics of the four levels of measurement. The nominal level of measurement uses categories to capture the variation. There are no mathematical relationships among these categories. For example, let's say respondents are asked to indicate the primary mode of transportation they used this morning and given six choices: subway, bus, personal car, walking, ride-sharing service, and others. There would be no mathematical relationships among these five categories even if they were assigned numerals: subway=1, bus=2, personal car=3, walking=4, and ride-sharing service=5 or other=6. In this context, we wouldn't be able to say that 1<2<3<4<5<6. In addition, concerning the idea of a natural zero, which is the total absence of a variable (not absence of a category), here we wouldn't be able to say that the mode of transportation this morning can be absent because they got to their desti-

nation using some specific mode. The absence of a variable is only possible when its count is zero, and this is only possible for the ratio level of measurement. How many cups of coffee did you drink this morning? If the respondent answers zero, then this variable is absent for this respondent. For the other levels of measurement, not choosing a response category or disagreeing with a statement does not indicate the absence of the entire variable but simply a reaction to information about this variable. For example, if a respondent is asked to indicate whether they agree or disagree on a five-point scale: "Strongly Disagree," "Disagree," "Neither Agree nor Disagree," "Agree" or "Strongly Agree" to the following statement: "I enjoy drinking coffee." Let's say they choose "Strongly Disagree." This would not indicate the absence of a respondent's liking of coffee but rather a level of dislike for coffee.

It is worth noting, not surprisingly, that there has been a historical disagreement among researchers regarding whether response scales correspond to an ordinal or interval level of measurement. The reality is that they are somewhere in between but closer to an interval than they are to an ordinal level (see Pedhazur & Pedhazur Schmelkin, 1991). And so, in this book, consistent with psychology and related social science literature, we will consider response scales to be interval-level measures.

Precision and the level of measurement

Use the following guide when considering how precisely you need to capture the concepts that you are attempting to measure:

First, consider the type of variable this concept represents (e.g., belief, attitude, intention, behavior, etc.). Second, determine the maximum amount of reasonably possible variation for this concept. Third, use the level of measurement that permits you to capture the maximum amount of variation possible (see suitability column in Table 3.6). Always do so unless you have a methodologically sound argument for not doing so.

What would qualify as a methodologically sound argument? Let's say you're trying to capture social media platform usage among respondents. Since this is a behavior and can theoretically be counted, the corresponding principle would be to capture this concept using a ratio level of measurement. Doing so, for example, would consist of asking your respondents to provide you with the number of hours and minutes they spent on each of the following platforms in the past 24 hours: Instagram, Facebook, X, and YouTube. And this count would provide you with the most precise estimate of usage. However, when you pause and think about it for a moment, respondents don't really keep track of the exact time they spend on social media. Social media use seems almost automated as people sporadically check their feeds numerous times a day. So, asking for the number of hours and minutes by relying on respondent memories would be unreasonable and would surely result in erroneous estimates. The more precise way of doing so would be to ask respondents to access each social media app on their phone, look up the usage counter provided by the app, then simply copy the amount of usage time provided by the app counter. However, asking a participant to do so would be very time-consuming since most social media app users have no idea where to find this information. It would take many minutes of valuable data collection time to provide respondents with video instructions on how to do so. Given the preceding, a researcher might still decide that relying on the respondents' memories is the most time efficient way of getting a glimpse at their relative frequency of using specific social media platforms. In this case, it would be reasonable for a researcher to argue that, even though the concept they are trying to measure is a behavior, capturing this concept using an interval level of measurement would be more methodologically reasonable than using a ratio level. Instead of asking for the number of hours and minutes, a researcher might ask for the frequency a respondent used each of the social media platforms in the past 24 hours. The example below shows how a researcher might ask the respondents to do so:

How often did you use each of the following social media platforms in the past 24 hours?

	Never	Rarely	Sometimes	Frequently	Very Frequently
Instagram					
Facebook					
X (formerly Twitter)					
YouTube					

While capturing the variation of usage in the manner given in the example above would not be the most precise way, it would still give the researcher a respondent's relative frequency of using the four social media platforms. It is more reasonable to expect respondents to be able to recall the relative frequency of their usage of social media platforms than the precise number of hours and minutes of using each social media platform. More information on the use of scales and respondents' recall abilities will be provided in Chapters 5 through 8.

A Self-Report Measurement Mindset (SRMM)

For every research project that involves understanding the collective human thought-process regarding a specific topic, a researcher must first determine the important concepts to measure. The most reliable sources for determining which variables are essential for a given study are the literature review related to the topic being investigated by the study and an established theoretical framework pertaining to the topic. One cannot rule out brainstorming with a research team as a source of potentially important variables. And, of course, for those researchers working on a client project, another source of important concepts will surely be the client. Once a researcher determines the concepts important to measure in their study, the mindset depicted in

Figure 3.7 needs to kick in when considering how to capture each concept through self-report measurement. The mindset is not about asking questions but about using questions as indicators of what you need to measure. Figure 3.7 illustrates the main components of the Self-Report Measurement Mindset (SRMM).

Figure 3.7 depicts what I call a self-report measurement mindset.

a. For every concept a researcher needs to measure, the first task is to define it clearly. Defining it, at a very minimum, will (1) Clarify the meaning of what the concept represents to the researchers; (2) Help researchers determine how simple or complex a specific concept is and how invisible it is; (3) Help researchers ensure the meaning of each measure used for the concept is overlapping with the definition given to that concept.

b. Once a concept has been clearly defined, it is important to pause and consider whether the concept, as described, is reasonable to measure based on who you plan on measuring. Whether a concept is reasonable to measure will depend on many factors, such as how self-aware about this concept are the people whom you plan on measuring. For example, asking how many burgers a person has eaten in the past year would not be reasonable, given the limits of human memory. Asking someone to tell you about some economic condition using jargon from the field of economics would not be reasonable unless the person is an economist and understands the jargon (see Chapters 5 through 8).

c. Once a concept has been defined and found reasonable to capture, the researcher needs to determine if it is likely to be a simple concept that is relatively visible, such as age, hair color, etc., or a complex concept that is more invisible, such as those involving a belief, an attitude, a feeling, etc. This determination about how visible or invisible a concept is will lead the researchers toward one of two routes: a path for more visible concepts and another for more invisible concepts.

d. For both routes, the task will be to find a way to externalize the concept. Externalization will be done with a single indicator if the concept is more visible and multiple indicators if the concept is more invisible. Here, you also need to start thinking about a suitable measurement level for this concept's indicators.

e. Regardless of whether to use a single indicator or multiple indicators, the formulation of these should be guided by principles of measurement extracted from the body of knowledge of self-report science (see Chapters 5 through 8).

f. When using a single indicator for a concept, the researcher can only hope that the indicator reflects the true nature of the invisible concept they set out to capture and that the errors due to measurement (EDM) are not substantial. This is since, for single indicators, there are no readily available tools to help the researchers determine the extent of errors due to measurement. Researchers proceed with their data analysis solely because they have faith in their measures but without evidence that their measures are not error plagued.

g. When using multiple indicators, a researcher can test the validity and reliability of their indicators by using a set of analytic tools that quantify the extent of errors

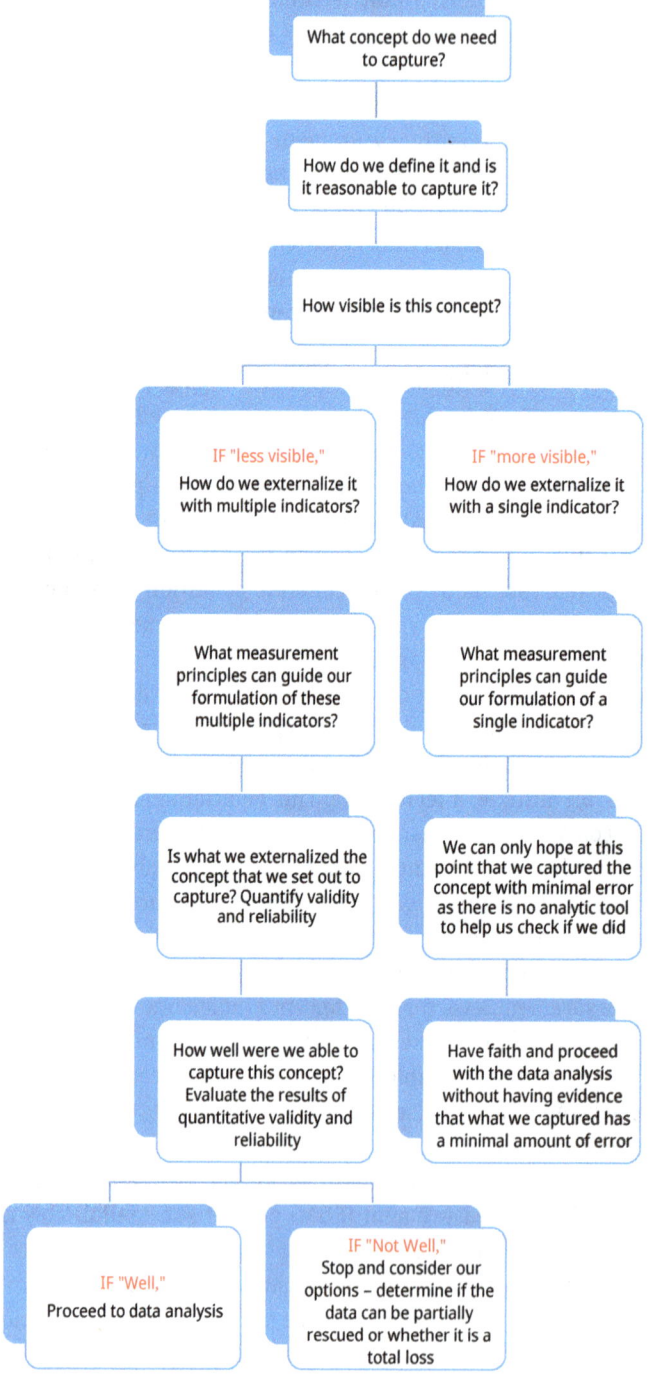

Figure 3.7: A Self-Report Measurement Mindset (SRMM). Source: Author.

due to measurement (see Chapter 9). If the analytic tools reveal an acceptable level of errors due to measurement (EDM), then they can proceed with their statistical analyses. If the analytic tools reveal an unacceptable amount of EDM, the researchers must stop and evaluate their options. Depending on how widespread the unacceptable amount of EDM is, researchers might: (1) Lose lower quality indicators of specific constructs but still retain their ability to capture those constructs with the remaining higher quality indicators; (2) Realize that all indicators of a specific construct were of low quality and lose their ability to capture that construct entirely; (3) Realize that all indicators of all constructs were of low quality and become unable to move forward with any data analyses. Fortunately, the first two outcomes are the most common, and the last outcome is extremely rare, though not impossible. In the extremely rare case where the third outcome occurs, there usually are more problems with the study than errors due to measurement.

The need for principles of self-report measurement

With pre-planning and multiple indicators, a researcher can quantify the validity and reliability of measures used to capture invisible concepts. The tools used for quantifying validity and reliability enable a researcher to pinpoint whether a measure they are using is of lower or higher quality than others and determine which measures to keep and which ones to discard. Being able to do so allows a researcher to determine if they were successful in capturing what they set out to capture and, therefore, able to proceed with their statistical analyses. The quantification of validity and reliability will be demonstrated by example in Chapter 9. While it is great that we can quantify validity and reliability, such quantification is only possible after the data has been collected. This is so since before the data is collected, we can only guess how respondents will interpret the measures we are asking them to react. We won't be able to know for sure how they interpreted the measures until after we get the data. And, by the time data collection is completed, there is very little a researcher can do if they find out that their measures have unacceptable levels of validity and reliability. Their only option then would be to redo the study, and this outcome is neither reasonable nor desirable.

Can I do anything to reduce the possibility of errors due to measurement (EDM) in my study before my data is collected?

Violating the assumptions in Tables 3.3 and Table 3.4 contributes to errors due to measurement (EDM), and the more EDM is involved in a study, the less able the researcher will be to move forward with their statistical analyses plan that would reveal the collective thought-process they wish to uncover. Our obsession should be to do everything we can to ensure the assumptions about the participant and about the measures are upheld. There is a strong need for sound advice on how to do so. Where would such advice come from? Fortunately, there are many studies spanning almost one hundred years, and the findings of many of these studies address the assumptions listed in Tables 3.3. and Table 3.4. Chapter 4 details the methodology I used to extract information from this body of knowledge and arrive at principles and expectations researchers can use as a guide when developing their self-report measures and avoid high levels of errors due to measurement.

References

Buskirk, T. D. (2020). Big Data. In P. Atkinson, S. Delamont, A. Cernat, J.W. Sakshaug, & R.A. Williams (Eds.), *SAGE Research Methods Foundations*. https://www.doi.org/10.4135/9781526421036943171

Carmines, E.G. & Zeller, R.A. (1979). *Reliability and Validity Assessment*. Thousand Oaks, CA: Sage.

DuBois, P.H. (1970). *A History of Psychological Testing*. Boston, MA: Allyn and Bacon.

Elasmar, M. (2019). *Validity and Reliability Challenges when Extracting Public Opinion Trends from Social Media Expressions*. In World Association for Public Opinion Research (WAPOR) Conference. Ontario, Canada.

Frey, B. (2018). *The SAGE encyclopedia of educational research, measurement, and evaluation* (Vols. 1–4). Thousand Oaks, CA: SAGE Publications, Inc. doi: 10.4135/9781506326139

Gulliksen, H. (1950). *Theory of Mental Tests*. New York: Wiley.

Heaton, G.B. (1975). *Writing English Language Tests*. Second edition. London: Longman.

Ignatow, G. & Mihalcea, R. (2018). Opinion mining. In *An introduction to text mining* (pp. 187–198). SAGE Publications, Inc, https://www.doi.org/10.4135/9781506336985

Jin, W., Kim, J., & Kim, S. (2020). Factor Analysis. In P. Atkinson, S. Delamont, A. Cernat, J.W. Sakshaug, & R.A. Williams (Eds.), *SAGE Research Methods Foundations*. https://www.doi.org/10.4135/9781526421036943172

Lavrakas, P. J. (2008). *Encyclopedia of survey research methods* (Vols. 1–0). Thousand Oaks, CA: Sage Publications, Inc. doi: 10.4135/9781412963947

Lord, F.M. & Novick, M.R. (1968). *Statistical Theory of Mental Test Scores*. Reading, MA: Addison-Wesley.

Maruyama, G. M. (1998). What does it mean to model hypothesized causal processes with nonexperimental data? In *Basics of structural equation modeling* (pp. 3–14). SAGE Publications, Inc., https://www.doi.org/10.4135/9781483345109

McNabb, D. E. (2014). Measurement error. In *Nonsampling error in social surveys* (pp. 97–113). SAGE Publications, Inc., https://www.doi.org/10.4135/9781483352923

Nunnally, J.C. (1978). *Psychometric Theory*. New York, NY: McGraw-Hill.

Rook, D.W. and Fisher, R.J. (1995). Normative influences on impulsive buying behaviors. *Journal of Consumer Research, 22*, 305–313.

Salkind, N. J. (2010). *Encyclopedia of research design* (Vols. 1–0). Thousand Oaks, CA: SAGE Publications, Inc. doi: 10.4135/9781412961288

Spearman, C. (1904). ""General intelligence"", objectively determined and measured. *American Journal of Psychology, 15*, 201–293.

Spector, P.E. (1992). *Summated Rating Scale Construction*. Thousand Oaks, CA: Sage.

Pedhazur, E. & Pedhazur Schmelkin, L. (1991). *Measurement, Design and Analysis*. Hillsdale, NJ: Erlbaum.

Stevens, S. S. (1946). On the Theory of Scales of Measurement. *Science, 103,(2684)*, 677–680.

Tourangeau, R. Rips, L.J. and Rasinski, K. (2000). *The Psychology of Survey Response*. New York, NY: Cambridge University Press.

Yang, B. Cardie, C. (2012). Extracting Opinion Expressions with semi-Markov Conditional Random Fields. In *Proceedings of the 2012 Joint Conference on Empirical Methods in Natural Language Processing and Computational Natural Language Learning*, pages 1335–1345, Jeju Island, Korea.

Yang, B. & Cardie, C. (2013). Joint Inference for Fine-grained Opinion-extraction. In *Proceedings of the 51st Annual Meeting of the Association for Computational Linguistics*, pages 1640–1649.

Yang, B. and Cardie, C. (2014). Joint Modeling of Opinion Expression Extraction and Attribute Classification. *Transactions of the Association for Computational Linguistics*, 2: 505–516, Sofia, Bulgaria.

Chapter 4
What can a researcher do to meet the self-report measurement assumptions?

Objectives of Chapter 4: This chapter provides an overview of the methodology that I used to systematically collect the articles that are used in Chapter 5 through 8 of this book. This methodology can be used by other researchers to build upon the principles and expectations I extracted from the literature that I found. Chapters 5 through 8 dig deeply into the scientific literature pertaining to specific aspects of self-report measurement. Each body of literature deals with an aspect researchers are very likely to encounter when developing self-report measures across various disciplines and within academia and industry. For several decades, aided by a continuously changing team of graduate students, I have been collecting articles investigating these aspects and summarizing their findings with an eye on learning what works for preempting errors when using self-report measurement.

Methodology for articles consulted

Type of articles consulted

An article was read and logged if it met the following criteria:
1. Does the article investigate at least one aspect of self-report measurement?
2. Does the article appear in a peer-reviewed academic journal?
3. Does the article include a methodology section that follows the method of science?
4. By reading this article, can we determine what its authors found?
5. By reading this article, can we identify takeaways that affect the practice of self-report measurement?

Sources of articles

The articles were found using a combination of the following search strategies:
1. Database searches of Sociological Abstracts, Psych-Info, Google Scholar, ABI-Inform International, and JSTOR.
2. Examination of the reference pages of relevant articles to identify additional cited articles that might be relevant.

Information extraction and organization

Articles addressing the same aspect of self-report measurement were stored in the same spreadsheet to systematically extract information from each article and allow quality control checks. After an article was deemed to fit the criteria for inclusion, the following details about it were recorded in the spreadsheet:
1. An APA Reference for the manuscript
2. What did the authors set out to investigate?
3. What method(s) did the authors use?
4. What did they find?
5. What does this mean for a researcher who uses self-report measurement?

Storing this information in this specific way allowed quality control checks. Multiple research assistants were asked to review each article summary to determine whether it agreed with each other's reading. When two assistants did not agree with the same summary when reading the same article, a third research assistant was asked to read the article and find a solution to the disagreement. As progress was made in compiling all this information, new waves of research assistants were asked to review summaries made by previous research assistants. Doing so helped confirm that the summaries reflected the readings of the articles by multiple graduate research assistants over the years. Each new group of graduate assistants was also asked to search for additional articles that could be added to the existing summaries. The number of articles about the same aspect of self-report measurement grew through iteration, and their summaries got progressively clearer over time.

Type of knowledge contribution

By going through the summaries about a specific aspect of self-report measurement, I noticed the bodies of knowledge varied greatly in size. Some topics were the subject of numerous studies, while others received less attention. There were also findings for particular aspects of self-report measurement that were consistent across studies and some not so consistent across studies. Some findings could be translated into actions, while others simply yielded important information about what researchers can expect to happen but did not result in recommended actions. The more studies existed about a specific aspect and the more consistent the findings across these studies, the more confident I became in their implications for self-report measurement. As a result, two types of outcomes stemmed from summarizing these studies:

Principles – These consist of definite guides to actions that would help those who adopt them preempt the introduction of errors due to measurement in their studies. Principles were extracted for specific aspects of self-report measurement if there were relatively numerous studies about those aspects and if enough findings across these studies pointed to a same outcome. In addition, only findings that can be translated into actions that a researcher can take – what to do or what not to do – were the basis for principles.

Expectations – These consist of important information for researchers to know and specific outcomes they can anticipate when utilizing self-report measurement. However, they do not constitute a guide to action.

Narrative for each aspect of self-report measurement

While I am sure there are readers who appreciate a more formal and detailed writing style when looking at a summary of a body of knowledge, and some who like to see all the spreadsheets in which the studies were logged, I am equally confident there are others who prefer the essence of these summaries. I thought about which approach to use in this book and chose the latter. Each chapter about a specific aspect of self-report measurement begins with a synopsis followed by the takeaways of principles and expectations. Any reflections or commentary on my end are clearly labeled to differentiate such editorial content from the information extracted from the literature.

Connecting the knowledge gained to the assumptions

Chapter 3 of this book identified assumptions about respondents and measures. It was noted that researchers need to ensure these assumptions are upheld for their self-report measures to yield the type of data that is valid and reliable and thus suitable for subsequent analyses. These appear in Table 3.3 and 3.4 of Chapter 3 of this book and are reproduced in Tables 4.1 and 4.2 below:

Table 4.1: Assumptions made about respondents for self-report measures to achieve their intended purpose.

When reacting to a measure or answering a question, the respondent	
Assumption A	Is willing to disclose information about themselves
Assumption B	Is truthful and not deliberately lying
Assumption C	Interprets each measure/question the way the researcher intended and in the same way that others who are also being measured are interpreting them
Assumption D	Can correctly recall needed information from memory to react to each measure/question

Table 4.1 (continued)

When reacting to a measure or answering a question, the respondent	
Assumption E	Can easily move from one measure/question to another when multiple measures/questions are included
Assumption F	Is self-aware
Assumption G	Is not influenced by one or more aspects of the questions/measures to which they are asked to react

Table 4.2: Assumptions made about the measures so that they can achieve their intended purpose.

Each measure developed by the researcher should ...	
Assumption H	Fully capture the concept or an aspect of the concept that it is intended to capture
Assumption I	Precisely capture the aspect of the concept that it is intended to capture
Assumption J	Capture a single concept and no other
Assumption K	Be consistent in its capturing of the concept that it was designed to capture

The principles and expectations, extracted and summarized in the following chapters directly affect whether these assumptions are upheld. The two tables above will be repeated at the beginning of each chapter to make it easier to see how the information covered in a chapter is related to one or more of the assumptions listed. The assumptions that are relevant to the contents of a specific chapter will be bolded in the tables placed at the beginning of each chapter. Doing so will make it easier for the reader to connect which assumptions are addressed by which chapter and why the information provided in each chapter is essential to their ability to use self-report measures successfully.

Limitations

The work presented here is a foundation for others to build and improve. The aspects of self-report measurement addressed in Chapters 5, 6, 7, and 8 are certainly not exhaustive. They are those about which a substantial number of articles exist. Despite the best intentions, the articles found, many of which are cited in the following chapters, are not comprehensive. The principles and expectations might not apply to all situations that involve self-report measurement. Every research project is different, and respondents are not expected to react homogeneously to the same self-report measurement across study contexts regardless of their level of education, demographics, areas of specialty, and other individual characteristics. However, the information in the chapters can serve as a "lowest common denominator" guide for researchers to preempt errors due to measurement in the study they are planning.

Chapter 5
Principles and expectations: Statement content and placement

Objectives of chapter 5: You will need to make many decisions regarding the content and placement of measures in a questionnaire. In terms of content, these decisions include whether a measure can consist of more than a single concept, whether a measure should be long or short, and whether a measure should allow participants to react by providing freestyle text or simply choosing from among predetermined response categories. Regarding placement, these decisions include where to locate measures that vary in focus in a questionnaire. While there are undoubtedly other decisions you will need to consider regarding the content and placement of measures, this chapter addresses the aspects about which there appears to be a consensus in the corresponding literature.

Which assumptions are addressed in this chapter?

Table 5.1: Assumptions made about respondents for self-report measures to achieve their intended purpose.

When reacting to a measure or answering a question, the respondent	
Assumption A	**Is willing to disclose information about themselves**
Assumption B	Is truthful and not deliberately lying
Assumption C	**Interprets each measure or question the way the researcher intended and in the same way that others who are also being measured are interpreting them**
Assumption D	Can correctly recall needed information from memory to react to each measure or question
Assumption E	**Can easily move from one measure/question to another**
Assumption F	Is self-aware
Assumption G	**Is reacting to a measure without being influenced by any aspect of the measure itself other than the content that directly overlaps with the invisible concept that needs to be captured**

The assumptions bolded in Tables 5.1 and 5.2 above are affected by violations of the principles provided in the sections of this chapter. The more confusing is the content of measures, the less likely a participant will be to continue reacting to the measures, the more their reactions will be influenced by something other than what the researcher set out to measure, the more likely the researcher will be capturing something different than what they set to measure and the more likely the researcher will obtain inconsistent measures.

Table 5.2: Assumptions made about the measures for self-report measures to achieve their intended purpose.

Each measure developed by the researcher should . . .	
Assumption H	Fully capture the concept or an aspect of the concept that it is intended to capture
Assumption I	Precisely capture the aspect of the concept that it is intended to capture
Assumption J	**Capture a single concept and no other**
Assumption K	**Consistently capture the concept that it was designed to capture**

Section 5.1: Can I use a measure or question that simultaneously captures two different ideas?

Definition of terms – What is a double-barreled measure?

"Double-barreled" refers to questions or measures simultaneously addressing two ideas or issues. This is typically done using conjunctions such as "and" and "or" within the same measure (Bartkus, Mills, & Olsen, 2015).

Examples of double-barreled measures

"Husbands should help their wives with the dishes and care for the children" (Blood, 1955, p. 402).
"We should be grateful for the leaders who tell us exactly what we shall do and how" (Menold, 2020, p.6)
Study findings across multiple disciplines consistently demonstrate that double-barreled measures are a significant source of measurement error. Double-barreled measures may lead to greater response latency and may confuse respondents as they attempt to determine how they should answer (Bassili & Scott, 1996). As such, they most probably also increase the response burden. Along the same lines, some respondents might have difficulty understanding or responding to double-barreled questions because of increased cognitive demands, because response choices do not answer all parts of the question, because they are not sure which part of the question to respond to, or because the different parts of the question are not related (Blood, 1955; Herzberg & Brähler, 2006; Schult, Schneider, & Sparfeldt, 2016; Williams, et al., 2009). Some participants might pay attention to the whole item. Others might only read the first descriptor, leading to inaccurate responses, and others may also want to respond differently to each part of the question (Morgan, Amtmann, Abrahamson,

Kajlich, & Hafner, 2014; Schult et al., 2016). All these potential problems lead researchers to recommend that double-barreled questions be split into two or more distinct questions.

Expectations

- Double-barreled questions may lead to greater response latency (Bassili & Scott, 1996).
- Some respondents might have difficulty understanding or responding to double-barreled questions because of increased cognitive demands because response choices do not answer all parts of the question, because they are not sure which part of the question to respond to, or because the parts of the question are not related (Blood, 1955; Herzberg & Brähler, 2006; Schult et al., 2016; Williams et al., 2009).
- Participants may want to respond differently to each part of a double-barreled question (Morgan et al., 2014).
- A source of bias with double-barreled questions is how participants weigh descriptors. Some participants might pay attention to the whole item, while others might only read the first descriptor (Schult et al., 2016).
- Participants may only focus on one of two stimuli included in a double-barreled item, which decreases the validity of the measures (Menold, 2020).

Principles

- Researchers should not use double-barreled measures/questions.
- Split double-barreled questions into two (or more) questions, each with a distinct focus (Bassili & Scott, 1996; Blood, 1955; Herzberg & Brähler, 2006; Lee & Pershing, 2002; Morgan et al., 2014; Schult et al., 2016; Williams et al., 2009).

Commentary

The confusion that double-barreled measures are sure to create will also likely fatigue the respondent. A mentally tired respondent is less likely to continue self-reporting. So, using double-barreled measures violates several of the assumptions pointed out in the first chapter. Fundamentally, double-barreled measures violate the core of the validity definition. At its core, validity is the extent to which a measure captures what it was designed to capture and nothing else (paraphrased from Heaton, 1975, p. 159). A measure that captures more than a single concept is capturing something other than what it was designed to capture, making it invalid. Unfortunately, despite the consistency of study findings pointing out that using double-barreled measures introduces a large amount of error in measurement, I still see them present in academic and industry studies. The easiest way to solve a measure that contains more than one concept is to split it into two measures. For example, instead of using a single measure for "Husbands should help their wives with the dishes and care for the children" (Blood, 1955, p. 402), the two measures become: Husbands should help their wives with the dishes. Husbands should help their wives care for the children.

In addition to measures containing two different concepts or ideas, researchers should also watch out for implicit double-barreled occurrences. An explicit double-barreled statement can be easily spotted by analyzing its contents. The following is an example of an implicit double-barreled occurrence: A researcher is tasked with measuring a new design of handbags by showing participants these new handbags and then asking them to tell the researcher how much they like their design. When showing the handbags, if the researcher displays the brand name, participants will use their preexisting knowledge about the brand when evaluating the design of the handbags. Therefore, their reactions to the design would not be solely a function of how much they like a specific design. Their reactions would be tainted by their existing impressions of the brand. In this case, even if the measure to which a consumer is asked to react has a single explicit concept, the handbag brand is another concept affecting the consumer's reaction, making the measure implicitly double-barreled.

References and additional readings

Bartkus, K.R., Howell, R.D., Hills, S.D., & Blackham, J. (2009). The quality of guest comment cards: An empirical study of U.S. lodging chains. *Journal of Travel Research, 48*(2), 162–176. doi:10.1177/0047287509332331

Bartkus, K.R., Mills, R., & Olsen, D. (2015). Clarifications on the design of customer comment cards: Question type, question wording, and writing space. *Journal of Hospitality Marketing & Management, 24*(2), 216–228. doi:10.1080/19368623.2014.885402

Bassili, J.N., & Scott, B.S. (1996). Response latency as a signal to question problems in survey research. *Public Opinion Quarterly, 60*(3), 390–399. doi:10.1086/297760

Blood, R.J. (1955). Respondent reactions to ambiguous items in an attitude scale. *The Journal Of Abnormal and Social Psychology, 50*(3), 402–403. doi:10.1037/h0045233

Christodoulou, C., Junghaenel, D., DeWalt, D., Rothrock, N., & Stone, A. (2008). Cognitive interviewing in the evaluation of fatigue items: Results from the Patient-Reported Outcomes Measurement Information System (PROMIS). *Quality of Life Research, 17*(10), 1239–1246. doi:10.1007/s11136-008-9402-x

Heaton, G.B. (1975). *Writing English Language Tests*. Second edition. London: Longman

Herzberg, P.Y., & Brähler, E. (2006). Assessing the big-five personality domains via short forms: A cautionary note and a proposal. *European Journal Of Psychological Assessment, 22*(3), 139–148. doi:10.1027/1015-5759.22.3.139

Hunt, S.D., Sparkman, Richard D., Jr, & Wilcox, J.B. (1982). The pretest in survey research: Issues and preliminary findings. *Journal of Marketing Research, 19*(2), 269–273. doi:10.2307/3151627

Lee, S.H., & Pershing, J.A. (2002). Dimensions and design criteria for developing training reaction evaluations. *Human Resource Development International*, 5(2), 175–197. doi:10.1080/13678860110053678

Menold, Natalja. (2020). Double-barreled questions: An analysis on the similarity of elements and on the measurement quality. *Journal of Official Statistics*, 36(4), 855–886. doi:10.2478/jos-2020-0041

Morgan, S., Amtmann, D., Abrahamson, D., Kajlich, A., & Hafner, B. (2014). Use of cognitive interviews in the development of the PLUS-M item bank. *Quality of Life Research*, 23(6), 1767–1775. doi:10.1007/s11136-013-0618-z

Schult, J., Schneider, R., & Sparfeldt, J.R. (2016). Assessing personality with multi-descriptor items. *European Journal of Psychological Assessment*, 1(1), 1–9. doi:10.1027/1015-5759/a000368

Williams, R.T., Heinemann, A.W., Bode, R.K., Wilson, C.S., Fann, J.R., & Tate, D.G. (2009). Improving measurement properties of the Patient Health Questionnaire-9 with rating scale analysis. *Rehabilitation Psychology*, 54(2), 198–203. doi:10.1037/a0015529

Section 5.2: How long should my measures be?

Definition of terms – What is the measure's length?

In the context of self-report measurement, the length of a measure consists of the number of words used in a question or statement to which a respondent is asked to react. These questions or statements are usually followed by a set of response choices or a scale that enables the respondent to express their reaction. This section does not include the studies that investigate the optimal number of response choices or points a response scale should have, as these are covered in different chapters in this book. This section solely focuses on the number of words used in a question or statement a respondent is asked to read or hear and to which this respondent is then asked to react.

In brief

The length of a measure, whether it be in the form of a question or statement "is expressed in the number of words ranging from 6 to 30. A short question text is defined as a text of 10 words or less, and a long question text is a text of more than 10 words" (Scherpenzeel & Saris, 1997, p. 365).

The relevant body of knowledge suggests questions should be of a medium length (~20 words) (Andrews, 1984; Payne, 1950) and be simply worded (Payne, 1950). Shorter survey questions are most effective when the goal is to maximize question comprehension (Holbrook et al., 2006; Johnson et al., 2006), reduce question complexity (Flesch, 1948), and generate high reliability as compared to longer survey questions (Alwin & Beattie, 2016). Longer questions are best suited for situations requiring high-level thinking (Holbrook et al., 2006) and generate high validity compared to shorter survey questions (Laurent, 1972; Scherpenzeel & Saris, 1997). Education is the most significant demographic moderator for validity and reliability in question length. Validity and reliability were highest among higher-educated respondents when the question length was increased. Conversely, validity and reliability were highest among uneducated populations when the question length was decreased (Knauper et al., 1997; Marquis et al., 1972). There are two situations where measures that consist of more words will result in better data quality:

1. When adding words assists in the recall of information being asked: An example of this appears in an article by Laurent (1972), though not used to illustrate the same point: The shorter measure is "Have you ever had trouble hearing" (p. 299) and the longer measure is "Trouble hearing is the last item of this list. We are looking for some information about it. Have you ever had any trouble hearing?" (p. 299). Another example is found in Cannell et al. (1981). The shorter measure is "What health problems have you had in the past year" (p. 405). The longer measure is "The next question asks about health problems during the last year. This is something we are asking everyone in the survey. What health problems have you had in the past year" (p. 406). In both these contexts, the longer measure is used to prime memory and help the respondent more easily retrieve information by progressive introduction of the information the researcher needs.
2. When adding words clarifies meaning: An example of this appears in an article by Blair et al. (1977), though not used to precisely illustrate this exact point. The shorter measure is "In the past year, how often did you become intoxicated while drinking any kind of alcoholic beverage?" followed by a frequency response scale (p. 318). The longer measure consists of two parts. The first part is:

> Sometimes people drink a little too much beer, wine, or whiskey so that they act different from usual. What word do you think we should use to describe people when they get that way, so that you will know what we mean and feel comfortable talking about it? (p. 318)

The first part would allow the respondent to express in their own words the effect of drinking too much and thus better understand this concept since they expressed themselves. After receiving a response to the first part of this measure, the second part asks:

> Occasionally, people drink on an empty stomach or drink a little too much and become (respondent's word). In the past year, how often did you become (respondent's word) while drinking any kind of alcoholic beverage? (p. 318).

This was then followed by a frequency response scale. Shorter measures tend to work better outside these specialized contexts than longer ones.

Expectations

The length of a measure/question influences validity and reliability.
- Longer questions produce higher validity, and shorter questions produce higher reliability.
- Longer measures increase comprehension difficulties.
- Longer questions increase response time and cognitive burden on respondents.
- Longer questions improve reporting for people with higher education (12 grades+) and reduce reporting quality for people with lower education (<12 grade).

Principles

- Use measures/questions that are medium length (~ 20 words).
- To maximize comprehension, use shorter measures/questions when participants are less educated and longer ones when subjects are more educated.
- Decrease question length when asking low-complexity questions and increase question length when asking high-complexity questions.
- Decrease the length of questions to lower the cognitive burden placed on participants.
- Consider using longer measures when aiding recall and/or when meaning needs to be clarified and narrowed.

Commentary

Given the above, researchers using choice modeling and similar techniques that utilize entire paragraphs as measures face a dilemma, as the commonly used paragraphs far exceed the 20-word optimal length for measures. When a researcher has no choice but to use paragraph-length measures, they must ensure their respondents are highly educated and highly motivated to focus on reading each measure carefully.

References and additional readings

Alwin, D. & Beattie, B. (2016). The KISS principle in survey design: question length and data quality. Sociological Methodology, 46(1), 121–152. doi: 10.1177/0081175016641714

Andrews, F. (1984). Construct validity and error components of survey measures: A structural modeling approach. Public Opinion Quarterly. 48 (2), 409–441. doi: 10.1086/268840

Blair, E., Sudman, S., Bradburn, N.M. & Stocking, C. (1977). How to ask questions about drinking and sex: response effects in measuring consumer behavior. Journal of Marketing Research, 14(3), 316–321.

Cannell, C., Oksenberg, L. & Converse, J. (1977) Striving for response accuracy: Experiments in new interviewing techniques. *Journal of Marketing Research. 14*(3), 306–315.

Cannell, C.F., Miller, Peter, V. & Oskenberg, L. (1981). Research on interviewing techniques *Sociological Methodology 12*, 389–437

Converse, J.M. (1976). Predicting no opinion in the polls. *American Association for Public Opinion Research, 40*(4), 515–530.

Dijkstra, W., Koomen, W. (1975). Effects of question length on verbal behavior in a bias-reduced interview situation. European Journal of Social Psychology,*5*(3), 399–403.ISSN: 00462772.

Flesch, Rudolf. (1948) A new reliability yardstick. *Journal of Applied Psychology, 32*(3), 221–233.

Gibson, J. & Kim, B. (2007). Measurement error in recall surveys and the relationship between household size and food demand. [Article]. *American Journal of Agricultural Economics, 89*(2), 473–489. doi: 10.1111/j.1467-8276.2007.00978.x

Holbrook, A., Cho, Y.I., & Johnson, T. (2006). The impact of question and respondent characteristics on comprehension and mapping difficulties. *Public Opinion Quarterly, 70*(4), 565–595. doi: doi:10.1093/poq/nfl027

Johnson, T.P., Young, I.K., Cho, Y., Holbrook, A., O'Rourke, D., Warnecke, R.B., & Chaves, N. (2006) "Cultural Variability in the Effects of Question Design Features on Respondent Comprehension of Health Surveys." *Annals of Epidemiology, 16* (9), 661–668.

Knauper, B., Belli, R., Hill, D., & Herzog, A. (1997). Question difficulty and respondent's cognitive ability: the effect on data quality. Journal of Official Statistics, *13*(2), 181–199.

Laurent, Andre (1972) Effects of Question Length on Reporting Behavior in the Survey Interview *Journal of the American Statistical Association, 67,* 338, 298–305.

Lenzer, T., Kaczmirek, L., & Galesic, M. (2011). Seeing through the eyes of the respondent: an eye-tracking study on survey question comprehension. International Journal of Public Opinion Research, *23*(3), 1–22.

Mangione, T., Fowler, F. & Louis, T. (1992). Question characteristics and interviewer effects. Journal of Official Statistics, *8*(3), 293–307.

Marquis, Kent H., Cannell, Charles, F., Laurent, Andre. (1972). Reporting Health Events in Household Interview: Effects of reinforcement, question length and reinterviews. US Department of Health, Education, and Welfare. Health Resource Administration, National Center for Health Statistics. Rockville, Maryland.

Morgan, S., Amtmann, D., Abrahamson, D., Kajlich, A., & Hafner, B. (2014). Use of cognitive interviews in the development of the PLUS-M item bank. *Quality of Life Research, 23*(6), 1767–1775. doi:10.1007/s11136-013-0618-z

Payne, Stanley L. (1950) "Case study in question complexity." *The Public Opinion Quarterly. 13* (4), 653–658. http://dx.doi.org/10.1086/266124

Scherpenzeel, A. & Saris, W. (1997). The validity and reliability of survey questions: a meta-analysis of MTMM studies. Sociological Methods & Research, *25*(3), 341–383.https://doi.org/10.1177/0049124197025003004

Wikman, A. & Warneryd, B. (1990) "Measurement Errors in Survey Questions: Explaining Response Variability." *Social Indicators Research. 22* (2), 199–212.

Willis, G. B. (1991). The use of verbal report methods in the development and testing of survey questionnaires. *Applied Cognitive Psychology, 5,* 251–267. doi: 0888-4080/91/030251-17

Yan, T. & Tourangeau, R. (2008). Fast times and easy questions: The effects of age, experience and question complexity on web survey response times. *Applied Cognitive Psychology. 22,* 51–68 DOI: 10.1002/acp1331

Section 5.3: Should I worry about the order in which my questions/measures are presented to a respondent?

Definition of terms – What is an order effect in measurement?

Question order refers to "the order . . . in which survey questions are asked" and, depending on the situation, may also include the context in which they are asked (Bishop, Oldendick, & Tuchfarber, 1982).

In brief

Studies have found that how measures are ordered can affect how respondents answer survey questions; however, the effects vary across research disciplines. Question order and placement effects include: responding to later questions based on how much effort was given to previous questions (Pustejovsky & Spillane, 2009, p. 222), "consistency/carryover/assimilation" (answering later questions more similarly to earlier questions because they have that information readily available in their mind) (Bickart, 1993, p. 52), "backfire/contrast" (answering differently from previous answers) (Bickart, 1993, p. 53), "part-whole" (when general and specific questions are asked together, respondents may exclude the specific reasons from the general question) (Willits & Ke, 1995, p. 392) (See also Bickart, 1993; Pustejovsky & Spillane, 2009; Schuman, Presser, & Ludwig, 1981; Schwarz, Strack, & Mai, 1991; Strack, Martin, & Schwarz, 1988; Tourangeau et al., 1989; Tourangeau et al., 1991).

Question order and context effects may be more pronounced among the less educated or those who are least informed on the topic of the survey/research (Alspach & Bishop, 1991; Benton & Daly, 1991; Bishop, Oldenick, & Tuchfarber, 1982; Rimal & Real, 2005; Sigelman, 1981). To lessen the question order effects when designing a questionnaire, you can randomize the order of questions, place neutral/unrelated questions in between, or put more general questions before specific questions (Bowling & Windsor, 2008; Crespi & Morris, 1984; Dietz & Jasinski, 2007; Hjortskov, 2017; McClendon & O'Brien, 1988; McFarland, 1981; Moy et al., 2001; Pustejovsky & Spillane, 2009; Ramirez & Straus, 2006; Schuman, Presser, & Ludwig, 1981; Schuman, Kalton, & Ludwig, 1983; Siminski, 2008; Tourangeau, Rasinski, & Bradburn, 1991; Willits & Ke, 1995; Willick & Ashley, 1971).

Expectations

- When specific questions are asked before general questions, there are order effects (Bowling & Windsor, 2008; McFarland, 1981; McClendon & O'Brien, 1988;

Moy et al., 2001; Schuman, Presser, & Ludwig, 1981; Schwarz, Strack, & Mai, 1991; Tourangeau et al., 1991; Willits & Ke, 1995;).
- Order effects can be one or more of the following: "consistency/carryover/assimilation" (Bickart, 1993, p. 52), "question scope redefinition" (Pustejovsky & Spillane, 2009, p. 223), "meaning change/ part-whole" (Willits & Ke, 1995, p. 392), "backfire/contrast" (Bickart, 1993, p. 53).
- Question order effects are generally more pronounced among less educated respondents and those who are least informed about the topic of the research (Alspach & Bishop, 1991; Benton & Daly, 1991; Bishop, Oldenick, & Tuchfarber, 1982; Rimal & Real, 2005; Sigelman, 1981).
- Questions on political party affiliation (Republican/Democrat/other) are generally not influenced by question order, most likely because partisanship is a well-ingrained attitude (McAllister & Wattenberg, 1995).

Principles

- Randomize the order of measures in a questionnaire to lessen question order effects and put more general questions before specific questions (Bowling & Windsor, 2008; Crespi & Morris, 1984; Dietz & Jasinski, 2007; Hjortskov, 2017; McClendon & O'Brien, 1988; McFarland, 1981; Moy et al., 2001; Pustejovsky & Spillane, 2009; Ramirez & Straus, 2006; Schuman, Presser, & Ludwig, 1981; Schuman, Kalton, & Ludwig, 1983; Siminski, 2008; Tourangeau, Rasinski, & Bradburn, 1991; Willick & Ashley, 1971; Willits & Ke, 1995).

Commentary

Order effect errors will happen. The best approach is to do everything in your power to preempt these effects. For example, randomize measures among others with the same level of specificity (i.e., general with general, specific with specific, etc.). Use a measurement approach that would enable you to quantitatively pinpoint the measures affected by one type of order effect and remove the affected measures from the analysis. Unfortunately, order effect errors are challenging to catch in the aftermath of data collection unless you use multiple indicators for each construct you are trying to capture (see Chapters 1 and 3). With multiple-item measures, you can quantify the validity and reliability of measures and pinpoint and remove the measures associated with more errors, including those that might have been affected by others preceding them (see techniques described in Chapter 9).

References and additional readings

Alspach, S.E., & Bishop, G.F. (1991). Question-order effects of presidential approval ratings on gubernatorial approval ratings: A research note. *Social Forces, 69*(4), 1241–1248. doi:10.2307/2579311

Ayidiya, S.A., & McClendon, M.J. (1990). Response effects in mail surveys. *Public Opinion Quarterly, 54*(2), 229–247. doi:10.1086/269200

Bartels, L.M. (2002). Question order and declining faith in elections. *Public Opinion Quarterly, 66*(1), 67–79. doi:10.1086/338349

Benton, J.E., & Daly, J.L. (1991). A question order effect in a local government survey. *Public Opinion Quarterly, 55*(4), 640–642. doi:10.1086/269285

Bickart, B.A. (1993). Carryover and Backfire effects in marketing research. *Journal of Marketing Research, 30*(1), 52–62. doi:10.2307/3172513

Bishop, G., Hippler, H., Schwarz, N. & Strack, F. (1988). A comparison of response effects in self-administered and telephone surveys. *Telephone Survey Methodology*, 321–340. No doi available.

Bishop, G.F., Oldendick, R.W., & Tuchfarber, A.J. (1982). Political information processing: question order and context effects. *Political Behavior, 4*(2), 177–200. doi:10.1007/BF00987188

Bishop, G.F., Oldendick, R.W., & Tuchfarber, A.J. (1984). Interest in political campaigns: The influence of question order and electoral context. *Political Behavior, 6*(2), 159–169. doi:10.1007/BF01207760

Bishop, G.F., Oldendick, R.W., & Tuchfarber, A.J. (1985). The importance of replicating a failure to replicate: Order effects on abortion items. *Public Opinion Quarterly, 49*(1), 105–114. doi:10.1086/268904

Bowling, A., & Windsor, J. (2008). Theory and method: The effects of question order and response-choice on self-rated health status in the English Longitudinal Study of Ageing (ELSA). *Journal of Epidemiology and Community Health, 62*(1), 81–85. doi:10.136/jech.2006.05821

Bradburn, N.M., & Mason, W.M. (1964). The effect of question order on responses. *Journal of Marketing Research, 1*(4), 57–64. doi:10.2307/3150380

Clancy, K. & Wachsler, R.A. (1971). Positional Effects in Shared-Cost Surveys. *The Public Opinion Quarterly, 35*(2), 258–265. doi:10.1086/267898

Colasanto, D., Singer, E., & Rogers, T.F. (1992). Context effects on responses to questions about AIDS. *Public Opinion Quarterly, 56*(4), 515–518. doi:10.1086/269340

Crespi, I., & Morris, D. (1984). Question order effect and the measurement of candidate preference in the 1982 Connecticut elections. *The Public Opinion Quarterly, 48*(3), 578–591. doi:0033-362X/84/0048-5782

Dietz, T.L. & Jasinski, J.L. (2007). The Effect of Item order on partner violence reporting: An examination of four versions of the revised conflict tactics scales. *Social Science Research, 36*(1), 353–373. doi:10.1016/j.ssresearch.2006.04.006

Hart, T.C. (1998). Causes and consequences of juvenile crime and violence: Public attitudes and question-order effect. *American Journal of Criminal Justice, 23*(1), 129–143. doi:10.1007/BF02887287

Hjortskov, M. (2017). Priming and context effects in citizen satisfaction surveys. *Public Administration, 95*(9), 912–926. doi:10.1111/padm.12346

McAllister, I., & Wattenberg, M.P. (1995). Measuring levels of party identification: Does question order matter? *Public Opinion Quarterly, 59*(2), 259–268. doi:0033-362x/95/5902-000750250

McClendon, M.J., & O'Brien, D.J. (1988). Question-order effects on the determinants of subjective well-being. *The Public Opinion Quarterly, 52*(3), 351–364. doi: 0033-362X/88/00

McFarland, S.G. (1981). Effects of question order on survey responses. *Public Opinion Quarterly, 45*(2), 208–215. doi: 0033-362x/81/0045-208

Moore, D.W. (2002). Measuring new types of question-order effects: Additive and subtractive. *Public Opinion Quarterly, 66*(1), 80–91. doi: 0033-362x/2002/6601-0005

Moy, P., Scheufele, D.A., Eveland, W.P., & McLeod, J.M. (2001). Support for the death penalty and rehabilitation: Question order or communication effect? *Journal of Applied Social Psychology, 31*(11), 2230–2255. doi: 10.1111/j.1559-1816.2001.tb00173.x

Pustejovsky, J.E., & Spillane. J.P. (2009). Question-order effects in social network name generators. *Social Networks, 31*(4), 221–229. doi:10.1016/j.socnet.2009.06.001

Ramirez, I.L., & Straus, M.A. (2006). The effect of question order on disclosure of intimate partner violence: An experimental test using the conflict tactics scales. *Journal of Family Violence, 21*(1), 1–10. doi:10.1007/s10896-005-9000-4

Rimal, R.N., & Real, K. (2005). Assessing the perceived importance of skin cancer: How question-order effects are influenced by issue involvement. *Health Education & Behavior, 33*(2), 398–412. doi:10.1177/1090198104272341

Schuman, H., Presser, S., & Ludwig, J. (1981). Context effects on survey responses to questions about abortion. *Public Opinion Quarterly, 45*(2), 216–223. doi: 0033-362X/81/0045-216

Schuman, H., & Ludwig, J. (1983). The norm of even-handedness in surveys as in life. *American Sociological Review, 48*(1), 112–120. doi:10.2307/2095149

Schuman, H., Kalton, G., & Ludwig, J. (1983). Context and contiguity in survey questionnaires. *Public Opinion Quarterly, 47*(1), 112–115. doi: 0033-362X/83/0047-112

Schwarz, N., & Hippler, H. (1995). Subsequent questions may influence answers to preceding questions in mail surveys. *The Public Opinion Quarterly, 59*(1), 93–97. doi: 0033-362X/95/5901-0004

Schwarz, N., Strack, F., & Mai, H. (1991). Assimilation and contrast effects in part-whole question sequences: A conversational logic analysis. *The Public Opinion Quarterly, 55*(1), 3–23. doi:10.1086/269239

Sigelman, L. (1981). Question-order effects on presidential popularity. *Public Opinion Quarterly, 45*(2), 199–207. doi:10.1086/268650

Siminski, P. (2008). Order effects in batteries of questions. *Quality & Quantity: International Journal of Methodology, 42*(4), 477–490. doi:10.1007/s11135-006-9054-2

Strack, F., Martin, L. L., & Schwarz, N. (1988). Priming and communication: Social determinants of information use in judgments of life satisfaction. *European Journal Of Social Psychology, 18*(5), 429–442. doi:10.1002/esjsp.2420180505

Tourangeau, R., Rasinski, K. A., & Bradburn, N. (1991). Measuring happiness in surveys: A test of the subtraction hypothesis. *Public Opinion Quarterly, 55*(2), 255–266. doi:10.1086/269256

Tourangeau, R., Rasinski, K.A., Bradburn, N., & D'Andrade, R. (1989). Carryover effects in attitude surveys. *The Public Opinion Quarterly, 53*(4), 495–524. doi: 0033-362X/89/0053-04/

Van de Walle, S. & Van Ryzin, G. (2011). The order of questions in a survey on citizen satisfaction with public services: Lessons from a split-ballot experiment. *Public Administration, 89*(4): 1436–1450. doi:10.1111/j.1467-9299.2011.01922.x.

Willick, D.H., & Ashley, R.K. (1971). Question order and the political party preferences of college students and their parents. *The Public Opinion Quarterly, 35*(2), 189–199. doi:10.1086/267890

Willits, F.K., & Ke, B. (1995). Part-whole question order effects: Views of rurality. *The Public Opinion Quarterly, 59*(3), 392–403. doi: 0033-362X/95/5903-0006$02.50

Wilson, D.C., Moore, D.W., McKay, P.F., & Avery, D.R. (2008). Affirmative action programs for women and minorities: Expressed support affected by question order. *Public Opinion Quarterly, 72*(3), 514–522. doi:10.1093/poq/nfn031

Section 5.4: When is it best to use open-ended measures?

Definition of terms – What is an open-ended measure?

An open-ended question is a format "which allows individuals to respond to [a] query in their own words," as opposed to traditional closed-ended formats, which "[force] people to choose among a fixed set of responses" (Geer, 1988, p. 365). Regardless of the survey mode, the general format of open-ended questions is the presentation of the question followed by an expectation that the respondent will freely respond verbally by writing or typing in a distinct answer box rather than selecting from a particular list of responses.

In brief

A measure is open-ended when the respondent can provide a free-form answer to a question without being constrained by a researcher's pre-selected response options (Geer, 1988). Open-ended measures are qualitative and provide subjective information that can then be interpreted by the researcher (Geer, 1988). Although several methodologies utilize open-ended questions exclusively, open-ended measures often appear alongside closed-ended questions, which are questions for which researchers provide the respondents with predetermined selectable responses from which they can choose.

Open-ended measures have an extensive range of uses. Arguably, they are most helpful when they enable researchers to discover reactions they failed to consider initially, and that wouldn't otherwise be found due to the answer constraints of closed-ended questions. Because of this strength of open-ended questions, there is a strong consensus that open-ended questions are helpful in pilot studies to develop more detailed and exhaustive closed-ended measures (Falthzik & Carroll, 1971; Fee, 1981; Krause, 2002; Schuman & Presser, 1979). While some researchers worry that open-ended questions will elicit more responses from educated versus less educated respondents, Geer (1988) found no such differences. Another study showed that open-ended questions effectively capture respondents' concerns about salient topics, making them suitable for use in studies of public opinion about politics (Geer, 1991).

Using open-ended questions can come with several disadvantages. In general, it was found that open-ended questions are less effective than closed-ended questions (MacQueen, Chen, Ramirez, Nnko, & Earp, 2014; Shelby, Lamdan, Siegel, Hrywna, & Taylor, 2006). This is particularly true when measuring reports of sensitive behaviors (Gmel & Lokosha, 2000; Ivis, Bondy, & Adlaf, 1997). However, Blair et al. (1977) found open-ended questions more effective in eliciting responses about sensitive topics.

Open-ended questions can be cumbersome to answer compared to closed-ended questions. They are often more effective when the respondent is interested enough in the subject matter to commit the energy to respond. A growing body of research focuses on approaching and overcoming the problems associated with open-ended questions. This literature is interested in how visual, graphical, and language cues might improve response quality in open-ended questions. One example of these cues is the size of the closed-ended answer box, where respondents can list their responses. Studies have shown mixed results on whether or not the size of the box can improve response length and quality, but encouraging findings show increasing the size of answer boxes can elicit longer responses and responses with more opinion statements (Behr, Bandilla, Kaczmirek, & Braun, 2013; Emde & Fuchs, 2012; Maloshonok & Terentev, 2016; Stern, Smyth, & Mendez, 2012; Smyth, Dillman, Christian, & McBride, 2009; Zuell, Menold, and Körber, 2014). The motivational text preceding an open-ended measure has increased a respondent's willingness to provide a free-form response. Such motivational text typically specifies that the answer to the open-ended question is critical to the researcher's study and encourages the respondent not to rush while providing their answer Zuell, Menold, and Körber (2014). Additionally, sparse research suggests that including a visual counter representing how many characters a respondent has left while answering an open-ended question can increase the number of longer answers (Emde & Fuchs, 2012).

The other notable concern about open-ended questions is discrepancies between the respondent's intended meaning and a researcher's interpretation of their response. This issue happens during the coding phase, where the researcher analyzes open-ended questions to assign meaning to qualitative data. Errors at this stage can significantly contribute to further errors in data analysis. Research has shown consistently that there often exist moderate to significant differences in how coders interpret open-ended responses (Durbin & Stuart, 1954; Frisbie & Sudman, 1968; Kammeyer & Roth, 1971; Kalton & Stowell, 1979; Woodward & Franzen, 1948). As a result of these findings, it is suggested that coders be highly trained and highly supervised to improve the coding process. Computer coding has also been proposed to reduce these errors and has been demonstrated to have similar reliability in coding as humans, but the method has pros and cons. While computers don't get tired or bored and can commit equal attention to all responses, they were not as successful as humans in recognizing specific nuances in language and its meaning. The advent of artificial intelligence (AI), beginning in 2023, and its application to the field of expression coding will undoubtedly revolutionize how open-ended questions will be analyzed. As this chapter is being written, it is already possible to code open-ended text with AI reliably and even quantify the expressions embedded into open-ended text (see Chapter 10 for details).

Expectations

1. Open-ended measures might be less effective in measuring sensitive topics/behaviors (Gmel & Lokosha, 2000; Ivis, Bondy, & Adlaf, 1997).
2. Using open-ended measures can increase people's likelihood to respond to satisfaction surveys (Riiskjær, Ammentorp, & Kofoed, 2012).
3. Open-ended answers might be less useful due to question miscomprehension (MacQueen, Chen, Ramirez, Nnko, & Earp, 2014).
4. Open-ended measures often result in missing data (Friborg & Rosenvinge, 2013).
5. Open-ended measures might reveal latent narrative structures regarding certain ideas (Krause, 2002).
6. Increasing the size of the answer box in open-ended questions might improve response length and quality (Behr, Bandilla, Kaczmirek, & Braun, 2013; Emde & Fuchs, 2012; Maloshonok & Terentev, 2016; Smyth, Dillman, Christian, & McBride, 2009; Stern, Smyth, & Mendez, 2012; Zuell, Menold, and Körber, 2015).
7. Providing respondents with motivational instructions can improve response quality (Zuell et al., 2015).
8. Researchers can expect significant discrepancies in how coders interpret open-ended responses (Durbin & Stuart, 1954; Frisbie & Sudman, 1968; Kalton & Stowell, 1979; Kammeyer & Roth, 1971; Woodward & Franzen, 1948).

Principles

1. Use open-ended measures when pilot testing to develop more comprehensive closed-ended measures.
2. Provide respondents with motivational instructions to improve response quality
3. Increase the size of the answer box in open-ended questions, as this might improve response length and quality
4. Train and supervise coders of open-ended responses very carefully to reduce errors in the coding process.
5. Use open-ended measures when providing close-ended response categories can potentially bias participant responses.
6. Use open-ended measures when significant time and money resources are available to ensure proper and thorough coding of what respondents have written.

Commentary

Two of the biggest challenges I found when using open-ended measures are the time and resources it takes to code text. Add to those the uncertainty regarding whether to consider two similar expressions made by two separate respondents as equivalent.

The main advantage of open-ended measures is the ability to get what is at the top of a respondent's mind without biasing them with prompted response categories. Starting in 2023, the arrival of AI assistants marks a shift in how open-ended responses can be coded. Chapter 10 demonstrates a methodology that can be used to extract thought-process building blocks for open-ended text. Using AI to code the contents of open-ended responses will undoubtedly make the coding task more efficient and less costly. Limitations in understanding nuances of language still exist but will most likely improve over time as AI further develops.

References and additional readings

Allison, L.D., Okum, M.A., & Dutridge, K.S. (2002). Assessing volunteer motives: a comparison of an open-ended probe and Likert rating scales. *Journal of Community & Applied Social Psychology, 12*(4), 243–255. doi:10.1002/casp.677

Behr, D., Bandilla, W., Kaczmirek, L., & Braun, M. (2013). Cognitive probes in web surveys. *Social Science Computer Review, 32*(4), 524–533. doi:10.1177/0894439313485203

Bell, D.W., Esses, V.M., & Maio, G.R. (1996). The utility of open-ended measures to assess intergroup ambivalence. *Canadian Journal of Behavioural Science, 28*(1), 12–18. doi:10.1037/0008-400X.28.1.12

Blair, E., Sudman, S., Bradburn, N., & Stocking, C. (1977). How to ask questions about drinking and sex: response effects in measuring consumer behavior. Journal of Marketing Research, 14(3), 316–321. doi: 10.2307/3150769

Brewer, P.R. (2002). Framing, value words, and citizens' explanations of their issue opinions. *Political Communication, 19*(3), 303–316. doi:10.1080/01957470290055510

Durbin, J., & Stuart, A. (1954). An experimental comparison between coders. *Journal of Marketing, 19*(1), 54. doi:10.2307/1246894

Ehrlich, H.J., & Rinehart, J.W. (1965). A brief report on the methodology of stereotype research. *Social Forces, 43*(4), 564–575. doi:10.2307/2574464

Emde, M., & Fuchs, M. (2012). Using adaptive questionnaire design in open-ended questions: A field experiment. Paper presented at the American Association for Public Opinion Research (AAPOR) 67th Annual Conference, San Diego, USA.

Falthzik, A.M., & Carroll, S.J. (1971). Rate of return for closed versus open-ended questions in a mail questionnaire survey of industrial organizations. *Psychological Reports, 29*(3 suppl), 1121–1122. doi:10.2466/pr0.1971.29.3f.1121

Fee, J. (1981). Symbols in survey questions: Solving the problems of multiple word meanings. *Political Methodology, 7*(2), 71–95. No doi available.

Friborg, O., & Rosenvinge, J.H. (2013). A comparison of open-ended and closed questions in the prediction of mental health. *Quality and Quantity, 47*(3), 1397–1411. doi:10.1007/s11135-011-9597-8

Frisbie, B., & Sudman, S. (1968). The use of computers in coding free responses. *Public Opinion Quarterly, 32*(2), 216. doi:10.1086/267600

Geer, J. (1988). What do open-ended questions measure? *The Public Opinion Quarterly, 52*(3), 365–371. doi:10.1086/269113

Geer, J. (1991). Do open-ended questions measure "salient" issues? *The Public Opinion Quarterly, 55*(3), 360–370. doi:10.1086/269268

Gmel, G. & Lokosha, O. (2000). Self-reported frequency of drinking assessed with a closed- or open-ended question format: a split-sample study in Switzerland. *Journal of Studies on Alcohol, 61*(3), 450–454. doi:10.15288/jsa.2000.61.450

Holland, J.L., & Christian, L.M. (2008). The influence of topic interest and interactive probing on responses to open-ended questions in web surveys. *Social Science Computer Review, 27*(2), 196–212. doi:10.1177/0894439308327481

Ivis, F., Bondy, S., & Adlaf, E. (1997). The effect of question structure on self-reports of heavy drinking: Closed-ended versus open-ended questions. *Journal of Studies on Alcohol, 58*(6), 622–624. doi:10.15288/jsa.1997.58.622

Kalton, G., & Stowell, R. (1979). A study of coder variability. *Applied Statistics, 28*(3), 276. doi:10.2307/2347199

Kammeyer, K.C., & Roth, J.A. (1971). Coding responses to open-ended questions. *Sociological Methodology, 3,* 60. doi:10.2307/270818

Kealy, M.J., & Turner, R.W. (1993). A test of the equality of closed-ended and open-ended contingent valuations. *American Journal of Agricultural Economics, 75*(2), 321. doi:10.2307/1242916

Krause, N. (2002). A comprehensive strategy for developing closed-ended survey items for use in studies of older adults. *The Journals of Gerontology Series B: Psychological Sciences and Social Sciences, 57*(5). doi:10.1093/geronb/57.5.s263

MacQueen, K.M., Chen, M., Ramirez, C., Nnko, S.E.A., & Earp, K.M. (2014). Comparison of closed-ended, open-ended, and perceived informed consent comprehension measures for a mock HIV prevention trial among women in Tanzania. *PLoS ONE, 9*(8), e105720. doi:10.1371/journal.pone.0105720

Maloshonok, N., & Terentev, E. (2016). The impact of visual design and response formats on data quality in a web survey of MOOC students. *Computers in Human Behavior, 62,* 506–515. doi:10.1016/j.chb.2016.04.025

Miller, P.V., & Cannell, C.F. (1982). A study of experimental techniques for telephone interviewing. *Public Opinion Quarterly, 46*(2), 250. doi:10.1086/268717

Riiskjær E., Ammentorp J., & Kofoed P. (2012) The value of open-ended questions in surveys on patient experience: number of comments and perceived usefulness from a hospital perspective. *International Journal for Quality in Health Care, 24*(5) 509–516; doi:10.1093/intqhc/mzs039

Schuman, H., & Presser, S. (1979). The open and closed question. *American Sociological Review, 44*(5), 692–712. doi:10.2307/2094521

Shelby, R A., Lamdan, R.M., Siegel, J.E., Hrywna, M., & Taylor, K.L. (2006) Standardized versus open-ended assessment of psychosocial and medical concerns among African American breast cancer patients. *Psycho-Oncology, 15*(5), 382–397. doi:10.1002/pon.959

Smyth, J.D., Dillman, D.A., Christian, L.M., & Mcbride, M. (2009). Open-ended questions in web surveys. *Public Opinion Quarterly, 73*(2), 325–337. doi:10.1093/poq/nfp029

Stern, M.J., Smyth, J.D., & Mendez, J. (2012). The effects of item saliency and question design on measurement error in a self-administered survey. *Field Methods, 24*(1), 3–27. doi:10.1177/1525822x11419478

Stoneman, P., Sturgis, P., & Allum, N. (2012). Exploring public discourses about emerging technologies through statistical clustering of open-ended survey questions. *Public Understanding of Science, 22*(7), 850–868. doi:10.1177/0963662512441569

Wind, Y., Denny, J., & Cunningham, A. (1979). A comparison of three brand evaluation procedures. *Public Opinion Quarterly, 43*(2), 261. doi:10.1086/268516

Woodward, J.L., & Franzen, R. (1948). A study of coding reliability. *Public Opinion Quarterly, 12*(2), 253. doi:10.1086/265947

Zuell, C., Menold, N., & Körber, S. (2014). The influence of the answer box size on item nonresponse to open-ended questions in a web survey. *Social Science Computer Review, 33*(1), 115–122. doi:10.1177/0894439314528091

Chapter 6
Principles and expectations: Response category characteristics

Objectives of Chapter 6: You need to make many decisions regarding response categories used to capture study participant reactions to self-report measures or questions. These decisions include whether to include a "neutral" category or a "don't know" option, whether the order in which you present the response categories matters, and the number of points to use on a scale. While there are undoubtedly other decisions you will need to make regarding response categories, this chapter addresses the key aspects emanating from a convergence across many studies, and this convergence can serve as guidance.

Which assumptions are addressed in this chapter?

Table 6.1: Assumptions made about respondents for self-report measures to achieve their intended purpose.

When reacting to a measure or answering a question, the respondent . . .	
Assumption A	Is willing to disclose information about themselves
Assumption B	Is truthful and not deliberately lying
Assumption C	Interprets each measure/question the way the researcher intended and in the same way that others who are also being measured are interpreting them
Assumption D	Can correctly recall needed information from memory to react to each measure/question
Assumption E	Can easily move from one measure/question to another
Assumption F	Is self-aware
Assumption G	**Is reacting to a measure without being influenced by any aspect of the measure itself other than the content that directly overlaps with the invisible concept that needs to be captured.**

The assumptions in bold in Tables 6.1 and 6.2 are affected by violations of the principles provided in the sections of this chapter. The more limited or confusing the response categories are, the less likely a participant will continue reacting to the measures, and their reactions will be more likely influenced by something other than what the researcher set out to measure. Thus, the more likely the researcher will be to capture something different than what they set to measure and the less precise and consistent the reactions to the measures will be.

Table 6.2: Assumptions made about the measures for self-report measures to achieve their intended purpose.

Each measure developed by the researcher should . . .	
Assumption H	Fully capture the concept or an aspect of the concept that it is intended to capture
Assumption I	**Precisely capture the aspect of the concept that it is intended to capture**
Assumption J	Capture a single concept and no other
Assumption K	**Is consistent in its capturing of the concept that it was designed to capture**

Section 6.1: Should I give my respondents the option of saying "I don't know"?

Definition of terms – What is a "Don't Know" response category?

In the context of self-report research, "[Don't Know] responses reflect the outcome of meta-cognitive monitoring of the contents of memory, as they represent one way by which responding to questions is avoided when confidence in potential answers is low" (Scorbia et al., 2008, p. 255). In other words, a "don't know" is a response option provided to the respondent in case they cannot make up their mind and choose from among a set of definite response categories, and/or they just don't have enough information about the topic to which a self-report measure is asking them to react.

In brief

"Don't Know" (DK) is a response alternative that should be considered a distinct response category and should not be considered a "no" or throwaway in analysis (Andrews, 1984). A DK response option in a questionnaire improves the overall validity and reliability of data (Andrews, 1984; Courtenay & Weidemann, 1985). However, a DK option and its analytical interpretation should be used cautiously. Respondents have an inconsistent understanding of DK (Faulkenberry & Mason, 1978; Feick, 1989; Scoboria et al., 2008).

Some researchers use filters to communicate that it's ok for a respondent to acknowledge they don't know enough and indicate so in their response. In this context, a 'filter' means a statement the researcher provides before asking specific questions. An example of such a filter that encourages respondents to choose "don't know" is: "Many people don't know the answers to these questions, so if there is some you don't know, just tell me, and we'll go on." (Mondak & Davis, 2001, p. 210). However, such filters can negatively impact the validity and reliability of data by inadvertently creating an overestimation of "don't know" and an underestimation of respondent knowledge (Bishop et al., 1983; Hippler & Schwarz, 1989; Luskin & Bullock, 2011; McClendon,

1986; McClendon & Alwin, 1993; Mondak & Davis, 2001; Schuman & Presser, 1979). These filters, when strongly worded (Hippler & Schwarz, 1989), when used in combination with high complexity questions (Hippler & Schwarz, 1989), and/or when used with question/measure content distant/less familiar to respondents (Bishop et al., 1983) can result in a higher level of DK responses than would have occurred otherwise. Strongly worded filters that imply the respondent needs expertise or complex knowledge of a subject before answering specific questions increase the rate of DK responses (Hippler & Schwarz, 1989). To reduce DK responses, researchers should ensure that respondents are familiar with or interested in the topic being measured (Converse, 1976; Francis & Busch, 1975; Pickery & Loosveldt, 2001), measures should be grouped thematically (Lam et al., 2002), and item complexity should be limited both for the respondent and, when applicable, also for the interviewer (Haener & Adamowicz, 1998; Pickery & Loosveldt, 2001).

Generally, respondent familiarity or interest in the question topic (Francis & Busch, 1975; Pickery & Loosveldt, 2001), education (Francis & Busch, 1975), and gender (Francis & Busch, 1975; Rapoport, 1985) are the most influential respondent characteristics that impact the rate of DK responses. Respondents who are female (Francis & Busch, 1975; Rapoport, 1985), less educated (Converse, 1976; Francis & Busch, 1975), and less interested (Converse, 1976; Francis & Busch, 1975; Pickery & Loosveldt, 2001) in the topic are more likely to produce a DK response.

McClendon & Alwin (1993) differentiate between the two types of errors possible with a don't know response category. They attribute these errors to two types of respondents they label floaters and non-floaters . A floater is a respondent who can express an opinion on a question/measure but would choose the DK option if offered. A non-floater is a respondent who does not have an opinion yet will express one and typically will not select the DK option if offered (McClendon & Alwin, 1993). In sum, there is the real possibility a respondent might choose the "don't know" category as an alternative to putting cognitive effort into reacting to a question. There is also the possibility that respondents will not choose the "don't know" option even though they either don't have enough information to react to a specific measure or don't have a definite reaction.

Expectations

- A "don't know" response option in a survey tends to increase the validity and reliability of the data (Andrews, 1984; Courtenay & Weidemann, 1985).
- However, strongly worded filters specifically encouraging "don't know" responses will negatively impact the validity and reliability of the data (Bishop et al., 1983; Hippler & Schwarz, 1989; Luskin & Bullock, 2011; McClendon, 1986; McClendon & Alwin, 1993; Mondak & Davis, 2001; Schuman & Presser, 1979;).

- Respondents have inconsistent interpretations of the response alternative "don't know" (Faulkenberry & Mason, 1978; Feick, 1989; Scoboria et al., 2008).
- Respondents unfamiliar with or interested in the measured topic are likelier to choose the "don't know" response category (Francis & Busch, 1975; Pickery & Loosveldt, 2001).
- Respondents who are less educated are more likely to choose the "don't know" response category (Francis & Busch, 1975).
- Female respondents are more likely to choose the "don't know" response category (Francis & Busch, 1975; Rapoport, 1985).

Principles

- Consider including a "don't know" response option when asking respondents about fact-based information with which they might not be familiar. When you include a "don't know" option, check if doing so has impacted the gender and level of education representation in the response patterns obtained from your measures.
- Do not discard "don't know" responses, and do not consider these as a form of expressing "no" or being "neutral."
- When choosing to include a "don't know" response category, do not precede it with a strongly worded filter. This might encourage participants to choose this response category when they have enough information to express an opinion.
- Limit the complexity of your measures and group them thematically to reduce the occurrence of "don't know" responses unrelated to a lack of knowledge.
- If choosing to include a "don't know" response category, clarify what the "don't know" option means in your study without using a strongly worded qualification.

Commentary

In my mind, whether to include a "don't know" option depends on which error you prefer to have. There will always be a proportion of participants unwilling to put the effort into responding. The argument often made is that these respondents would automatically choose the "don't know" option, so this option should not be given. But this argument misses the point: if they are unwilling to put in the effort, would you rather them choose "don't know" or make up an answer? I would rather they choose the "don't know" option since doing so won't distort the tail-ends of the data distribution I will be analyzing. In my opinion, given the broad interpretation of what "don't know" means among respondents, it would be a good idea, if possible, to replace the "don't know" with "I don't have information to express an opinion about this." This reminds me of a recent prompt I received when scrolling through my status update on a major social media network. I was asked to express how much I find a specific brand "reliable." The problem is I had never heard of the brand. I was not given a way to tell the researchers I was not responding because I didn't have enough information about the brand to express an opinion. I simply kept scrolling. Wouldn't it have been more beneficial for the researcher collecting the data to give me a way of telling them that I am not expressing an opinion because I don't know enough about this brand? Without such information, my lack of response will probably be interpreted as my unwillingness to express an opinion about the brand.

References and additional readings

Andrews, F. (1984). Construct validity and error components of survey measures: A structural modeling approach. *The Public Opinion Quarterly, 48*(2), 409–442. doi:10.1086/2688/40

Bishop, G., Oldendick, R., & Tuchfarber, A. (1983). Effects of filter questions in public opinion surveys. *The Public Opinion Quarterly, 47*, 528–546. doi:10.1086/268810

Coombs, C., & Coombs, L. (1976). "Don't know": item ambiguity or respondent uncertainty? *The Public Opinion Quarterly, 40*(4), 497–514. doi:10.1086/268336

Converse, J. (1976). Predicting no opinion in the polls. *The Public Opinion Quarterly, 40*(4), 515–530. doi:10.1086/268337

de Leeuw, E.D., Hox, J.J., & Boevé, A. (2015). Handling do-not-know answers: Exploring new approaches in online and mixed-mode surveys. *Social Science Computer Review, 34*(1), 1–17. doi:10.1177/0894439315573744

Faulkenberry, G.D., & Mason, R. (1978) Characteristics of no opinion and no opinion response groups. *The Public Opinion Quarterly, 42*(4), 533–543. doi:10.1086/268478

Feick, L. (1989). Latent class analysis of survey questions that include don't know responses. *The Public Opinion Quarterly, 53*(4), 525–547. doi:10.1086/269170

Francis, J., & Busch, L. (1975) What we now know about "I don't knows." *The Public Opinion Quarterly, 39*(2), 207–218. doi:10.1086/268217

Gilljam, M., & Granberg, D. (1993). Should we take don't know for an answer? *The Public Opinion Quarterly, 57*, 348–357. doi:10.1086/269380

Haener, M., & Adamowicz, W. (1998). Analysis of "don't know" response to referendum contingent valuation questions. *Agricultural and Resource Economics Review, 27*(2), 218–230. doi:10.1017/S1068280500006535

Hippler, H., & Schwarz, N. (1989). 'No opinion' filters: a cognitive perspective. *International Journal of Public Opinion Research, 1*(1), 77–87. doi:10.1093/ijpor/1.1.77

Lam, T., Green, K., & Bordignon, C. (2002). Effects of item grouping and position of the "don't know" option on questionnaire response. *Field Methods, 14*(4), 418–432. doi:10.1177/152582202237730

Leigh, J.H., & Martin, C.R. (1987) 'Don't know' item nonresponse in a telephone survey: Effects of question form and respondent characteristics. *Journal of Marketing Research, 24*(4), 418–424. doi:10.2307/3151390

Luskin, R., & Bullock, J. (2011). "Don't know" means "don't know": DK responses and the public's level of political knowledge. *The Journal of Politics, 73*(2), 547–557. doi:10.1017/S0022381611000132

McClendon, M. J. (1986) Unanticipated effects of no-opinion filters on attitudes and attitude strength. *Sociological Perspectives, 29*, 379–395. doi:10.2307/1389026

McClendon, M.J., & Alwin, D.F. (1993) No-opinion filters and attitude measurement reliability. *Sociological Methods & Research, 21*(4), 438–464. doi:10.1177/0049124193021004002

Mondak, J.J., & Davis, B.C. (2001) Asked and answered: Knowledge levels when we will not take "don't know" for an answer. *Political Behavior, 23*(3), 199–224. doi:10.1023/A:1015015227594s

Pickery, J. & Loosveldt, G. (2001). An exploration of question characteristics that mediate interviewer effects on item nonresponse. *Journal of Official Statistics, 17*(3), 337–350. No doi available.

Rapoport, R. (1982). Sex differences in attitude expression: a generational explanation. *The Public Opinion Quarterly, 46*(1), 86–96. doi:10.1086/268701

Rapoport, R. (1985). Like mother, like daughter: intergenerational transmission of DK response rates. *The Public Opinion Quarterly, 49*(2), 198–208. doi:10.1086/268914

Schuman, H., & Presser S. (1979). The assessment of "no opinion" in attitude surveys. *Sociological Methodology, 10*, 241–275. doi:10.2307/270773

Scoboria, A., Mazzoni, G., & Kirsch, I. (2008). "Don't know" responding to answerable and unanswerable questions during misleading and hypnotic interviews. *Journal of Experimental Psychology, 14*(3), 255–265. doi:10.1037/1076-898X.14.3.255

Wang, H. (1997). Treatment of "don't-know" responses in contingent valuation surveys: a random valuation model. *Journal of Environmental Economics and Management, 32*, 219–232. doi:10.1006/jeem.1996.0965

Waterman, A., Blades, M., & Spencer, C. (2004). Indicating when you do not know the answer: the effect of question format and interviewer knowledge on children's 'don't know' responses. *British Journal of Developmental Psychology, 22*, 335–348. doi:10.1348/0261510041552710

Section 6.2: Should I include a neutral response category in my response scales?

Definition of terms – What is a neutral response category?

A neutral response category, typically located in the middle of a response scale, such as "Neither Agree nor Disagree" or "Neither Likely nor Unlikely," is offered as an alternative to the options of the same scale that elicit a respondent's explicit proclamations of opinion certainty. The "neutral" option is distinct from "not sure" or "don't know" reactions that generally indicate a lack of sufficient knowledge about the topic being investigated.

In brief

Interpretations of middle response categories vary among respondents (DuBois & Burns, 1975; Edwards, 1946; González-Romá & Espejo, 2003; Kulas, Stachowski, & Haynes, 2008; Tourangeau, Couper, & Conrad, 2004). Two different interpretations of the middle response categories are possible: neutral responses (representing an opinion directly in the middle) or essentially "opt-out" responses (i.e., "no opinion," "not sure," "not applicable," "indifferent," "irrelevant," etc.). Given the possible diverse interpretations of what a middle response category represents, it is difficult to read a respondent's mind and know which interpretation they used when selecting "neutral" as a reaction to a survey question. Because of this ambiguity, the middle response category is often used as a catch-all to mean any of the above interpretations.

The tendency of a respondent to select a neutral response varies based on many factors (Bishop, 1987; Harzing, 2006; Klopfer & Madden, 1980; Presser & Schuman, 1980; Roberts & Smith, 2014; Si & Cullen, 1998; Sturgis, Weems & Onwuegbuzie, 2001; Velez & Ashworth, 2007). A neutral response category's presence (or lack thereof) is most influential to respondents with weaker opinions on a subject (Presser and Schuman, 1980). The propensity to select a neutral response option is influenced both by question characteristics and respondent attributes. The less clear a question appears, the more likely it will elicit a neutral response (Velez & Ashworth, 2007). The more cognitively difficult a question appears, the more likely it will elicit a neutral response (Valez & Ashworth, 2007). Respondent attributes also influence the likelihood of selecting a neutral response. Some cultures are more likely to choose a neutral response than others. For example, Asian cultures have a higher percentage of neutral responses than Western cultures (Si & Cullen, 1998). Native speakers (relative to the language used in the instrument) are more likely to answer with stronger opinions than non-native speakers (Harzing, 2006).

Respondents cope in various ways when people have a neutral opinion on a topic, and a middle response category is not offered. Respondent coping mechanisms include: (1) Assigning greater weights to attributes of a topic to come to a positive or negative judgment; (2) Responding in a socially desirable way to appease an interviewer/researcher; or (3) Selecting an opt-out response (Converse, 1976; Duncan & Stenbeck, 1988; Faulkenberry & Mason, 1978; Garland, 1991; Kalton, Roberts, & Holt, 1980; Krosnick et al., 2002; Nowlis, Kahn, & Dhar, 2002). To differentiate the meanings of neutral response categories from opt-out responses (i.e., "no opinion," "don't know," "cannot decide," "not sure," etc.), opt-out response categories should be separated from the response scale verbally and/or visually, as applicable.

The literature on the number of response categories (see Section 4 in this chapter) appears to prefer the inclusion of a neutral midpoint to capture the variation among respondents better. However, some researchers believe that more research needs to be conducted before guidance on always including a neutral category becomes definite (Adelson & McCoach, 2010; Alwin & Krosnick, 1991; Kieruj et al., 2010; Scherpenzeel et al., 1997; Weijters et al., 2010).

Expectations

- Interpretations of the middle response category vary among respondents and are perceived as relatively ambiguous (DuBois & Burns, 1975; Edwards, 1946; González-Romá & Espejo, 2003; Kulas, Stachowski, & Haynes, 2008; Tourangeau, Couper, & Conrad, 2004). Respondents often use the middle response category as a "catch-

all" to mean a variety of responses: neutral, no opinion, not sure, not applicable, indifferent, irrelevant, etc.
- Respondents with weaker positions on a topic will be more influenced by the presence of middle response categories than respondents with more substantial et a positions on a topic, as well as education, linguistic, and cultural factors (Bishop, 1987; Harzing, 2006; Klopfer & Madden, 1980; Presser & Schuman, 1980; Si & Cullen, 1998; Sturgis, Roberts, & Smith, 2014; Velez & Ashworth, 2007; Weems & Onwuegbuzie, 2001).
- A greater percentage of respondents will select a neutral response when explicitly offered (compared to if respondents must come up with it on their own).
- The less clear a question is perceived, the higher the percentage of neutral responses it will receive, and the more complex a question is perceived to be, the higher the percentage of neutral responses it will receive.
- Respondents often use neutral responses to avoid cognitive effort or social embarrassment by selecting a neutral response compared to "don't know."

Principles

- Do not include a neutral response category if you have special limiting circumstances associated with your study participants or know your participants can express a valenced reaction about the topic you are researching.
- Barring any exceptional circumstances with your participants or the topic being researched, consider including a neutral response option in the response scales you are using that asks participants to agree, like, or express similar valenced reactions.
- Position a neutral response category explicitly and visually as the midpoint of a response scale.
- When including "opt-out" responses (no opinion, not sure, etc.), separate these visually from the main categories of your response scales to differentiate them from the midpoint option.
- Be sure to use clear and simple wording to reduce cognitive burden and, in turn, reduce unwarranted selections of the neutral option.

Commentary

My perspective on whether to include or not include a neutral response is that it is a tradeoff between two sources of error. It might encourage respondents to select the neutral category even though they might have a valenced opinion on the matter the question asks about. In this case, this respondent's valenced opinion would not be captured by selecting a neutral response. Not including a neutral option might force a respondent to choose a valenced opinion even though they might not have one. In this case, causing a participant to express a valenced opinion when they have none, if not randomly distributed, would result in variation patterns that incorrectly reflect the true variation in responses among the measured participants. So, which error would you rather have? Between the two, I would prefer not to capture an opinion at all rather than one that forcefully expresses a valence when the participant feels neutral about the topic of the question being asked.

In addition to the preceding, a researcher cannot consider including a neutral response without determining whether the data they are collecting will be analyzed using techniques that go beyond descriptives and assume continuous data. There is strong evidence that response scales of five or more categories approach the qualities of continuous data (see Section 4), and including a neutral response is often necessary to achieve five or more gradations in response scales. However, we cannot ignore one primary concern in the neutral response literature: study participants frequently choose the neutral response category when offered.

References and additional readings

Adelson, J., McCoach, D. (2010). Measuring the mathematical attitudes of elementary students: The effects of a 4-point or 5-point likert-type scale. *Educational and Psychological Measurement, 70*(5), 796–807. doi:10.1177/0013164410366694

Alwin, D., & Krosnick, J. (1991). The reliability of survey attitude measurement. *Sociological Methods & Research, 20*(1), 139–181. doi:10.1177/0049124191020001005

Bishop, G. (1987). Experiments with the middle response alternative in survey questions. *The Public Opinion Quarterly, 51*(2), 220–232. doi:10.1086/269030

Converse, J. (1976). Predicting no opinion in the polls. *The Public Opinion Quarterly, 40*(4), 515–530. doi:10.1086/268337

DuBois, B., & Burns, J. (1975). An analysis of the meaning of the question mark response category in attitude scales. *Educational and Psychological Measurement, 35*, 869–884. doi:10.1177/001316447503500414

Duncan, O., & Stenbeck, M. (1988). No opinion or not sure? *The Public Opinion Quarterly, 52*(4), 513–525. doi:10.1086/269127

Edwards, A. (1946). A critique of 'neutral' items in attitude scales constructed by the method of equal appearing intervals. *Psychological Review, 53*(3), 159–169. doi:10.1037/h0054184

Faulkenberry, D., & Mason, R. (1978). Characteristics of nonopinion and no opinion response groups. *The Public Opinion Quarterly, 42*(4), 533–543. doi:10.1086/268478

Garland, R. (1991). The mid-point on a rating scale: is it desirable? *Marketing Bulletin, 2*, 66–70. Retrieved from http://marketing-bulletin.massey.ac.nz.

González-Romá, V., & Espejo, B. (2003). Testing the middle response categories <Not sure>, <In between> and <?> in polytomous items. *Psicothema, 15*(2), 278–284. No doi available.

Harzing, A. (2006). Response styles in cross-national survey research. *International Journal of Cross Cultural Management, 6*(2), 243–266. doi: 10.1177/1470595806066332

Hernández, A., Drasgow, F., & González-Romá, V. (2004). Investigating the functioning of a middle category by means of a mixed-measurement model. *Journal Of Applied Psychology, 89*(4), 687–699. doi:10.1037/0021-9010.89.4.687

Kalton, G., Roberts, J., & Holt, D. (1980). The effects of offering a middle response option with opinion questions. *Journal of the Royal Statistical Society. Series D (The Statistician), 29*(1), 65–78. doi:10.2307/2987495

Klopfer, F., & Madden, T. (1980). The middlemost choice on attitude items: Ambivalence, neutrality, or uncertainty? *Personality and Social Psychology Bulletin, 6*(1), 97–101. doi:10.1177/014616728061014

Krosnick, J., Holbrook, A., Berent, M., Carson, R., Hanemann, M., Kopp, R., Mitchell, R., Presser, S., Ruud, P., Smith, V., Moody, W., Green, M., & Conaway, M. (2002). The impact of "no opinion" response options on data quality: Non-attitude reduction or an invitation to satisfice? *The Public Opinion Quarterly, 66*(3), 371–403. doi:10.1086/341394

Kulas, J., Stachowski, A., & Haynes, B. (2008). Middle response functioning in likert-responses to personality items. *Journal of Business and Psychology, 22*(3), 251–259. doi:10.1007/s10869-008-9064-2

Madden, T., & Klopfer, F. (1978). The "cannot decide" option in Thurstone-type attitude scales. *Educational and Psychological Measurement, 38*(2), 259–264. doi:10.1177/001316447803800207

Nowlis, S., Kahn, B., & Dhar, R. (2002). Coping with ambivalence: The effect of removing a neutral option on consumer attitude and preference judgments. *Journal of Consumer Research, 29*(3), 319–334. doi:10.1086/344431

Presser, S., & Schuman, H. (1980). The measurement of a middle position in attitude surveys. *The Public Opinion Quarterly, 44*(1), 70–85. doi:10.1086/268567

Si, S., & Cullen, J. (1998). Response categories and potential cultural bias: Effects of an explicit middle point in cross-cultural surveys. *The International Journal of Organizational Analysis, 6*(3), 218–230. doi:10.1108/eb02888

Sturgis, P., Roberts, C., & Smith, P. (2014). Middle alternatives revisited: How the neither/ nor response acts as a way of saying "I don't know"? *Sociological Methods & Research, 43*(1), 15–38. doi: 10.1177/0049124112452527

Tourangeau, R., Couper, M., & Conrad, F. (2004). Spacing, position, and order: Interpretive heuristics for visual features of survey questions. *The Public Opinion Quarterly, 68*(3), 368–393. doi:10.1093/poq/nfh035

Velez, P., & Ashworth, S. (2007). The impact of item readability on the endorsement of the midpoint response in surveys. *Survey Research Methods, 1*(2), 69–74. doi:10.18148/srm/2007.v1i2.76

Weems, G., & Onwuegbuzie, A. (2001). The impact of midpoint responses and reverse coding on survey data. *Measurement and Evaluation in Counseling and Development, 34*(3), 166–176. doi:10.1080/07481756.2002.12069033

Section 6.3: Should I worry about the order in which the response choices are presented to a respondent?

Definition of terms – What is the order of response choices?

Response order is "the order in which the response alternatives are presented" in a questionnaire or survey (Bishop & Smith, 2001, p. 479).

In brief

The placement of a response category relative to other response categories can often result in one of two known effects. The first is associated with response categories that are listed first. It is frequently the case that because they are listed first, they are more prioritized by the respondent. This is known as the primacy effect. The second is associated with response categories that are listed last, and, as such, they are more prominent in a respondent's memory. This is a recency effect (Krosnick & Alwin, 1987).

Most studies on response order have found that primacy effects are more likely to occur in visually presented surveys, such as with show cards or Likert-type scales (Becker, 1954; Belson, 1966; Chan, 1991; Duffy, 2003; Friedman et al., 1993; Galesic et al., 2008; Malhotra, 2008; Malhotra, 2009; Nicholls et al., 2006). This may occur because items presented first can establish a cognitive framework for respondents to judge later items. The earlier items are processed more deeply by participants, leading them to remember them and be more likely to choose those options (Krosnick & Alwin, 1987). Recency effects often happen in oral surveys (Chang & Krosnick, 2010; Holbrook et al., 2007; Krosnick & Schuman, 1988; McClendon, 1986). Recency effects may also be more likely when the questions or response options are longer rather than shorter, such as a complete sentence rather than a word or phrase (Bishop & Smith, 2001; Holbrook et al., 2007; McClendon, 1986). Recency effects may be more common in orally presented surveys because when response options are read aloud, the later items are more readily available in the participants' minds (Krosnick & Alwin, 1987). Some studies have shown that more complex and more complicated to understand questions can lead to more significant response order effects (Holbrook et al., 2007; McClendon, 1986), while others have shown that easier questions may lead to greater effects because respondents may not be motivated to pay attention (Malhotra, 2009).

Researchers have also found that highly motivated participants will show less response order effects (Krosnick & Alwin, 1987; Weng & Cheng, 2000). Self-administered surveys may lead to fewer response order effects because respondents can read through all the response options in any order they choose (Ayidiya & McClendon, 1990; Bishop et al., 1988; Chang & Krosnick, 2010). Respondents who may be more prone to response order effects include older, less educated, and less cognitively complex participants (Holbrook et al., 2007; Knauper, 1999; Krosnick & Alwin, 1987; Malhotra, 2008; Malhotra, 2009; McClendon, 1986). Respondents with favorable attitudes or firmly held beliefs may be less prone to response order effects (Friedman et al., 1993; Krosnick & Schuman, 1988).

Expectations

- Likert-type scales are prone to primacy effects (Chan, 1991; Friedman et al., 1993; Nicholls et al., 2006), especially among lower-educated, older, and less cognitively complex individuals.
- Orally presented surveys are prone to recency effects (Chang & Krosnick, 2010; Holbrook et al., 2007; Krosnick & Schuman, 1988; McClendon, 1986).

- Recency effects may be more likely when the questions or response options are longer rather than shorter, such as a complete sentence rather than a word or phrase (Bishop & Smith, 2001; Holbrook et al., 2007; McClendon, 1986).
- With visually presented surveys, researchers should expect a primacy effect. Respondents are more likely to choose items at the beginning of a list or on the left side of the page/screen, including Likert-type scales (Becker, 1954; Belson, 1966; Chan, 1991; Friedman et al., 1993; Duffy, 2003; Nicholls et al., 2006; Malhotra, 2008; Malhotra, 2009).
- Questions that are more difficult to understand may be more prone to response order effects (McClendon, 1986; Holbrook et al., 2007).
- Older respondents are more likely to experience response order effects (Knauper, 1999; Holbrook et al., 2007).
- Less cognitively complex people are more likely to experience response order effects (Holbrook et al., 2007; Knauper, 1999; Krosnick & Alwin, 1987).
- Less educated respondents are more likely to experience response order effects (Holbrook et al., 2007; McClendon, 1986; Krosnick & Alwin, 1987; Malhotra, 2008; Malhotra, 2009).
- Respondents with favorable attitudes or firmly held beliefs may experience less response order effects (Friedman et al., 1993; Krosnick & Schuman, 1988).
- Highly motivated respondents may be less prone to response order effects (Krosnick & Alwin, 1987; Weng & Cheng, 2000).
- Response order effects are less likely in self-administered surveys (Bishop et al., 1988; Chang & Krosnick, 2010).

Principles

- Provide clear and straightforward but very visible instructions about reading all options before selecting from among the provided responses.
- Provide shorter lists of response categories whenever possible without affecting your ability to capture the variation you seek.
- Consider rotating the order of response choices between different questionnaire sections (Krosnick & Alwin, 1987; Duffy, 2003; Holbrook et al., 2007). When choosing to do so, be sure to provide very conspicuous and prominent instructions to the respondents about the order of responses being rotated.
- Use simple and straightforward language for the measures and their corresponding response categories and limit the length of the self-report data collection session (Duffy, 2003; Holbrook et al., 2007; Krosnick & Alwin, 1987; Malhotra, 2009).

Commentary

Two recurring questions that I get asked in the context of ordering a response scale are: does it make a difference if I order my response scale categories is an ascending order (e.g. from Strongly Disagree to Strongly Agree) or a descending order? And, how do I make sure the participants are paying attention to the nuances among response categories? When deciding whether to organize agreement or likelihood response scales from negative to positive or positive to negative or low to high or high to low, remember there is a human tendency to proceed in an ascending order rather than in a descending order. For example, counting in an ascending order is easier than a descending order. As such, it is possible that the ascending order would be easier to process and result in less burden for respondents. With respect to whether study participants are paying attention and reading the response categories, some researchers think It is useful to use one or more attention checks. For a discussion of the various techniques of attention checks, please see Berinsky, Margolis and Sances, (2014), Meade & Craig, (2012), and Chapter 8 in this book.

References and additional readings

Ayidiya, S.A., & McClendon, M.J. (1990). Response effects in mail surveys. *Public Opinion Quarterly, 54*(2), 229–247. doi:10.1086/269200

Barnette, J.J. (2000). Effects of stem and likert response option reversals on survey internal consistency: If you feel the need, there is a better alternative to using those negatively worded stems. *Educational and Psychological Measurement, 60*(3), 361–370. doi:10.1177/00131640021970592

Becker, S.L. (1954). Why an order effect. *Public Opinion Quarterly, 18*(3), 271–278. doi:10.1086/266516

Belson, W.A. (1966). The effects of reversing the presentation order of verbal rating scales. *Journal of Advertising Research, 6*(4), 30–37. doi:10.1080/01411926.2010.544712

Berinsky, A. J., Margolis, M. F., & Sances, M. W. (2014). Focusing on the fundamentals: The use of attention checks to detect inattentive respondents in survey research. *Political Analysis, 22*(1), 1–23.

Bishop, G., Hippler, H., Schwarz, N. & Strack, F. (1988). A comparison of response effects in self-administered and telephone surveys. *Telephone Survey Methodology,* 321–340. No doi available.

Bishop, G., & Smith, A. (2001). Response-order effects and the early Gallup split-ballots. *Public Opinion Quarterly, 65*(4), 479–505. doi:10.1086/323575

Chan, J.C. (1991). Response-order effects in Likert-type scales. *Educational and Psychological Measurement, 51*(3), 531–540. doi:10.1177/0013164491513002

Chang, L. & Krosnick, J. (2010). Comparing oral interviewing with self-administered computerized questionnaires: An experiment. *Public Opinion Quarterly, 74*(1), 154–167. doi:10.1093/poq/nfp090

Duffy, B. (2003). Response order effects – How do people read? *International Journal of Market Research, 45*(4), 457–466. No doi available.

Friedman, H.H., Herskovitz, P.J., & Pollack, S. (1993). The biasing effects of scale-checking styles on response to a Likert scale. Proceedings of the American Statistical Association Annual Conference: Survey Research Methods, 792–795. Retrieved from https://www.amstat.org/Sections/Srms/Proceedings/papers/1993_133.pdf.

Galesic, M., Tourangeau, R., Couper, M.P., & Conrad, F.G. (2008). Eye-tracking data: New insights on response order effects and other cognitive shortcuts in survey responding. *Public Opinion Quarterly, 72*(5), 892–913. doi:10.1093/poq/nfn059

Holbrook, A.L., Krosnick, J.A., Moore, D., & Tourangeau, R. (2007) Response order effects in dichotomous categorical questions presented orally: The impact of question and respondent attributes. *Public Opinion Quarterly, 71*(3), 1–25. doi:10.1093/opq/nfm024

Knauper, B. (1999). The impact of age and education on response order effects in attitude measurement. *Public Opinion Quarterly, 63*(3), 347–370. doi:10.1086/297724

Krosnick, J., & Alwin, D. (1987). An evaluation of a cognitive theory of response-order effects in survey measurement. *Public Opinion Quarterly, 51*(2), 201–219. doi:10.1086/269029

Krosnick, J.A., & Schuman, H. (1988). Attitude intensity, importance, and certainty and susceptibility to response effects. *Journal of Personality and Social Psychology, 54*(6), 940–952. doi:10.1037/0022-3514.54.6.940

Malhotra, N. (2008). Completion time and response order effects in web surveys. *Public Opinion Quarterly, 72*(5), 914–934. doi:10.1093/poq/nfn050

Malhotra, N. (2009). Order effects in complex and simple tasks. *Public Opinion Quarterly, 73*(1), 180–198. doi:10.1093/poq/nfp008

McClendon, M.J. (1986). Response-order effects for dichotomous questions. *Social Science Quarterly, 67*(1), 205–211. No doi available.

Meade, A. W., & Craig, S. B. (2012). Identifying careless responses in survey data. *Psychological Methods, 17*(3), 437–455.

Nicholls, M.E., Orr, C.A., Okubo, M., & Loftus, A. (2006). Satisfaction guaranteed the effect of spatial biases on responses to Likert scales. *Psychological Science, 17*(12), 1027–1028. doi:10.1111/j.1467-9280.2006.01822.x

Rammstedt, B., & Krebs, D. (2007). Does response scale format affect the answering of personality scales? Assessing the big five dimensions of personality with different response scales in a dependent sample. *European Journal Of Psychological Assessment, 23*(1), 32–38. doi:10.1027/1015-5759.23.1.32

Weng, L.J., & Cheng, C.P. (2000). Effects of response order on Likert-type scales. *Educational and Psychological Measurement, 60*(6), 908–924. doi:10.1177/00131640021970989

Section 6.4: How many points should I use for my response scales?

Definition of terms – Number of response scale points?

In the context of self-report research, respondents are often asked to read statements, provided a gradation of possible reactions to these statements, and then asked to choose the reaction that best matches their thoughts or feeling about each statement. The gradation of reactions is known as a response scale. Each point on the response scale represents a degree of intensity corresponding to a reaction to a statement or other stimulus provided by the researcher (see Alwin, 1992). For example, respondents might be asked to express their agreement to a statement on a scale that ranges from "Strongly Disagree", "Disagree", Neither Agree nor Disagree, Agree, and Strongly Agree or indicate how often they use a specific service on a scale of "Never," "Rarely," "Sometimes," "Frequently," or "Very Frequently." The question researchers usually ask about response scales deals with the number of gradations or points these scales should optimally have. The most common types of response scales include those known as Likert type. These include agreement scales (from "Strongly Disagree" to "Strongly Agree"), likelihood scales (from "Very Unlikely" to "Very Likely"), liking scales ("Don't Like At All" to "Like Very Much"), and others that follow a similar style. Another widely used scale is known as semantic differential. These scales ask respondents to express their reactions along a continuum of points at each end of which is one of a set of bipolar adjectives. For example, "Dislike"–"Like"; "Old Fashion"–"Trendy"; "Ugly"–"Beautiful", etc.

In brief

Most studies under this category aim to find the optimal number of response categories that yield the most valid and reliable data. Overall, there is no consensus in the research community regarding this optimal number. However, many studies show this optimal number between five and seven points. Much of the research on response category stems from the "Information Theory Hypothesis," which states that reliability (and in some cases, validity) increases as the number of response categories increases. This is "based on the idea that since more information can be transmitted via response scales of greater length, respondents can more reliably convey their subjective states using scales with more categories" (Alwin, 1992, p. 111). Many studies confirmed the Information Theory Hypothesis and, instead of choosing an optimal number of response categories, simply found that reliability increases with the number of categories (Alwin, 1992; Bendig et al., 1953; Halpin et al., 1994; Maydeu-Olivares et al., 2009). There must be a cap to the Information Theory Hypothesis where reliability reaches a threshold before leveling off and potentially even dropping.

Overall, scales with fewer response categories (less than 15) are just as effective as continuous scales or scales ranging from 0–100 (Cicchetti et al., 1985; McKelvie, S., 1978; Scherpenzeel et al., 1997). The most common findings indicate that reliability levels out at either 5-point (Adelson et al., 2010; Bandalos et al., 1996; Jenkins et al., 1977; Lissitz et al., 1975 McKelvie, S., 1978; Revilla et al., 2013; Scherpenzeel et al., 1997; Weijters et al., 2010), 6-point (Matell et al., 1972; McKelvie, 1978; Moore et al., 2002; Moors, 2008) or 7-point (Bandalos et al., 1996; Cicchetti et al., 1985; Courneya et al., 2006; Hofmans et al., 2007; Matell et al., 1972; Preston et al., 2000; Ramsay, 1973; Scherpenzeel et al., 1997; Weijters et al., 2010) response scales, and thus 5-, 6-, or 7-point response categories are considered optimal.

Alternatively, fewer articles found no relationship between the number of response categories and validity or reliability scores (Bendig, 1954; Brown et al., 1991; Jacoby & Matell, 1971). Though there has not been total agreement in the research community about the optimal number of response categories, there is agreement that more verbal cues (labeling each response category) as opposed to strictly endpoint labeling increases data quality (for example, including all three of the following labels: "I know a great deal about this country," "I know something about this country," "I know very little about this country" (Bendig et al., 1953, p. 88) as opposed to just the first and last labels (Bendig et al., 1953; Boote, 1981; Weijters et al., 2010; Weng, 2004).

Expectations

- Some research indicates that reliability increases with the number of categories following the Information Theory Hypothesis (Alwin, 1992; Bendig et al., 1953; Halpin et al., 1994; Maydeu-Olivares et al., 2009).
- Some research indicates no relationship between the number of response categories and a measure's reliability (Bendig, 1954; Brown et al., 1991; Jacoby & Matell, 1971).
- A large number of studies indicates the optimal number of response categories that maximize validity and reliability is 5- to 7-points (Adelson et al., 2010; Bandalos et al., 1996; Cicchetti et al., 1985; Courneya et al., 2006; Hofmans et al., 2007; Jacoby & Matell, 1971; Jenkins et al., 1977; Lissitz et al., 1975; McKelvie, 1978; Moore et al., 2002; Moors, 2008; Preston et al., 2000; Ramsay, 1973; Revilla et al., 2013; Scherpenzeel et al., 1997; Weijters et al., 2010).
- Completely labeled scales, or scales with endpoint and midpoint labels (as opposed to just labeling the endpoints), are associated with better data quality (Bendig, 1953; Bendig & Hughes, 1953; Boote, 1981; Weng, 2004; Weijters et al., 2010).

Principles

- Generally, using 5-, 6-, or 7-point response scales will yield the highest levels of validity and reliability.
- Whenever possible, completely label response scales (as opposed to strictly labeling endpoints or simply providing numbers).

Commentary

In addition to the evidence that converges around using scales that are 5- to 7-point in length to maximize validity and reliability, there is another critical reason for using scales that have at least five points. A scale with fewer than five points violates the assumption of continuous data required by most statistics beyond simple descriptive techniques. A scale with fewer than five response categories would thus prevent or make it very difficult for a researcher to use higher-order statistical tools when analyzing their data (for a discussion, see Clarifio & Perla, 2007).

The finding that there is a correlation between the number of scale points and the reliability of a measure captured by this scale is interesting. It is important to remember that, when it comes to humans, the number of scale points they can distinguish has its limits. In an unpublished experiment, I found that, when given a 100-point scale designed to capture the certainty of consumers' intention to adopt a new technology, respondents overwhelmingly chose three points along a range of 100 possible points. These three points were 0, 50 and 100. The study participants mentally reduced the 100-point scale to three points, which is highly problematic from the point of view of fully capturing the variation and being able to analyze the data using advanced statistical tools. So, the 5-to-7-point finding seems to be optimal for humans. When it comes to machines, however, this limitation is not present, and Chapter 10 demonstrates the use of a 19-point scale for coding sentiment present in social media text with the help of AI.

References and additional readings

Adelson, J.L., & McCoach, D.B. (2010). Measuring the mathematical attitudes of elementary students: The effects of a 4-point or 5-point Likert-type scale. *Educational and Psychological Measurement, 70*(5), 796–807. doi:10.1177/0013164410366694

Alwin, D.F. (1992). Information transmission in the survey interview: Number of response categories and the reliability of attitude measurement. *Sociological Methodology, 22*, 83–118. doi:10.2307/270993

Alwin, D.F. (1997). Feeling thermometers versus 7-point scales. Which are better? *Sociological Methods and Research, 25*(3), 318–341. doi:10.1177/0049124197025003003

Bandalos, D.L., & Enders, C.K. (1996). The effects of nonnormality and number of response categories on reliability. *Applied Measurement in Education, 9*(2), 151–160. doi:10.1207/s15324818ame0902_4

Bendig, A.W. (1953). The reliability of self-ratings as a function of the amount of verbal anchoring and of the number of categories on the scale. *Journal of Applied Psychology, 37*(1), 38–41. doi:10.1037/h0057911

Bendig, A.W. (1954). Reliability of short rating scales and the heterogeneity of the rated stimuli. *Journal Of Applied Psychology, 38*(3), 167–170. doi:10.1037/h0059072

Bendig, A.W., & Hughes II, J. B. (1953). Effect of amount of verbal anchoring and number of rating-scale categories upon transmitted information. *Journal of Experimental Psychology, 46*(2), 87. doi: 10.1037/h0062482

Boote, A.S. (1981). Reliability testing of psychographic scales. *Journal of Advertising Research, 21*(5), 53–60. No doi available.

Brown, G., Widing, R.E., & Coulter, R.L. (1991). Customer evaluation of retail salespeople utilizing the SOCO scale: A replication, extension, and application. *Journal of the Academy of Marketing Science, 19*(4), 347–351. doi:10.1007/BF02726510

Chang, L. (1994). A psychometric evaluation of 4-point and 6-point likert-type scales in relation to reliability and validity. *Applied Psychological Measurement, 18*(3), 205–215. doi:10.1177/014662169401800302

Cicchetti, D., Showalter, D., Tyrer, P. (1985). The effect of number of rating scale categories on levels of interrater reliability: A Monte Carlo investigation. *Applied Psychological Measurement, 9*(1), 31–36. doi:10.1177/014662168500900103

Carifio, J., & Perla, R. J. (2007). Ten common misunderstandings, misconceptions, persistent myths and urban legends about Likert scales and Likert response formats and their antidotes. *Journal of Social Sciences, 3*(3), 106–116. https://doi.org/10.3844/jssp.2007.106.116

Courneya, K.S., Conner, M., & Rhodes, R.E. (2006). Effects of different measurement scales on the variability and predictive validity of the 'two-component' model of the theory of planned behavior in the exercise domain. *Psychology & Health, 21*(5), 557–570. doi:10.1080/14768320500422857

Halpin, G., Halpin, G., & Arbet, S. (1994). Effects of number and type of response choices on internal consistency reliability. *Perceptual And Motor Skills, 79*(2), 928–930. doi:10.2466/pms.1994.79.2.928

Hofmans, J., Theuns, P., & Mairesse, O. (2007). Impact of the number of response categories on linearity and sensitivity of self-anchoring scales: A functional measurement approach. *Methodology: European Journal Of Research Methods For The Behavioral And Social Sciences, 3*(4), 160–169. doi:10.1027/1614-2241.3.4.160

Jacoby, J., & Matell, M.S. (1971). Three point Likert scales are good enough. *Journal Of Marketing Research, 8*(4), 495–500. doi:10.2307/3150242

Jenkins, G., & Taber, T.D. (1977). A Monte Carlo study of factors affecting three indices of composite scale reliability. *Journal Of Applied Psychology, 62*(4), 392–398. doi:10.1037/0021-9010.62.4.392

Kieruj, N.D., & Moors, G. (2010). Variations in response style behavior by response scale format in attitude research. *International Journal of Public Opinion Research, 22*(3), 320–342. doi:10.1093/ijpor/edq001

Lehmann, D., & Hulbert, J. (1972). Are three-point scales always good enough? *Journal of Marketing Research, 9*(4), 444–446. doi:10.1177/002224377200900416

Lissitz, R., & Green, S. (1975). *Journal of Applied Psychology, 60*(1), 10–13. doi:10.1037/h0076268

Masters, J.R. (1974). The relationship between number of response categories and reliability of Likert-type questionnaires. *Journal of Educational Measurement, 11*(1), 49–53. doi:10.1111/j.1745-3984.1974.tb00970.x

Matell, M.S., & Jacoby, J. (1972). Is there an optimal number of alternatives for Likert-scale items? Effects of testing time and scale properties. *Journal Of Applied Psychology, 56*(6), 506–509. doi:10.1037/h0033601

Maydeu-Olivares, A., Kramp, U., García-Forero, C., Gallardo-Pujol, D., & Coffman, D. (2009). The effect of varying the number of response alternatives in rating scales: Experimental evidence from intra-individual effects. *Behavior Research Methods, 41*(2), 295–308. doi:10.3758/BRM.41.2.295

McCallum, D.M., Keith, B.R., & Wiebe, D.J. (1988). Comparison of response formats for multidimensional health locus of control scales: Six levels versus two levels. *Journal of Personality Assessment, 52*(4), 732–736. doi:10.1207/s15327752jpa5204_12

McKelvie, S.J. (1978). Graphic rating scales: How many categories? *British Journal of Psychology, 69*(2), 185–202. doi:10.1111/j.2044-8295.1978.tb01647.x

Moors, G. (2008). Exploring the effect of a middle response category on response style in attitude measurement. *Quality and Quantity, 42*(6), 779–794. doi:10.1007/s11135-006-9067-x

Preston, C., & Colman, A. (2000) Optimal number of response categories in rating scales: Reliability, validity, discriminating power, and respondent preferences. *Acta Psychologica, 104*(1),1–15. doi:10.1016/S0001-6918(99)00050-5

Ramsay, J. (1973). The effect of number of categories in rating scales on precision of estimation of scale values. *Psychometrika, 38*(4), 513–532. doi:10.1007/BF02291492

Revilla, M.A., Saris, W.E., & Krosnick, J.A. (2013). Choosing the number of categories in agree–disagree scales. *Sociological Methods & Research, 43*(1), 73–97. doi:10.1177/0049124113509605

Scherpenzeel, A.C., & Saris, W.E. (1997). The validity and reliability of survey questions: A meta-analysis of MTMM studies. *Sociological Methods and Research, 25*(3), 341–383. doi: 10.1177/0049124197025003004

Schwarz, N., Hippler, H., Deutsch B., Strack, F. (1985). Response scales: Effects of category range on reported behavior and comparative judgments. *Public Opinion Quarterly, 49*(3), 388–395. doi:10.1086/268936

Weijters, B., Cabooter, E., & Schillewaert, N. (2010). The effect of rating scale format on response styles: The number of response categories and response category labels. *International Journal Of Research In Marketing*, *27*(3), 236–247. doi:10.1016/j.ijresmar.2010.02.004

Weng, L. (2004). Impact of the number of response categories and anchor labels on coefficient alpha and test-retest reliability. *Educational and Psychological Measurement*, *64*(6), 956–972. doi:10.1177/0013164404268674

Chapter 7
Principles and expectations: Motivation to self-report

Objectives of Chapter 7: You will need to make many decisions when motivating study participants to self-report. These decisions include how to contact participants, the type of appeals you use when inviting them to participate, whether to personalize your communication with them, the kinds of incentives you might use to encourage them to participate, whether you need to alleviate their concerns over the privacy of their self-disclosures and what to anticipate regarding their level of interest in the topic of your research. While there are undoubtedly other decisions you must consider when motivating study participants, this chapter addresses the aspects aligned in a substantial proportion of the corresponding literature.

Which assumptions are addressed in this chapter?

Table 7.1: Assumptions made about respondents for self-report measures to achieve their intended purpose.

When reacting to a measure or answering a question, the respondent	
Assumption A	**Is willing to disclose information about themselves**
Assumption B	Is truthful and not deliberately lying
Assumption C	Interprets each measure/question the way the researcher intended and in the same way that others who are also being measured are interpreting them
Assumption D	Can correctly recall needed information from memory to react to each measure/question
Assumption E	Can easily move from one measure/question to another when multiple measures/questions are included
Assumption F	Is self-aware
Assumption G	Is not influenced by one or more aspects of the questions/measures to which they are asked to react

The assumption bolded in Table 7.1 is affected by violations of the principles provided in the sections of this chapter. The premise of self-report measurement depends on an individual's willingness to self-report. If someone invited to participate in a study decides not to participate, this decision terminates the possibility of collecting information from this individual. While this topic has most commonly been covered under the non-response rubric that falls under sampling, I look at it in this book from a mea-

Table 7.2: Assumptions made about the measures so that they can achieve their intended purpose.

Each measure developed by the researcher should . . .	
Assumption H	Fully capture the concept or an aspect of the concept that it is intended to capture
Assumption I	Precisely capture the aspect of the concept that it is intended to capture
Assumption J	Capture a single concept and no other
Assumption K	Be consistent in its capturing of the concept that it was designed to capture

surement viewpoint. The more motivated an individual is to self-report, the more likely they will reveal helpful information captured through their completed self-report measures. What can a researcher do to maximize the chances that individuals are willing to self-report and be candid when they do? This chapter goes over findings from the relevant literature.

Section 7.1: Can the way I contact respondents influence their willingness to self-report?

Definition – What is contacting respondents?

Contact is defined by Merriam-Webster (2019) as "an establishing of communication with someone or an observing or receiving of a significant signal from a person or object" (par. 7). In the context of surveys, the primary contact researchers make with a respondent happens at the point that the respondent receives the survey, be it a physical copy or a web link (Manfreda et al., 2008). Other types of contact are advance contact, which refers to any contact made with a potential respondent before the main contact, and follow-up contact, which refers to any subsequent contacts made with the respondent after the main contact, usually serving as a reminder to complete the survey for those who have not yet done so (Linsky, 1975).

It is necessary to note that most research discussed in this chapter does not explicitly evaluate the effectiveness of contact on respondents' motivation. Most researchers assess the effects of contact in terms of tangible response or cooperation rates. For our purposes, we will equate high or low levels of response and/or cooperation rates with corresponding high or low levels of effectiveness in increasing respondent motivation.

In brief

Extensive research has been conducted on the effectiveness of various methods and aspects of contacting survey respondents. There is plenty of evidence supporting the use of advance contact (Allen et al., 1980; Bosnjak et al., 2008; Cook et al., 2000; De Leeuw et al., 2007; Dillman et al., 1976; Duncan, 1979; Edwards et al., 2002; Fan & Yan, 2010; Ford, 1967; Fox et al., 1988; Goldstein & Jennings, 2002; Hembroff et al., 2005; Jones & Lang, 1980; Kanuk & Berenson, 1975; Kaplowitz et al., 2004; Larson & Poist, 2004; Link & Mokdad, 2005; Linsky, 1975; Mitchell & Nugent, 1991; Porter & Whitcomb, 2007; Robertson et al., 2000; Stafford, 1966; Walker & Burdick, 1977; Yammarino et al., 1991; Yu & Cooper, 1983).

There are also many studies supporting the use of follow-up contact (Boyle et al., 2012; Blumberg et al., 1974; Duncan, 1979; Etzel & Walker, 1974; Nichols & Meyer, 1966; Kanuk & Berenson, 1975; Linsky, 1975; Roscoe et al., 1975; Jones & Lang, 1980; Swan et al., 1980; Furse et al., 1981; Powers & Alderman, 1982; Yu & Cooper, 1983; De Leeuw & Hox, 1988; Fox et al., 1988; James & Bolstein, 1990; Yammarino et al., 1991; Dillman et al., 1994; Asch et al., 1997; Fox et al., 1998; Edwards et al., 2002; Schonlau et al., 2003; Kaplowitz et al., 2004; Larson & Poist, 2004; Roose et al., 2007; Shih & Fan, 2007; Van Horn et al., 2009; Fan & Yan, 2010; Messer & Dillman, 2011).

For advance contact, several researchers have found telephone calls, letters, or electronic contacts (text messages or emails) to be most effective (Stafford, 1966; Linsky, 1975; Hembroff et al., 2005; Porter & Whitcomb, 2007; and Bosnjak et al., 2008). Specifically for follow-up contacts, there is evidence to support the use of telephone calls and postcards to motivate respondents (Linsky, 1975; Roscoe et al., 1975; Asch et al., 1997; Fox et al., 1998; Schonlau et al., 2003; and Messer & Dillman, 2011).

While most of the research in this chapter refers to postal or web surveys, Blohm et al. (2006) suggest that the principles regarding the success of advance contact may not apply to face-to-face interviews. These researchers found that interviewers who showed up to potential respondents' homes unannounced were more successful in obtaining completed interviews rather than those who called ahead to potential respondents to try to schedule an appointment (Blohm et al., 2006).

For mail surveys, several researchers have concluded that using higher classes of postage, especially in follow-up contacts, as well as providing respondents with an envelope with an actual stamp rather than with a business reply envelope are more effective than other forms of postage (Jeanne & Gullahorn, 1963; Blumberg et al., 1974; Kanuk & Berenson, 1975; Linsky, 1975; Tedin & Hofstetfer, 1982; Armstrong & Lusk, 1987; Fox et al., 1988; Edwards et al., 2002).

In terms of the contact process, the exact number of contacts made with a respondent is also essential: there seems to be a consensus among studies that researchers should plan to contact their respondents no more than three times, as too many contacts may lead to oversaturation and frustration which can decrease individuals' motivation to participate (Goulet, 1977; Heberlein & Baumgartner, 1978; Cook et al., 2000; Manfreda et al., 2008; Shih & Fan, 2009; Van Horn et al., 2009).

Similarly, the timing of contact is essential to a certain extent. While the time of day or day of the week does not appear to have any significant effects (Mitchell & Nugent, 1991), follow-up contacts should be sent earlier rather than later, ideally no later than three days after receipt of the survey, with more variation in the timing of subsequent follow-up contacts are made (Nichols & Meyer, 1966; and Crawford et al., 2001).

While most of the literature dates back to when telephone and mail surveys were the standard modes of data collection, several more recent studies have found that when conducting web surveys, electronic contacts such as text messages or emails are effective both when used alone and when combined and with traditional postal contacts (Bosnjak et al., 2008; Manfreda et al., 2008; and Millar & Dillman, 2011).

Expectations

- In general, contacting respondents in advance will increase their motivation to participate in a survey when the time comes. One potential exception may be if the researcher has a very homogenous sample rather than one that is diverse and represents several different groups of people (Parsons & Medford, 1972).
- The most effective types of advance contact to increase respondent motivation are telephone calls, letters, and, in recent years, text messages and emails.
- Follow-up contact with respondents is a highly reliable method of increasing their motivation to participate in surveys.
- Follow-up postcards and telephone calls have traditionally been the most effective follow-up methods for increasing respondent motivation.
- For postal surveys, respondents are more motivated to respond to those sent with higher classes of mail, most commonly first-class. However, forms of "special delivery" are effective as well.
- Additionally, when participants are asked to return surveys by mail, using return envelopes with actual stamps is more motivating than using business reply envelopes.
- Contacting a respondent too often leads to oversaturation and can adversely affect motivation to participate in a survey.
- Generally, the time of day or day of the week a respondent is contacted does not affect motivation to participate in surveys.

Principles

- Make advance contact with the potential respondent through telephone calls, letters, postcards or electronic contact about four or five days before sending the self-report measures (e.g. survey) (Stafford, 1966; Ford, 1967; Kanuk & Berenson, 1975; Linsky, 1975; Dillman et al., 1976; Walker & Burdick, 1977; Duncan, 1979; Allen et al., 1980; Jones & Lang, 1980; Yu & Cooper, 1983; Fox et al., 1988; Mitchell & Nugent, 1991; Yammarino et al., 1991; Cook et al., 2000; Robertson et al., 2000;

Edwards et al., 2002; Goldstein & Jennings, 2002; Kaplowitz et al., 2004; Larson & Poist, 2004; Hembroff et al., 2005; Link & Mokdad, 2005; De Leeuw et al., 2007; Porter & Whitcomb, 2007; Bosnjak et al., 2008; and Fan & Yan, 2010).
- Follow up with potential respondents or send a reminder via a telephone call or a postcard, with the first follow-up contact ideally made three days after sending the survey, and any subsequent follow-ups varied in their timing. Additionally, after the first follow-up, be sure to provide the respondent with a new copy of the survey (Nichols & Meyer, 1966; Blumberg et al., 1974; Etzel & Walker, 1974; Kanuk & Berenson, 1975; Linsky, 1975; Roscoe et al., 1975; Duncan, 1979; Jones & Lang, 1980; Swan et al., 1980; Furse et al., 1981; Powers & Alderman, 1982; Yu & Cooper, 1983; De Leeuw & Hox, 1988; Fox et al., 1988; James & Bolstein, 1990; Yammarino et al., 1991; Dillman et al., 1994; Asch et al., 1997; Fox et al., 1998; Edwards et al., 2002; Schonlau et al., 2003; Kaplowitz et al., 2004; Larson & Poist, 2004; Roose et al., 2007; Shih & Fan, 2007; Van Horn et al., 2009; Fan & Yan, 2010; Messer & Dillman, 2011; and Boyle et al., 2012).
- When expecting participants to return completed self-report measures by regular mail, opt for first-class (or generally any higher class) mail and reply envelopes with actual stamps rather than business reply envelopes (Jeanne & Gullahorn, 1963; Blumberg et al., 1974; Kanuk & Berenson, 1975; Linsky, 1975; Tedin & Hofstetfer, 1982; Armstrong & Lusk, 1987; Fox et al., 1988; Edwards et al., 2002).
- For web surveys, use electronic contacts (text messages or emails), either alone or a combination of electronic and postal contacts (Bosnjak et al., 2008; Manfreda et al., 2008; Millar & Dillman, 2011).
- In general, plan to contact respondents no more than three times to prevent oversaturating them and decreasing their motivation (Goulet, 1977; Heberlein & Baumgartner, 1978; Cook et al., 2000; Manfreda et al., 2008; Shih & Fan, 2009; Van Horn et al., 2009).

Commentary

Important goals of contacting respondents are to establish rapport, establish the credibility of the organization collecting the information, and reduce uncertainty about confidentiality, privacy, and other concerns associated with filling out questionnaires.

References and additional readings

Allen, C. T., Schewe, C. D., & Wijk, G. (1980). More on self-perception theory's foot technique in the pre-call/mail survey setting. *Journal of Marketing Research, 17*(4), 498. doi:10.2307/3150502

Armstrong, J. S., & Lusk, E. J. (1987). Return postage in mail surveys a meta-analysis. *Public Opinion Quarterly, 51*(2), 233–248. doi:10.1086/269031

Asch, D. A., Jedrziewski, M. K., & Christakis, N. A. (1997). Response rates to mail surveys published in medical journals. *Journal of Clinical Epidemiology, 50*(10), 1129–1136.10.1016/s0895-4356(97)00126-1

Birnholtz, J. P., Horn, D. B., Finholt, T. A., & Bae, S. J. (2004). The effects of cash, electronic, and paper gift certificates as respondent incentives for a web-based survey of technologically sophisticated respondents. *Social Science Computer Review, 22*(3), 355–362. doi:10.1177/0894439304263147

Blohm, M., Hox, J., & Koch, A. (2006). The influence of interviewers' contact behavior on the contact and cooperation rate in face-to-face household surveys. *International Journal of Public Opinion Research, 19*(1), 97–111. doi:10.1093/ijpor/edh120

Blumberg, H. H., Fuller, C., & Hare, A. P. (1974). Response rates in postal surveys. *Public Opinion Quarterly, 38*(1), 113. doi:10.1086/268140

Bosnjak, M., Neubarth, W., Couper, M. P., Bandilla, W., & Kaczmirek, L. (2008). Prenotification in web-based access panel surveys: The influence of mobile text messaging versus e-mail on response rates and sample composition. *Social Science Computer Review, 26*(2), 213–223. doi:10.1177/0894439307305895

Boyle, T., Heyworth, J., Landrigan, J., Mina, R., & Fritschi, L. (2012). The effect of lottery scratch tickets and donation offers on response fraction: A study and meta-analysis. *Field Method, 24*(1), 112–132. doi:10.1177/1525822X11424549

Champion, D. J., & Sear, A. M. (1969). Questionnaire response rate: A methodological analysis. *Social Forces, 47*(3), 335–339. doi:10.2307/2575033

Contact [Def. 2c]. (2019). In *Merriam-Webster Online*. Retrieved April 8, 2019, from https://www.merriam-webster.com/dictionary/contact.

Cook, C., Heath, F., & Thompson, R. L. (2000). A meta-analysis of response rates in web- or internet-based surveys. *Educational and Psychological Measurement, 60*(6), 821–836. doi:10.1177/00131640021970934

Cox, E. P., III, Anderson, T., Jr., & Fulcher, D. G. (1974). Reappraising mail survey response rates. *Journal of Marketing Research, 11*(4), 413–417. doi:10.2307/3151287

Crawford, S. D., Couper, M. P., & Lamias, M. J. (2001). Web surveys: Perceptions of burden. *Social Science Computer Review, 19*(2), 146–162. doi:10.1177/089443930101900202

De Leeuw, E., Callegaro, M., Hox, J., Korendijk, E., & Lensvelt-Mulders, G. (2007). The influence of advance letters on response in telephone surveys: A meta-analysis. *Public Opinion Quarterly, 71*(3), 413–443. doi:10.1093/poq/nfm014

De Leeuw, E.D., & Hox, J.J. (1988). The effects of response-stimulating factors on response rates and data quality in mail surveys. *Journal of Official Statistics, 4*(3), 241–249. No doi available.

Deutskens, E., De Ruyter, K., Wetzels, M., & Oosterveld, P. (2004). Response rate and response quality of internet-based surveys: An experimental study. *Marketing Letters, 15*(1), 21–36. doi:10.1023/B:MARK.0000021968.86465.00

Dickson, J.P., & MacLachlan, D.L. (1996). Fax surveys: Return patterns and comparison with mail surveys. *Journal of Marketing Research, 33*(1), 108–113. doi:10.2307/3152017

Dillman, D.A., Christenson, J.A., Carpenter, E.H., & Brooks, R.M. (1974). Increasing mail questionnaire response: A four state comparison. *American Sociological Review, 39*(5), 744–756. doi:10.2307/2094318

Dillman, D.A., Gallegos, J.G., & Frey, J.H. (1976). Reducing refusal rates for telephone interviews. *Public Opinion Quarterly, 40*(1), 66–78. doi:10.1086/268268

Dillman, D.A., West, K.K., & Clark, J.R. (1994). Influence of an invitation to answer by telephone on response to census questionnaires. *Public Opinion Quarterly, 58*(4), 557–568. doi:10.1086/269447

Duncan, W. J. (1979). Mail questionnaires in survey research: A review of response inducement techniques. *Journal of Management, 5*(1), 39–55. doi:10.1177/014920637900500103

Edwards, P., Roberts, I., Clarke, M., DiGuiseppi, C., Pratap, S., Wentz, R., & Kwan, I. (2002). Increasing response rates to postal questionnaires: Systematic review. *BMJ, 324*(7347), 1183. doi:10.1136/bmj.324.7347.1183

Etzel, M. J., & Walker, B. J. (1974). Effects of alternative follow-up procedures on mail survey response rates. *Journal of Applied Psychology, 59*(2), 219–221. doi:10.1037/h0036456

Fan, W., & Yan, Z. (2010). Factors affecting response rates of the web survey: A systematic review. *Computers in Human Behavior, 26*(2), 132–139. doi:10.1016/j.chb.2009.10.015

Ford, N. M. (1967). The advance letter in mail surveys. *Journal of Marketing Research, 4*(2), 202–204. doi:10.2307/3149368

Fox, C. M., Boardley, D., & Robinson, K.L. (1998). Cost-effectiveness of follow-up strategies in improving the response rate of mail surveys. *Industrial Marketing Management, 27*(2), 127–133. doi:10.1016/s0019-8501(97)00043-6

Fox, R.J., Crask, M.R., & Kim, J. (1988). Mail survey response rate a meta-analysis of selected techniques for inducing response. *Public Opinion Quarterly, 52*(4), 467–491. doi:10.1086/269125

Furse, D.H., Stewart, D.W., & Rados, D.L. (1981). Effects of foot-in-the-door, cash incentives, and followups on survey response. *Journal of Marketing Research, 18*(4), 473. doi:10.2307/3151342

Goldstein, K. M., & Jennings, M. K. (2002). The effect of advance letters on cooperation in a list sample telephone survey. *Public Opinion Quarterly, 66*(4), 608–617. doi:10.1086/343756

Goulet, W. M. (1977). Efficacy of a third request letter in mail surveys of professionals. *Journal of Marketing Research, 14*(1), 112–114. doi:10.2307/3151068

Greer, T.V., & Chuchinprakarn, N. (1999). Business respondents' behavior: Main and interaction effects of delivery method, questionnaire length, and time of the week. *Journal of Business-to-Business Marketing, 6*(1), 59–88. doi:10.1300/J033v06n01_03

Greer, T.V., Chuchinprakarn, N., & Seshadri, S. (2000). Likelihood of participating in mail survey research: Business respondents' perspectives. *Industrial Marketing Management, 29*(2), 97–109. doi:10.1016/s0019-8501(98)00038-8

Hackler, J. C., & Bourgette, P. (1973). Dollars, dissonance, and survey returns. *Public Opinion Quarterly, 37*(2), 276–281. doi:10.1086/268085

Hayslett, M. M., & Wildemuth, B. M. (2004). Pixels or pencils? The relative effectiveness of web-based versus paper surveys. *Library & Information Science Research, 26*(1), 73–93. doi:10.1016/j.lisr.2003.11.005

Heberlein, T. A., & Baumgartner, R. (1978). Factors affecting response rates to mailed questionnaires: A quantitative analysis of the published literature. *American Sociological Review, 43*(4), 447–462. doi:10.2307/2094771

Hembroff, L. A., Rusz, D., Rafferty, A., McGee, H., & Ehrlich, N. (2005). The cost-effectiveness of alternative advance mailings in a telephone survey. *Public Opinion Quarterly, 69*(2), 232–245. doi:10.1093/poq/nfi021

Hopkins, K.D., & Podolak, J. (1983). Class-of-mail and the effects of monetary gratuity on the response rates of mailed questionnaires. *Journal of Experimental Education, 51*(4), 169–171. doi:10.1080/00220973.1983.11011857

James, J. M., & Bolstein, R. (1990). The effect of monetary incentives and follow-up mailings on the response rate and response quality in mail surveys. *Public Opinion Quarterly, 54*(3), 346–361. doi:10.1086/269211

Jeanne, E., & Gullahorn, J. T. (1963). An investigation of the effects of three factors on response to mail questionnaires. *Public Opinion Quarterly, 27*(2), 294–296. doi:10.1086/267170

Jones, W.H., & Lang, J.R. (1980). Sample composition bias and response bias in a mail survey: A comparison of inducement methods. *Journal of Marketing Research, 17*(1), 69–76. doi:10.2307/3151119

Jones, W. H., & Linda, G. (1978). Multiple criteria effects in a mail survey experiment. *Journal of Marketing Research, 15*(2), 280–284. doi:10.2307/3151263

Kanuk, L., & Berenson, C. (1975). Mail surveys and response rates: A literature review. *Journal of Marketing Research, 12*(4), 440–453. doi:10.2307/3151093

Kaplowitz, M.D., Hadlock, T. D., & Levine, R. (2004). A comparison of web and mail survey response rates. *Public Opinion Quarterly, 68*(1), 94–101. doi:10.1093/poq/nfh006

Kimball, A.E. (1961). Increasing the rate of return in mail surveys. *Journal of Marketing, 25*(6), 63–64. doi:10.2307/1248517

Klassen, R.D., & Jacobs, J. (2001). Experimental comparison of web, electronic and mail survey technologies in operations management. *Journal of Operations Management, 19*(6), 713–728. doi:10.1016/s0272-6963(01)00071-7

Labrecque, D.P. (1978). A response rate experiment using mail questionnaires. *Journal of Marketing, 42*(4), 82–83. doi:10.2307/1250090

Larson, P. D., & Poist, R. F. (2004). Improving response rates to mail surveys: a research note. *Transportation Journal*, 67–74. Retrieved from https://www.jstor.org/stable/20713582.

Link, M. W., & Mokdad, A. (2005). Advance letters as a means of improving respondent cooperation in random digit dial studies. *Public Opinion Quarterly, 69*(4), 572–587. doi:10.1093/poq/nfi055

Linsky, A. S. (1975). Stimulating responses of mailed questionnaires: a review. *Public Opinion Quarterly, 39*(1), 82–101. doi:10.1086/268201

Manfreda, K. L., Bosnjak, M., Berzelak, J., Haas, I., & Vehovar, V. (2008). Web surveys versus other survey modes. *International Journal of Market Research, 50*(1), 79–104. doi:10.1177/147078530805000107

McCrohan, K. F., & Lowe, L. S. (1981). A cost/benefit approach to postage used on mail questionnaires. *Journal of Marketing, 45*(1), 130. doi:10.2307/1251726

McGinnis, M. A., & Hollon, C. J. (1977). Mail survey response rate and bias: The effect of home versus work address. *Journal of Marketing Research, 14*(3), 383–384. doi:10.2307/3150779

Messer, B. L., & Dillman, D. A. (2011). Surveying the general public over the internet using address-based sampling and mail contact procedures. *Public Opinion Quarterly, 75*(3), 429–457. doi:10.1093/poq/nfr021

Millar, M.M., & Dillman, D.A. (2011). Improving response to web and mixed-mode surveys. *Public Opinion Quarterly, 75*(2), 249–269. doi:10.1093/poq/nfr003

Mitchell, V.W., & Nugent, S. (1991). Industrial mail surveys: The costs and benefits of telephone pre-notification. *Journal of Marketing Management, 7*(3), 257–269. doi:10.1080/0267257x.1991.9964155

Nichols, R. C., & Meyer, M. A. (1966). Timing postcard follow-ups in mail-questionnaire surveys. *Public Opinion Quarterly, 30*(2), 306–307. doi:10.1086/267412

Parsons, R. J., & Medford, T. S. (1972). The effect of advance notice in mail surveys of homogeneous groups. *Public Opinion Quarterly, 36*(2), 258–259. doi:10.1086/267998

Porter, S.R., & Whitcomb, M.E. (2005). E-mail subject lines and their effect on web survey viewing and response. *Social Science Computer Review, 23*(3), 380–387. doi:10.1177/0894439305275912

Porter, S.R., & Whitcomb, M.E. (2007). Mixed-Mode contacts in web surveys: Paper is not necessarily better. *Public Opinion Quarterly, 71*(4), 635–648. doi:10.1093/poq/nfm038

Powers, D. E., & Alderman, D. L. (1982). Feedback as an incentive for responding to a mail questionnaire. *Research in Higher Education, 17*(3), 207–211. doi:10.1007/BF00976698

Robertson, B., Sinclair, M., & Forbes, A. (2000). The effect of an introductory letter on participation rates using telephone recruitment. *Australian and New Zealand Journal of Public Health, 24*(5), 552. doi:10.1111/j.1467-842x.2000.tb00512.x

Roose, H., Lievens, J., & Waege, H. (2007). The joint effect of topic interest and follow-up procedures on the response in a mail questionnaire: An empirical test of the leverage-saliency theory in audience research. *Sociological Methods & Research, 35*(3), 410–428. doi:10.1177/0049124106290447

Roscoe, A. M., Lang, D., & Sheth, J. N. (1975). Follow-up methods, questionnaire length, and market differences. *Journal of Marketing, 39*, 20–27. doi:10.2307/1250111

Schonlau, M., Asch, B.J., & Du, C. (2003). Web surveys as part of a mixed-mode strategy for populations that cannot be contacted by e-mail. *Social Science Computer Review 21*(2), 218–222. doi:10.1177/0894439303021002007

Shih, T. H., & Fan, X. (2007). Response rates and mode preferences in web-mail mixed-mode surveys: a meta-analysis. *International Journal of Internet Science, 2*(1), 59–82. doi:10.1177/1525822X08317085

Shih, T. H., & Fan, X. (2009). Comparing response rates in e-mail and paper surveys: A meta-analysis. *Educational Research Review, 4*(1), 26–40. doi:10.1016/j.edurev.2008.01.003

Singer, E., Van Hoewyk, J., & Maher, M.P. (2000). Experiments with incentives in telephone surveys. *Public Opinion Quarterly, 64*(2), 171–188. doi:10.1086/317761

Stafford, J.E. (1966). Influence of preliminary contact on mail returns. *Journal of Marketing Research, 3*(4), 410–411. doi:10.2307/3149860

Swan, J.E., Epley, D.E., & Burns, W.L. (1980). Can follow-up response rates to a mail survey be increased by including another copy of the questionnaire? *Psychological Reports, 47*(1), 103–106. doi:10.2466/pr0.1980.47.1.103

Tedin, K.L., & Hofstetfer, C.R. (1982). The effect of cost and importance factors on the return rate for single and multiple mailings. *Public Opinion Quarterly, 46*(1), 122–128. doi:10.1086/268704

Van Horn, P.S., Green, K.E., & Martinussen, M. (2009). Survey response rates and survey administration in counseling and clinical psychology: A meta-analysis. *Educational and Psychological Measurement, 69*(3), 389–403. doi:10.1177/0013164408324462

Vocino, T. (1977). Three variables in stimulating responses to mailed questionnaires. *Journal of Marketing, 41*(4), 76–77. doi:10.2307/1250238

Walker, B. J., & Burdick, R. K. (1977). Advance correspondence and error in mail surveys. *Journal of Marketing Research, 14*(3), 379–382. doi:10.2307/3150778

Yammarino, F. J., Skinner, S. J., & Childers, T. L. (1991). Understanding mail survey response behavior a meta-analysis. *Public Opinion Quarterly, 55*(4), 613–639. doi:10.1086/269284

Yu, J., & Cooper, H. (1983). A quantitative review of research design effects on response rates to questionnaires. *Journal of Marketing Research, 20*(1), 36–44. doi:10.2307/3151410

Section 7.2: How can I convince the respondent to self-report?

Definition of term – What are appeals?

The term "appeal" is generally defined as "the power of arousing a sympathetic response" (Merriam-Webster online dictionary, 2019). In self-report measurement, a sympathetic response is manifested in a respondent's willingness to participate in a study and self-report. In this context, the appeal involves the strategy or combination of techniques used by the researcher to elicit a respondent's willingness to self-report. This chapter explores the appeals that may yield high motivation among survey respondents. Appeals may include the language and tone used in cover letters or introductions, framing requests for follow-up questions, and any other strategy that may resonate with the respondent.

It is important note that most studies reviewed do not explicitly measure participant motivation. Most researchers evaluate the success of an appeal in terms of response rates. This chapter will equate high response rates with high motivation and vice versa.

Example of appeals

Houston and Nevin (1977) provide excellent examples of four different types of appeals: "Social utility appeal" asks for the assistance of the respondent to improve the understanding of consumers in general; "Help-the-sponsor appeal " asks for the respondent's help to enhance the quality of specific services that the respondent is already using; "Egoistic appeal " emphasizes the importance of the respondent and/or their opinions; and "Combined appeal " adds two or more the preceding strategies together to strengthen the argument used to encourage the respondent to react to self-report measures (Houston & Nevin, 1977, p. 375).

In brief

While some researchers argue that appeals have no significant effects on participation (Dillman, Christenson, Carpenter, & Brooks, 1974 and Jones & Lang, 1980), a myriad of research suggests otherwise. Studies suggest several factors related to appeal strategies must be considered to increase respondents' motivation to complete a survey.

Egoistic appeals, in which the importance of the respondent's opinion is emphasized, are the most effective (Slocum, Empey, & Swanson, 1956; Champion & Sear, 1969; Blumberg, Fullerm and Hare, 1974; Houston & Nevin, 1977; Childers, Pride, & Ferrell, 1980; and Porter & Whitcomb, 2003). However, the effectiveness of an egoistic appeal may be influenced by its combination with another appeal, such as the type of sponsorship of the survey (Houston & Nevin, 1977) or the inclusion of a deadline statement (Porter and Whitcomb, 2003). Concerning sponsorship, several studies have found that invited survey participants are more likely to respond to self-report measurement projects associated with governmental agencies or academic institutions, and adding the name and title of the person in charge of the survey seems to add credibility to it (see Porter & Whitcomb, 2003). In terms of setting a deadline, Porter and Whitcomb (2003) provide the following as an example: "The website will be closed at midnight on [specific date inserted here]" (p. 582).

Altruistic appeals, which are also known as social utility or help-the-sponsor appeals, are also effective in many cases (Slocum et al., 1956; Houston & Nevin, 1977; Jones & Linda, 1978; Mowen & Cialdini, 1980; Esslemont, Gendall, & Hoek, 1995; Schneider & Johnson, 1995; Grove, Singer, & Corning, 2000; Edwards, Roberts, Clarke, DiGuiseppi, Pratap, Wentz, & Kwan, 2002; and Trouteaud, 2004; Han, Albaum, Wiley, & Thirkell, 2009). As with egoistic appeals, the effectiveness of altruistic appeals may be swayed based on the type of survey sponsorship. This type of appeal works better if the sponsor is a credible nonprofit than a commercial organization (Houston & Nevin, 1977). It works better if the receiver of the altruism is society rather than a sponsor (Schneider & Johnson, 1995). It works better if the respondent already has a high level of community involvement (Grove, Singer, & Corning, 2000). Some researchers have argued against the use of altruistic appeals, stating they have no significant effects and harm response rates (Champion & Sear, 1969; Linsky, 1975; Roberts, McCrory, & Forthoffer, 1978; Yu & Cooper, 1983; and Blohn, Hox, & Koch, 2006). Schneider and Johnson (1995) found that altruistic appeals should be avoided in commercial surveys.

In addition to egoistic and altruistic appeals, some less traditional, less commonly researched appeals may affect respondents' motivation levels. One appeal is the scarcity appeal, which frames survey participation as a rare opportunity, operating under the assumption that rare opportunities are perceived as more valuable, a technique that yielded positive results for Grove, Cialdini, and Couper (1992). Another is the mandatory appeal, which presents a survey in such a way that the respondents feel they are required to participate. Not much research has been conducted on mandatory appeals. From what research is available, there are conflicting results on the effectiveness of mandatory appeals (Dillman, Singer, Clark, & Treat, 1996) since suggesting that mandatory participation will most likely lower a respondent's motivation to self-report (Biner, 1988).

Two additional appeals are the promise to give feedback on research results and the statement of a deadline within the request to participate. There is limited research on providing input to respondents as an effective type of appeal, but some found it compelling (Powers & Alderman, 1982). The effects of stating a deadline have been studied a bit more, and several researchers have found evidence that giving respondents a set deadline increases the overall willingness to participate in a survey, especially in the first wave (Henley, 1976; Roberts, McCrory, & Forthoffer, 1978; and Porter & Whitcomb, 2003). However, there is also the risk that if people miss the deadline, they will not respond (Blumberg, Fuller, & Hare, 1974; Henley, 1976).

Another category of appeals is those involved when a project has a second phase after a participant has completed the first phase. Study results show that the success of a researcher's ability to convince participants to provide additional information in phase two of a study will depend on the context, but three types of appeals have worked. The direct appeal (Goulet, 1977) consists of a request to take the survey, usually accompanied by some material or psychological incentive. The "loss framing tactic" highlights the respondent's loss of opportunity to provide feedback. An example is provided by Tourangeau and Ye (2009): "Unfortunately, the information you've already provided to us will be much less valuable unless you complete the second interview" (p. 340). Another technique is the "appeal to social norms" (Misra, Stokols, & Marino, 2011). Here, the researcher informs the respondent of what others usually do when invited to participate in the survey, creating social pressure to conform and participate. Misra, Sotkols, and Marino (2011) give an example of this: "Most years, over 75% of conference participants complete the survey. Please join your fellow participants in improving the quality of future conferences by filling out the survey . . .." (Misra, Stokols, & Marino, 2011, p. 92).

Expectations

- Different appeals may work better depending on different survey sponsors (e.g., an altruistic appeal such as social utility or help-the-researcher may work better for a university, and an egoistic appeal may work better for a for-profit research company).
- Egoistic appeals seem to be more effective at increasing motivation than altruistic appeals.
- The respondent's level of community involvement may increase the effectiveness of the altruistic appeal.
- Using the scarcity appeal to frame survey participation as a rare opportunity may increase respondent motivation.
- It is unclear whether mandatory appeals increase motivation to participate or deprive the respondent of their freedom, decreasing motivation to participate.
- Stating a deadline will increase participation, especially in the first wave of the survey, but response rates compared with surveys not stating a deadline ultimately converge in the long run.
- The success of appeals used for phase two of a study varies based on context, and no definitive patterns have been found.

Principles

- Use the egoistic appeal, which was found to be the most effective in various contexts and when combined with other appeals.
- Use the altruistic appeal when dealing with samples of individuals who score high on a community involvement index.
- Use the altruistic appeal when the survey is sponsored by a non-commercial entity (i.e., a university).
- Consider setting a deadline for participation, but be ready to offer extensions to those who did not initially participate.

Commentary

Since the use of many different types of appeals does not usually add to the cost of a study, it might be a good idea to consider using the egoistic appeal in combination with others.

References and additional readings

Appeal [Def. 3]. (n.d.). In Merriam-Webster Online. Retrieved February 24, 2019, from https://www.merriam-webster.com/dictionary/appeal.

Biner, P. M. (1988). Effects of cover appeal and monetary incentives on survey response: A reactance theory application. Basic and Applied Social Psychology, 9(2), 99–106. Doi: 10.1207/s15324834basp0902_3

Blohm, M., Hox, J., & Koch, A. (2006). The influence of interviewers' contact behavior on the contact and cooperation rate in face-to-face household surveys. International Journal of Public Opinion Research, 19(1), 97–111. doi: http://dx.doi.org/10.1093/ijpor/edh120

Blumberg, H. H., Fuller, C., & Hare, A. P. (1974). Response rates in postal surveys. Public Opinion Quarterly, 38(1), 113–123. Doi: 10.1086/268140

Champion, D. J., & Sear, A. M. (1969). Questionnaire response rate: A methodological analysis. Social Forces, 47(3), 335–339. doi: 10.2307/2575033

Childers, T. L., Pride, W. M., & Ferrell, O. C. (1980). A reassessment of the effects of appeals on response to mail surveys. Journal of Marketing Research, 17(3), 365–370. doi: 10.2307/3150535

Dillman, D. A., Singer, E., Clark, J. R., & Treat, J. B. (1996). Effects of benefits appeals, mandatory appeals, and variations in statements of confidentiality on completion rates for census questionnaires. Public Opinion Quarterly, 60(3), 376–389. doi: 10.1086/29775

Edwards, P., Roberts, I., Clarke, M., DiGuiseppi, C., Pratap, S., Wentz, R., & Kwan, I. (2002). Increasing response rates to postal questionnaires: systematic review. British Medical Journal, 324(7347), 1183. doi: 10.1136/bmj.324.7347.1183

Esslemont, D., Gendall, P., & Hoek, J. (1995). The effect of appeal, complexity and tone in a mail survey covering letter. Journal of the Market Research Society, 37(3), 251–264. doi:10.1177/147078539503700304

Goulet, W. M. (1977). Efficacy of a third request letter in mail surveys of professionals. Journal of Marketing Research, 14(1), 112–114. doi: 10.2307/3151068

Groves, R. M., Singer, E., & Corning, A. (2000). Leverage-saliency theory of survey participation: Description and an illustration. Public Opinion Quarterly, 64(3), 299–308. doi: 10.1086/317990

Han, V., Albaum, G., Wiley, J.B. & Thirkell, P. (2009). Applying theory to structure respondents' stated motivations for participating in web surveys. Qualitative Market Research: An International Journal, 12(4), 428–442. doi: 10.1108/13522750910993338

Henley, J.R. Jr. (1976). Response rates to mail questionnaires with a return deadline. The Public Opinion Quarterly, 40(3), pp. 374–374. doi:10.1086/268314

Houston, M. J., & Nevin, J. R. (1977). The effects of source and appeal on mail survey response patterns. Journal of Marketing Research, 14(3), 374–378. doi: 10.2307/3150777

Jones, W. H., & Lang, J. R. (1980). Sample composition bias and response bias in a mail survey: A comparison of inducement methods. Journal of Marketing Research, 17(1), 69–76. doi: 10.2307/3151119

Jones, W. H., & Linda, G. (1978). Multiple criteria effects in a mail survey experiment. Journal of Marketing Research, 15(2), 280–284. doi: 10.2307/3151263

Linsky, A. S. (1975). Stimulating responses of mailed questionnaires: A review. Public Opinion Quarterly, 39(1), 82–101. doi: 10.1086/268201

Misra, S., Stokols, D., & Marino, A. H. (2011). Using norm-based appeals to increase response rates in evaluation research: A field experiment. American Journal of Evaluation, 33(1), 88–98. doi: 10.1177/1098214011414862

Mowen, J. C., & Cialdini, R. B. (1980). On implementing the door-in-the-face compliance technique in a business context. Journal of Marketing Research, 17(2), 253–258. Doi: 10.2307/3150936

Porter, S. R., & Whitcomb, M. E. (2003). The impact of contact type on web survey response rates. Public Opinion Quarterly, 67(4). doi: 10.1086/378964

Powers, D. E., & Alderman, D. L. (1982). Feedback as an incentive for responding to a mail questionnaire. Research in Higher Education, 17(3), 207–211. doi: 10.1007/BF00976698

Roberts, R. E., McCrory, O. F., & Forthoffer, R. N. (1978). Further evidence on using a deadline to stimulate responses to a mail survey. Public Opinion Quarterly, 42(3), 407–410. Doi: 10.1086/268464

Schneider, K. C., & Johnson, J. C. (1995). Stimulating response to market surveys of business professionals. Industrial Marketing Management, 24(4), 265–276. Doi: 10.1016/0019-8501(94)00084-a

Slocum, W. L., Empey, L. T., & Swanson, H. S. (1956). Increasing response to questionnaires and structured interviews. American Sociological Review, 21(2), 221–225. doi: 10.2307/2088526

Tourangeau, R., & Ye, C. (2009). The framing of the survey request and panel attrition. Public Opinion Quarterly, 73(2), 338–348. doi: 10.1093/poq/nfp021

Trouteaud, A. R. (2004). How you ask counts: A test of internet-related components of response rates to a web-based survey. Social Science Computer Review, 22(3), 385–392. Doi: 10.1177/0894439304265650

Yu, J., & Cooper, H. (1983). A quantitative review of research design effects on response rates to questionnaires. Journal of Marketing Research, 20(1), 36–44. doi: 0.2307/3151410

Section 7.3: Does personalizing communication with respondents increase their willingness to self-report?

Definition of terms – What is personalization?

Personalization is defined by researchers in several ways, including "addressing the respondent by name and hand signing letters" (Linsky, 1975, p. 92) and using "typed envelopes, personally addressed letters and individualized greetings, and actual signatures on cover letters" (Duncan, 1979). Essentially, any tactic used to personalize the survey experience is meant to make it seem that the researcher is speaking directly to the respondent rather than to the impersonal masses being invited to participate in a study.

It is important to note most of the research studies in this chapter do not explicitly evaluate the effectiveness of personalization on respondents' motivations. Most researchers tend to assess the effects of personalization in terms of response or cooperation rates. For our purposes, we will equate higher or lower response or cooperation rates with corresponding high or low levels of effectiveness in increasing respondent motivation.

In brief

A good deal of research has been conducted on the use of personalization in survey procedures. Many of the same tactics have been carried over across different survey modes. For example, while there is mixed evidence regarding the use of personalization in mail surveys - many researchers found it effective (Blumberg et al., 1974; Carpenter, 1974; Cox et al., 1974; Dillman & Frey, 1974; Linsky, 1975; Duncan, 1979; Yu & Cooper, 1983; De Leeuw & Joop, 1988; Edwards et al., 2002; and Dillman et al., 2007), while others found it ineffective (Kimball, 1961; Mason et al., 1961; Andreasen, 1970; Kawash & Aleamoni, 1971; Dillman et al., 1974; Houston & Jefferson, 1975; Kanuk & Berenson, 1975; Labrecque, 1978; Pressley, 1978; Roberts et al., 1978; Golden et al., 1981; and Fox et al., 1988). One consistently effective personalization tactic is addressing the potential respondent by name, particularly in the salutation of cover letters and any correspondence throughout the process. While there is less research about personalization via telephone, findings are still worth noting. For example, Dillman and Frey (1974) found that calling potential respondents and addressing them by name before mailing them a survey increases their cooperation rate. A similar personalization tactic was also effective in a survey conducted entirely via the telephone (Dillman, Gallegos, & Frey, 1976). Addressing respondents by name is also an effective tactic of personalization when sending email invitations to a web survey (Cook et al., 2000; Heerwegh, 2005; Heerwegh & Loosveldt, 2006; Joinson & Reips, 2007; and Fan & Yan, 2010).

While there are many potential tactics for personalizing a survey, research has indicated that simply addressing a potential respondent by name can significantly increase motivation.

Expectations

- Historically, the effectiveness of personalizing mail invitations to participate in a study has been mixed. Some studies find it doesn't make a difference (Kimball, 1961; Mason et al., 1961; Andreasen, 1970; Kawash & Aleamoni, 1971; Dillman et al., 1974; Houston & Jefferson, 1975; Kanuk & Berenson, 1975; Labrecque, 1978; Pressley, 1978; Roberts et al., 1978; Golden et al., 1981; and Fox et al., 1988), while other studies find personalization to be effective in increasing a participant's willingness to participate in a survey (Blumberg et al., 1974; Carpenter, 1974; Cox et al., 1974; Dillman & Frey, 1974; Linsky, 1975; Duncan, 1979; Yu & Cooper, 1983; De Leeuw & Joop, 1988; Edwards et al., 2002; and Dillman et al., 2007).
- Addressing respondents by name in invitation cover letters has increased an individual's willingness to participate in a survey. When name personalization is not possible, another method of personalization that was also found to be effective includes referring to the respondent as a member of a group to which the respondent knows they belong (e.g., Harley Davidson bike owners) (Dillman et al., 2007).
- Additionally, preceding a mail questionnaire with a personalized phone call may be effective (Dillman & Frey, 1974). Along these lines, addressing respondents by name during the introductory portion of a telephone interview may encourage a willingness to participate in a survey and self-report (Dillman et al., 1976).

- There is strong evidence of the effectiveness of personalizing emails when inviting individuals to participate in a web survey (Cook et al., 2000; Heerwegh, 2005; Heerwegh & Loosveldt, 2006; Joinson & Reips, 2007; and Fan & Yan, 2010).

Principles

- Personalize letters and emails by addressing the participants by their names. Do so unless you have reason to believe the participants you are attempting to study are a special group that might prefer you not to know their names (see Andreasen, 1970).
- Consider handwritten notes when sending letters and postcards if doing so is within time and budget.
- When a phone number is available, consider making pre-contact by voice and addressing the potential respondent by their full name before mailing a questionnaire or emailing a link to a web survey.

Commentary

In my view, humanizing interactions between a researcher and respondents is always good practice. It doesn't take much effort or a lot of additional resources to do so, and I find it hard to believe there would be negative effects stemming from establishing a personalized rapport between a researcher and a potential participant in a study. I am always weary of letters that refer to me as "Dear subscriber" or "Dear respondent," as I don't feel these letters are talking to me. As such, I tend to pay less attention to these invitations than those that address me personally.

References and additional readings

Andreasen, A.R. (1970). Personalizing mail questionnaire correspondence. *Public Opinion Quarterly*, *34*(2), 273–277. doi:10.1086/267798

Bälter, K.A., Bälter, O., Fondell, E., & Lagerros, Y.T. (2005). Web-based and mailed questionnaires: a comparison of response rates and compliance. *Epidemiology*, *16*(4), 577–579. doi:10.1097/01.ede.0000164553.16591.4b

Blumberg, H.H., Fuller, C., & Hare, A.P. (1974). Response rates in postal surveys. *Public Opinion Quarterly*, *38*(1), 113. doi:10.1086/268140

Carpenter, E.H. (1974). Personalizing mail surveys: A replication and reassessment. *Public Opinion Quarterly*, *38*(4), 614–620. doi:10.1086/268188

Cook, C., Heath, F., & Thompson, R.L. (2000). A meta-analysis of response rates in web- or internet-based surveys. *Educational and Psychological Measurement*, *60*(6), 821–836. doi:10.1177/00131640021970934

Cox, E.P., III, Anderson, T., Jr. & Fulcher, D.G. (1974). Reappraising mail survey response rates. *Journal of Marketing Research, 11*(4), 413–417. doi:10.2307/3151287

De Leeuw, E.D., and Joop, J.H.. (1988). The effects of response-stimulating factors on response rates and data quality in mail surveys. *Journal of Official Statistics, 4*(3), 241–249. No doi available.

Dillman, D.A., Christenson, J.A., Carpenter, E.H., & Brooks, R.M. (1974). Increasing mail questionnaire response: A four state comparison. *American Sociological Review, 39*(5), 744–756. doi:10.2307/2094318

Dillman, D.A., & Frey, J.H. (1974). Contribution of personalization to mail questionnaire response as an element of a previously tested method. *Journal of Applied Psychology, 59*(3), 297–301. doi:10.1037/h0036534

Dillman, D.A., Gallegos, J.G., & Frey, J.H. (1976). Reducing refusal rates for telephone interviews. *Public Opinion Quarterly, 40*(1), 66–78. doi:10.1086/268268

Dillman, D.A., Lesser, V., Mason, R., Carlson, J., Willits, F., Robertson, R., & Burke, B. (2007). Personalization of mail surveys for general public and populations with a group identity: Results from nine studies*. *Rural Sociology, 72*(4), 632–646. doi:10.1526/003601107782638693

Duncan, W.J. (1979). Mail questionnaires in survey research: A review of response inducement techniques. *Journal of Management, 5*(1), 39–55. doi:10.1177/014920637900500103.

Edwards, P., Roberts, I., Clarke, M., DiGuiseppi, C., Pratap, S., Wentz, R., & Kwan, I. (2002). Increasing response rates to postal questionnaires: Systematic review. *BMJ, 324*(7347), 1183. doi:10.1136/bmj.324.7347.1183

Fan, W., & Yan, Z. (2010). Factors affecting response rates of the web survey: A systematic review. *Computers in Human Behavior, 26*(2), 132–139. doi:10.1016/j.chb.2009.10.015

Fox, R.J., Crask, M.R., & Kim, J. (1988). Mail survey response rate a meta-analysis of selected techniques for inducing response. *Public Opinion Quarterly, 52*(4), 467–491. doi:10.1086/269125

Golden, L.L., Anderson, W.T., & Sharpe, L.K. (1981). The effects of salutation, monetary incentive, and degree of urbanization on mail questionnaire response rate, speed and quality. *Advances in Consumer Research, 8*(1). No doi available.

Heerwegh, D. (2005). Effects of personal salutations in e-mail invitations to participate in a web survey. *Public Opinion Quarterly, 69*(4), 588–598. doi:10.1093/poq/nfi053

Heerwegh, D., & Loosveldt, G. (2006). An experimental study on the effects of personalization, survey length statements, progress indicators, and survey sponsor logos in web surveys. *Journal of Official Statistics, 22*(2), 191. No doi available.

Houston, M.J., & Jefferson, R.W. (1975). The negative effects of personalization on response patterns in mail surveys. *Journal of Marketing Research, 12*(1), 114–117. doi:10.2307/3150671

Joinson, A.N., & Reips, U.D. (2007). Personalized salutation, power of sender and response rates to web-based surveys. *Computers in Human Behavior, 23*(3), 1372–1383. doi:10.1016/j.chb.2004.12.011

Kanuk, L., & Berenson, C. (1975). Mail surveys and response rates: A literature review. *Journal of Marketing Research, 12*(4), 440–453. doi:10.2307/3151093

Kawash, M.B., & Aleamoni, L.M. (1971). Effect of personal signature on the initial rate of return of a mailed questionnaire. *Journal of Applied Psychology, 55*(6), 589–592. doi:10.1037/h0031936

Kimball, A.E. (1961). Increasing the rate of return in mail surveys. *Journal of Marketing, 25*(6), 63–64. doi:10.2307/1248517

Labrecque, D.P. (1978). A response rate experiment using mail questionnaires. *Journal of Marketing, 42*(4), 82–83. doi:10.2307/1250090

Linsky, A.S. (1975). Stimulating responses of mailed questionnaires: a review. *Public Opinion Quarterly, 39*(1), 82–101. doi:10.1086/268201

Marcus, B., Bosnjak, M., Lindner, S., Pilischenko, S., & Schütz, A. (2007). Compensating for low topic interest and long surveys: A field experiment on nonresponse in web surveys. *Social Science Computer Review, 25*(3), 372–383. doi:10.1177/0894439307297606

Mason, W.S., Dressel, R.J., & Bain, R.K. (1961). Living research: An experimental study of factors affecting response to a mail survey of beginning teachers. *Public Opinion Quarterly, 25*(2), 296–299. doi:10.1086/267022

Porter, S.R., & Whitcomb, M.E. (2003). The impact of contact type on web survey response rates. *Public Opinion Quarterly, 67*(4), 579–588. doi:10.1086/378964

Pressley, M.M. (1978). Care needed when selecting response inducements in mail surveys of commercial populations. *Journal of the Academy of Marketing Science, 6*(4), 336–341. doi:10.1007/bf02732317

Roberts, R.E., McCrory, O.F., & Forthofer, R.N. (1978). Further evidence on using a deadline to stimulate responses to a mail survey. *Public Opinion Quarterly, 42*(3), 407–410. doi:10.1086/268464

Vocino, T. (1977). Three variables in stimulating responses to mailed questionnaires. *Journal of Marketing, 41*(4), 76–77. doi:10.2307/1250238

Yu, J., & Cooper, H. (1983). A quantitative review of research design effects on response rates to questionnaires. *Journal of Marketing Research, 20*(1), 36–44. doi:10.2307/3151410

Section 7.4: Can I give respondents anything to encourage them to self-report?

Definition of terms – What are incentives?

According to Merriam-Webster (2019), an incentive is "something that incites or has a tendency to incite to determination or action" (par. 1). This term is used by many of the authors whose research is discussed here, but they may also use alternative but similar terms, such as "rewards." The incentives and rewards discussed in this section are both monetary and non-monetary. The distribution and timing methods will also be addressed: prepaid and enclosed rewards, promised and delayed rewards, and lotteries.

It is important to note that most of the research discussed in this chapter does not explicitly evaluate the effectiveness of incentives on respondents' motivation. Most researchers tend to evaluate the effects of incentives in terms of response or cooperation rates. For our purposes, we will equate high or low response or cooperation rates with corresponding high or low levels of effectiveness in increasing respondent motivation brought about by certain types of incentives.

In brief

Extensive research has been conducted on using incentives to raise survey response rates. There is a general consensus that the use of prepaid or enclosed monetary incentives is the most effective tactic (Shuttleworth, 1931; Kimball, 1961; Wotruba, 1966; Doob & Zabrack, 1971; Doob & Freedman, 1973; Hackler & Bourgette, 1973; Blumberg, Fuller, & Hare, 1974; Armstrong, 1975; Kanuk & Berenson, 1975; Robin & Walters, 1976; Goodstadt, Chung, Kronitz, & Cook, 1977; Pressley & Tullar, 1977; Chromy & Horvitz, 1978; Duncan, 1979; Friedman & San Augustine, 1979; Hansen, 1980; Furse, Stewart, &

Rados, 1981; Gunn & Rhodes, 1981; Furse & Stewart, 1982; Tedin & Hofstetfer, 1982; Hopkins & Podolak, 1983; Yu & Cooper, 1983; Furse & Stewart, 1984; Mizes, Fleece, & Roos, 1984; Paolillo & Lorenzi, 1984; Skinner, Ferrell, & Pride, 1984; Berk, Mathiowetz, Ward, & White, 1987; Berry & Kanouse, 1987; Biner, 1988; Fox, Crask, & Kim, 1988; Hopkins, 1988; Spry, Hovell, Sallis, Hofstetter, Elder, and Molgaard, 1989; James & Bolstein, 1990; Yammarino, Skinner, & Childers, 1991; Hopkins & Gullickson, 1992; Brennan, Seymour, & Gendall, 1993; Church, 1993; Armstrong & Yokum, 1994; Schneider & Johnson, 1995; Warriner, Goyder, Gjertsen, Hohner, & McSpurren, 1996; Groves, Singer, & Corning, 2000; Singer, Van Hoewyk, & Maher, 2000; Edwards, Roberts, Clarke, DiGuiseppi, Pratap, Wentz, & Kwan, 2002; Birnholtz, Horn, Finholt, & Bae, 2004; Delnevo, Abatemarco, & Steinberg, 2004; Deutskens, De Ruyter, Wetzels, & Oosterveld, 2004; Groves, Presser, & Dipko, 2004; Larson & Poist, 2004; Teisl, Roe, and Vayda, 2006; Dirmaier, Harfst, Koch, & Schulz, 2007; Wetzels, Schmeets, Van den Brakel, & Feskens, 2008; Dillman, Phelps, Tortora, Swift, Kohrell, Berck, & Messer, 2009; and Millar & Dillman, 2011).

In terms of specific amounts of money used for these incentives, research has generally shown that amounts between $1 and $5 are successful, perhaps up to as much as $25 (James & Bolstein, 1992). In general, larger incentives do not necessarily lead to increased effectiveness, except perhaps in the case of longitudinal studies (Collins, Ellickson, Hays, & McCaffrey, 2000; Edwards et al., 2002). Regarding timing placement, Huck and Gleason (1974) found that if multiple contacts are going to be made in the survey process, monetary incentives should be sent no later than during the first follow-up, or else this strategy will not be effective.

Researchers have also studied the effects of promised incentives when a researcher tells the respondents they will receive monetary compensation upon completing a survey. In general, promised incentives may increase motivation compared to no incentives at all, but many researchers note they are not as effective as prepaid and enclosed incentives (Schewe & Cournoyer, 1976; Spry et al., 1989; Collins et al., 2000; and Delnevo et al., 2004). However, other researchers found no success at all with promised incentives (Wotruba, 1966; Dohrenwend, 1970; Blumberg et al., 1974; Kanuk & Berenson, 1975; Paolillo & Lorenzi, 1984; Cook et al., 1985; and Berk et al., 1987).

Researchers are split in terms of lottery incentives, in which respondents are told that they are entered into lotteries and drawings for particular amounts of money or material prizes. Some found that lottery incentives are effective (Spry et al., 1989; Balakrishnan, Chawla, Smith, & Michalski, 1992; Kalantar & Talley, 1999; Deutskens et al., 2004; Tuten, Galesic, & Bosnjak, 2004; Robertson, Walkom, & McGettigan, 2005; Heerwegh, 2006; and Göritz & Wolff, 2007). However, approximately just as many found these incentives to be ineffective (Golden, Anderson, & Sharpe, 1981; Paolillo & Lorenzi, 1984; Koloski, Talley, Boyce, & Morris-Yates, 2001; O'Neil & Penrod, 2001; Cobanoglu & Cobanoglu, 2003; Wenemark, Vernby, & Norberg, 2010; Boyle, Heyworth, Landrigan, Mina, & Fritschi, 2012; and Evangelista, Poon, & Albaum, 2008). Interestingly,

Heerwegh (2006) found lottery incentives to be effective specifically with women compared to men. In terms of the money used in financial lotteries, $100 seems optimal for students (Porter & Whitcomb, 2003).

Charitable incentives, in which contributions are made to charitable causes (sometimes of the respondent's choice or a cause pre-selected by the company conducting research), are found to generally be ineffective (Robertson & Bellenger, 1978; Furse & Stewart, 1982; Brennan et al., 1993; Gendall & Healey, 2009; and Boyle et al., 2012). Meanwhile, gift incentives, such as ballpoint pens, are similar to promised incentives in that they are more effective than not using any incentive at all, but they are still not as effective as prepaid monetary incentives (Houston & Jefferson, 1975; Hansen, 1980; Nederhof, 1983; Willimack et al., 1995; and Gritz, 2004).

With regard to survey mode, there appears to be little difference in the effects of incentives between mail and online surveys. However, there is some evidence that prepaid incentives are less effective with online surveys and that promised incentives and lotteries may be more effective (Crawford, McCabe, Couper, & Boyd, 2001; Schonlau, Asch, & Du, 2003; Messer & Dillman, 2011).

Expectations

- Generally, prepaid monetary incentives are incredibly effective and the most effective out of any type of incentive to increase respondent motivation.
- Promised (or conditional) monetary incentives are generally more effective than no use of any incentive, but they are not as effective as prepaid monetary incentives. The same is true for gift incentives such as pens.
- There is about equal research for and against the use of lottery incentives . However, one article finds explicitly that while this type of incentive is not effective among men, it is effective among women (Heerwegh, 2006).
- Larger monetary incentives do not necessarily increase response rates. While there is no consensus around a specific amount, most experiments find success with incentives between $1 and $5, with the potential to use larger incentives in longitudinal studies.
- There is no substantial evidence to support the offer of charitable donations as an incentive.
- The success of incentives is generally similar between online and offline survey modes. However, there is some evidence that prepaid incentives are less effective with online surveys and that promised incentives and lotteries may be more effective.

Principles

- Use prepaid monetary incentives to increase respondent motivation (Shuttleworth, 1931; Kimball, 1961; Wotruba, 1966; Doob & Zabrack, 1971; Doob & Freedman, 1973; Hackler & Bourgette, 1973; Blumberg et al., 1974; Armstrong, 1975; Kanuk & Berenson, 1975; Robin & Walters, 1976; Goodstadt et al., 1977; Pressley & Tullar, 1977; Chromy & Horvitz, 1978; Duncan, 1979; Friedman & San Augustine, 1979; Hansen, 1980; Furse et al., 1981; Furse & Stewart, 1982; Tedin & Hofstetfer, 1982; Hopkins & Podolak, 1983; Yu & Cooper, 1983; Furse & Stewart, 1984; Mizes et al., 1984; Paolillo & Lorenzi, 1984; Skinner et al., 1984; Berk et al., 1987; Berry & Kanouse, 1987; Fox et al., 1988; Biner, 1988; Hopkins, 1988; James & Bolstein, 1990; Spry et al., 1987; Yammarino et al., 1991; Hopkins & Gullickson, 1992; Brennan et al., 1993; Church, 1993; Armstrong & Yokum, 1994; Schneider & Johnson, 1995; Warriner et al., 1996; Groves et al., 2000; Singer et al., 2000; Edwards et al., 2002; Birnholtz et al., 2004; Delnevo et al., 2004; Deutskens et al., 2004; Groves et al., 2004; Larson & Poist, 2004; Teisl et al., 2006; Dirmaier et al., 2007; Wetzels et al., 2008; Dillman et al., 2009; and Millar & Dillman, 2009).
- Use monetary incentives of between $1 and $5, but if a long-term study is being conducted, larger incentives of up to $25 may be effective (James & Bolstein, 1992; Collins et al., 2000).
- Use the monetary incentive at the earliest contact stage and no later than at the first follow-up (Huck & Gleason, 1974).

Commentary

Interestingly, the small amounts of prepaid incentives appear to still work in 2024, even though the value of $1 or $5 today is very different from when many of the earliest incentive studies were conducted. I say this because many of the leading survey institutions in the U.S. are still using these amounts. I speak as someone who has received several invitations to participate in surveys in the past year, each of which enclosed anywhere from $2 to $5 dollar cash incentives. I am guessing the value of the money sent is symbolic. When receiving it, participants might feel that, in return for the unexpected small gift, they would give the sender some of their time and participate in the self-report task to which they were invited.

References and additional readings

Armstrong, J. S. (1975). Monetary incentives in mail surveys. *Public Opinion Quarterly, 39*(1), 111–116. doi:10.1086/268203

Armstrong, J.S., & Yokum, J.T. (1994). Effectiveness of monetary incentives: Mail surveys to members of multinational professional groups. *Industrial Marketing Management, 23*(2), 133–136. doi:10.1016/0019-8501(94)90014-0

Asch, D.A., Jedrziewski, M.K., & Christakis, N.A. (1997). Response rates to mail surveys published in medical journals. *Journal of Clinical Epidemiology, 50*(10), 1129–1136. doi:10.1016/s0895-4356(97)00126-1

Baker, R., Blumberg, S.J., Beck, J.M., Couper, M.P., Courtright, M., Dennis, J.M., Dillman, D., Frankel, M.R., Garland, P., Groves, R.M., Kennedy, C., Krosnick, J., Lavrakas, P.J., Lee, S., Link, M., Piekarski, L., Rao, K., Thomas, R.K., & Zahs, D. (2010). Research Synthesis: AAPOR Report on Online Panels. *Public Opinion Quarterly, 74*(4), 711–781. doi:10.1093/poq/nfq048

Balakrishnan, P.V.S., Chawla, S.K., Smith, M.F., & Michalski, B.P. (1992). Mail survey response rates using a lottery prize giveaway incentive. *Journal of Direct Marketing, 6*(3), 54–59. doi:10.1002/dir.4000060308

Berk, M.L., Mathiowetz, N.A., Ward, E.P., & White, A.A. (1987). The effect of prepaid and promised incentives: Results of a controlled experiment. *Journal of Official Statistics, 3*(4), 449–457. doi:10.18148/srm/2008.v2i3.599

Berry, S.H., & Kanouse, D.E. (1987). Physician response to a mailed survey an experiment in timing of payment. *Public Opinion Quarterly, 51*(1), 102–114. doi:10.1086/269018

Biner, P. M. (1988). Effects of Cover Appeal and Monetary Incentives on Survey Response: A Reactance Theory Application. *Basic and Applied Social Psychology, 9*(2), 99–106. doi:10.1207/s15324834basp0902_3

Birnholtz, J., Horn, D.B., Finholt, T.A., & Bae, S.J. (2004). The effects of cash, electronic, and paper gift certificate as respondents incentives for a web-based survey of technologically sophisticated respondents. *Social Science Computer Review, 22*(3), 355–362. doi:10.1177/0894439304263147

Blumberg, H.H., Fuller, C., & Hare, A.P. (1974). Response rates in postal surveys. *Public Opinion Quarterly, 38*(1), 113. doi:10.1086/268140

Bosnjak, M., & Tuten, L.T. (2003). Prepaid and promised incentives in web surveys: An experiment. *Social Science Computer Review, 21*(2), 208–217. doi:10.1177/0894439303251569

Boyle, T., Heyworth, J., Landrigan, J., Mina R., & Fritschi, L. (2012). The effect of lottery scratch tickets and donation offers on response fraction: A study and meta-analysis. *Field Method, 24*(1), 112–132. doi:10.1177/1525822X11424549

Brennan, M., Seymour, P., & Gendall, P. (1993). The effectiveness of monetary incentives in mail surveys: Further data. *Marketing Bulletin, 4*, 43–51. doi:10.2307/2582116

Chromy, J. R., & Horvitz, D. G. (1978). The use of monetary incentives in national assessment household surveys. Journal of the American Statistical Association, 73(363), 473–478. doi:10.1080/01621459.1978.10480037

Church, A.H. (1993). Estimating the effect of incentives on mail survey response rates: A meta-analysis. *Public Opinion Quarterly, 57*(1), 62–79. doi:10.1086/269355

Cobanoglu, C., & Cobanoglu, N. (2003). The effect of incentives in web surveys: Application and ethical considerations. *International Journal of Market Research, 45*(4), 475–488. doi:10.1016/s0278-4319(02)00072-5

Collins, R.L., Ellickson, P. L., Hays, R. D., & McCaffrey, D.F. (2000). Effects of incentive size and timing on response rates to a follow-up wave of a longitudinal mailed survey. *Evaluation Review, 24*(4), 347–363. doi:10.1177/0193841X0002400401

Cook, C., Heath, F., & Thompson, R.L. (2000). A meta-analysis of response rates in web- or internet-based surveys. *Educational and Psychological Measurement, 60*(6), 821–836. doi: 10.1177/00131640021970934

Cook, J.R., Schoeps, N., & Kim, S. (1985). Program responses to mail surveys as a function of monetary incentives. *Psychological Reports, 57*(2), 366–366. doi:10.2466/pr0.1985.57.2.366

Crawford, S., McCabe, S., Couper, M. & Boyd, C. (2001). From mail to web: improving response rates and data collection efficiencies. Paper presented at the International Conference on Improving Surveys, Copenhagen, Denmark.

Delnevo, C.D., Abatemarco, D.J., & Steinberg, M B. (2004). Physician response rates to a mail survey by specialty and timing of incentive. *American Journal of Preventive Medicine, 26*(3), 234–236. doi:10.1016/j.amepre.2003.12.013

Denton, J.J., Tsai, C.Y., & Chevrette, P. (1988). Effects on survey responses of subjects, incentives, and multiple mailings. *The Journal of Experimental Education, 56*(2), 77–82. doi:10.1080/00220973.1988.10806469

Deutskens, E., De Ruyter, K., Wetzels, M., & Oosterveld, P. (2004). Response rate and response quality of internet-based surveys: An experimental study. *Marketing Letters, 15*(1), 21–36. doi:10.1023/B:MARK.0000021968.86465.00

Dillman, D.A., Gallegos, J. G., & Frey, J. H. (1976). Reducing refusal rates for telephone interviews. *Public Opinion Quarterly, 40*(1), 66–78. doi:10.1086/268268

Dillman, D.A., Phelps, G., Tortora, R., Swift, K., Kohrell, J., Berck, J., & Messer, B.L. (2009). Response rate and measurement differences in mixed-mode surveys using mail, telephone, interactive voice response (IVR) and the Internet. *Social Science Research, 38*(1), 1–18. doi:10.1016/j.ssresearch.2008.03.007

Dirmaier, J., Harfst, T., Koch, U., & Schulz, H. (2007). Incentives increased return rates but did not influence partial nonresponse or treatment outcome in a randomized trial. *Journal of Clinical Epidemiology, 60*(12), 1263–1270. doi:10.1016/j.jclinepi.2007.04.006

Dissonance. [Def. 1]. (2019). In *Merriam-Webster Online*. Retrieved April 17, 2019, from https://www.merriam-webster.com/dictionary/dissonance.

Dohrenwend, B.S. (1970). An experimental study of payments to respondents. *Public Opinion Quarterly, 34*(4), 621–624. doi:10.1086/267848

Doob, A.N., & Freedman, J L. (1973). Effects of sponsor and prepayment on compliance with a mailed request. *Journal of Applied Psychology, 57*(3), 346–347. doi:10.1037/h0034704

Doob, A.N., & Zabrack, M. (1971). The effect of freedom-threatening instructions and monetary inducement on compliance. *Canadian Journal of Behavioural Science/Revue Canadienne des Sciences du Comportement, 3*(4), 408–412. doi:10.1037/h0082283

Duncan, W. J. (1979). Mail questionnaires in survey research: A review of response inducement techniques. *Journal of Management, 5*(1), 39–55. doi:10.1177/014920637900500103

Edwards, P., Roberts, I., Clarke, M., DiGuiseppi, C., Pratap, S., Wentz, R., & Kwan, I. (2002). Increasing response rates to postal questionnaires: Systematic review. *BMJ, 324*(7347), 1183. doi:10.1136/bmj.324.7347.1183

Evangelista, F., Poon, P., & Albaum, G. (2008). Enhancing survey response rates: Lessons from a field experiment. *Proceedings*, Australia and New Zealand Marketing Academy Conference, Sydney, Australia. doi:10.1177/014920630202800202

Fan, W., & Yan, Z. (2010). Factors affecting response rates of the web survey: A systematic review. *Computers in Human Behavior, 26*(2), 132–139. doi:10.1016/j.chb.2009.10.015

Fox, R.J., Crask, M.R., & Kim, J. (1988). Mail survey response rate: A meta-analysis of selected techniques for inducing response. *Public Opinion Quarterly, 52*(4), 467–491. doi:10.1086/269125

Friedman, H.H., & San Augustine, A.J. (1979). The effects of a monetary incentive and the ethnicity of the sponsor's signature on the rate and quality of response to a mail survey. *Academy of Marketing Science, 7*(1–22), 95–100. doi:10.1007/bf02721916

Furse, D.H., & Stewart, D.W. (1982). Monetary incentives versus promised contribution to charity: New evidence on mail survey response. *Journal of Marketing Research, 19*(3), 375. doi:10.2307/3151572

Furse, D.H., & Stewart, D.W. (1984). Manipulating dissonance to improve mail survey response. *Psychology & Marketing, 1*(2), 79–94. doi:10.1002/mar.4220010208

Furse, D.H., Stewart, D.W., & Rados, D.L. (1981). Effects of foot-in-the-door, cash incentives, and followups on survey response. *Journal of Marketing Research, 18*(4), 473. doi:10.2307/3151342

Gelb, B.D. (1975). Incentives to increase survey returns: Social class considerations. *Journal Of Marketing Research, 12*(1), 107–109. doi:10.2307/3150669

Gendall, P., & Healey, B. (2009). The Effect of a promised contribution to charity on mail survey response. *International Journal of Market Research, 52*(5), 565. doi:10.2501/s147078531020148x

Golden, L.L., Anderson, W.T., & Sharpe, L.K. (1981). The effects of salutation, monetary incentive, and degree of urbanization on mail questionnaire response rate, speed and quality. *Advances in Consumer Research, 8*(1). No doi available.

Goodstadt, M.S., Chung, L., Kronitz, R., & Cook, G. (1977). Mail survey response rates: Their manipulation and impact. *Journal of Marketing Research, 14*(3), 391–395. doi:10.2307/3150782

Gritz, A. (2004). The impact of material incentives on response quantity, response quality, sample composition, survey outcome and cost in online access panels. *International Journal of Market Research, 46*(3), 327–346. doi: 10.1177147078530404600307

Göritz, A.S. (2006). Incentives in web studies: Methodological issues and a review. *International Journal of Internet Science, 1*(1), 58–70. No doi available.

Göritz, A.S., & Wolff, H.G. (2007). Lotteries as incentives in longitudinal web studies. *Social Science Computer Review, 25*(1), 99–110. doi:10.1177/0894439306292268

Groves, R.M., Cialdini, R.B., & Couper, M.P. (1992). Understanding the decision to participate in a survey. *Public Opinion Quarterly, 56*(4), 475–495. doi:10.1086/269338

Groves, R.M., Presser, S., & Dipko, S. (2004). The role of topic interest in survey participation decisions. *Public Opinion Quarterly, 68*(1), 2–31. doi:10.1093/poq/nfh002

Groves, R.M., Singer, E., & Corning, A. (2000). Leverage-saliency theory of survey participation: Description and an illustration. *Public Opinion Quarterly, 64*(3), 299–308. doi:10.1086/317990

Gunn, W.J., & Rhodes, I.N. (1981). Physician response rates to a telephone survey: Effects of monetary incentive level. *Public Opinion Quarterly 45*(1), 109–115. doi:10.1086/268638

Hackler, J.C., & Bourgette, P. (1973). Dollars, dissonance, and survey returns. *Public Opinion Quarterly, 37*(2), 276–281. doi:10.1086/268085

Han, V., Albaum, G., Wiley, J.B., & Thirkell, P. (2009). Applying theory to structure respondents' stated motivations for participating in web surveys. *Qualitative Market Research: An International Journal, 12*(4), 428–442. doi: 10.1108/13522750910993338

Hansen, R.A. (1980). A self-perception interpretation of the effect of monetary and nonmonetary incentives on mail survey respondent behavior. *Journal of Marketing Research, 17*(1), 77–83. doi:10.2307/3151120

Heerwegh, D. (2006). An investigation of the effect of lotteries on web survey response rates. *Field Methods, 18*(2), 205–220. doi:10.1177/1525822x05285781

Hopkins, K.D. (1988). Mail surveys of professional populations: The effects of monetary gratuities on return rates. *Journal of Experimental Education, 56*(4), 173–175. doi:10.1080/00220973.1988.10806483

Hopkins, K. D., & Gullickson, A. R. (1992). Response rates in survey research: A meta-analysis of the effects of monetary gratuities. *The Journal of Experimental Education, 61*(1), 52–62. doi:10.1080/00220973.1992.9943849

Hopkins, K.D., & Podolak, J. (1983). Class-of-mail and the effects of monetary gratuity on the response rates of mailed questionnaires. *Journal of Experimental Education, 51*(4), 169–171. doi:10.1080/00220973.1983.11011857

Houston, M.J., & Jefferson, R.W. (1975). The negative effects of personalization on response patterns in mail surveys. *Journal of Marketing Research, 12*(1), 114–117. doi:10.2307/3150671

Huck, S.W., & Gleason, E.M. (1974). Using monetary inducements to increase response rates from mailed surveys: A replication and extension of previous research. *Journal of Applied Psychology, 59*(2), 222–225. doi:10.1037/h0036457

Incentive [Def. 1]. (2019). In *Merriam-Webster Online*. Retrieved May 13, 2019, from https://www.merriam-webster.com/dictionary/incentive.

James, J.M., & Bolstein, R. (1990). The effect of monetary incentives and follow-up mailings on the response rate and response quality in mail surveys. *Public Opinion Quarterly, 54*(3), 346–361. doi:10.1086/269211

James, J.M., & Bolstein, R. (1992). Large monetary incentives and their effect on mail survey response rates. *Public Opinion Quarterly, 56*(4), 442–453. doi:10.1086/269336

Kalantar, J.S., & Talley, N.J. (1999). The effects of lottery incentive and length of questionnaire on health survey response rates: a randomized study. *Journal of Clinical Epidemiology, 52*(11), 1117–1122. doi:10.1016/s0895-4356(99)00051-7

Kanuk, L., & Berenson, C. (1975). Mail surveys and response rates: A literature review. *Journal of Marketing Research, 12*(4), 440–453. doi:10.2307/3151093

Kimball, A.E. (1961). Increasing the rate of return in mail surveys. *Journal of Marketing, 25*(6), 63–64. doi:10.2307/1248517

Koloski, N.A., Talley, N.J., Boyce, P.M., & Morris-Yates, A.D. (2001). The effects of questionnaire length and lottery ticket inducement on the response rate in mail surveys. *Psychology and Health, 16*(1), 67–75. doi:10.1080/08870440108405490

Larson, P.D., & Poist, R.F. (2004). Improving response rates to mail surveys: A research note. *Transportation Journal, 43*(4), 67–74. No doi available.

Linsky, A. S. (1975). Stimulating responses of mailed questionnaires: A review. *Public Opinion Quarterly, 39*(1), 82–101. doi:10.1086/268201

Messer, B. L., & Dillman, D. A. (2011). Surveying the general public over the internet using address-based sampling and mail contact procedures. *Public Opinion Quarterly, 75*(3), 429–457. doi:10.1093/poq/nfr021

Millar, M.M., & Dillman, D.A. (2011). Improving response to web and mixed-mode surveys. *Public Opinion Quarterly, 75*(2), 249–269. doi:10.1093/poq/nfr003

Mizes, J.S., Fleece, E.L., & Roos, C. (1984). Incentives for increasing return rates: Magnitude levels, response bias, amd format. *Public Opinion Quarterly, 48*(4), 794–800. doi:10.1086/268885

Nederhof, A.J. (1983). The effects of material incentives in mail surveys: Two studies. *Public Opinion Quarterly, 47*(1), 103–112. doi:10.1086/268770

O'Neil, K.M., & Penrod, S.D. (2001). Methodological variables in Web-based research that may affect results: Sample type, monetary incentives, and personal information. *Behavior Research Methods, Instruments, & Computers, 33*(2), 226–233. doi:10.3758/bf03195369

Paolillo, J.G., & Lorenzi, P. (1984). Monetary incentives and mail questionnaire response rates. *Journal of Advertising, 13*(1), 46–48. doi:10.1080/00913367.1984.10672874

Porter, S.R., & Whitcomb, M.E. (2003). The impact of lottery incentives on student survey response rates. *Research in Higher Education, 44*(4), 389–407. doi:10.1023/A:1024263031800

Pressley, M.M., & Tullar, W.L. (1977). A factor interactive investigation of mail survey response rates from a commercial population. *Journal of Marketing Research, 14*(1), 108–111. doi:10.2307/3151067

Robertson, D.H., & Bellenger, D.N. (1978). A new method of increasing mail survey responses: Contributions to charity. *Journal of Marketing Research, 15*, 632–633. doi:10.2307/3150635

Robertson, J., Walkom, E.J., & McGettigan, P. (2005). Response rates and representativeness: A lottery incentive improves physician survey return rates. *Pharmacoepidemiology and Drug Safety, 14*(8), 571–577. doi:10.1002/pds.1126

Robin, D.P., & Walters, C.G. (1976). The effect of return rate of messages explaining monetary incentives in mail questionnaire studies. *Journal of Business Communication, 13*(3), 49–54. doi:10.1177/002194367601300305

Schewe, C.D., & Cournoyer, N.G. (1976). Prepaid vs. promised monetary incentives to questionnaire response: Further evidence. *Public Opinion Quarterly, 40*(1), 105–107. doi:10.1086/268272

Schonlau, M., Asch, B.J., & Du, C. (2003). Web surveys as part of a mixed-mode strategy for populations that cannot be contacted by e-mail. *Social Science Computer Review, 21*(2), 218–222. doi:10.1177/0894439303021002007

Schneider, K.C., & Johnson, J.C. (1995). Stimulating response to market surveys of business professionals. *Industrial Marketing Management, 24*(4), 265–276. doi:10.1016/0019-8501(94)00084-a

Shih, T.H., & Fan, X. (2007). Response rates and mode preferences in web-mail mixed-mode surveys: a meta-analysis. *International Journal of Internet Science, 2*(1), 59–82. doi:10.1177/0894439309350698

Shih, T.H., & Fan, X. (2009). Comparing response rates in e-mail and paper surveys: A meta-analysis. *Educational Research Review, 4*(1), 26–40. doi:10.1016/j.edurev.2008.01.003

Shuttleworth, F.K. (1931). A study of questionnaire technique. *Journal of Educational Psychology, 22*(9), 652–658. doi:10.1037/h0074591

Singer, E., Van Hoewyk, J., & Maher, M P. (2000). Experiments with incentives in telephone surveys. *Public Opinion Quarterly, 64*(2), 171–188. doi:10.1086/317761

Skinner, S.J., Ferrell, O.C., & Pride, W.M. (1984). Personal and nonpersonal incentives in mail surveys: Immediate versus delayed inducements. *Journal of the Academy of Marketing Science, 12*(1–2), 106–114. doi:10.1007/bf02729490

Spry, V.M., Hovell, M.F., Sallis, J.G., Hofstetter, C.R., Elder, J.P., & Molgaard, C.A. (1989). Recruiting survey respondents to mailed surveys: Controlled trials of incentives and prompts. *American Journal of Epidemiology, 130*(1), 166–172. doi:10.1093/oxfordjournals.aje.a115309

Tedin, K.L., & Hofstetfer, C.R. (1982). The effect of cost and importance factors on the return rate for single and multiple mailings. *Public Opinion Quarterly, 46*(1), 122–128. doi:10.1086/268704

Teisl, M.F., Roe, B., & Vayda, M.E. (2006). Incentive effects on response rates, data quality, and survey administration costs. *International Journal of Public Opinion Research, 18*(3), 364–373. doi:10.1093/ijpor/edh106

Tuten, T.L., Galesic, M., & Bosnjak, M. (2004). Effects of immediate versus delayed notification of prize draw results on response behavior in web surveys: An experiment. *Social Science Computer Review, 22*(3), 377–384. doi:10.1177/0894439304265640

Warriner, K., Goyder, J., Gjertsen, H., Hohner, P., & McSpurren, K. (1996). Charities, no; Lotteries, no; Cash, yes. Main effects and interactions in a Canadian incentives experiment. *Public Opinion Quarterly, 60*(4), 542–562. doi:10.1086/297772

Wenemark, M., Vernby, Å., & Norberg, A.L. (2010). Can incentives undermine intrinsic motivation to participate in epidemiologic surveys? *European Journal of Epidemiology, 25*(4), 231–235. doi:10.1007/s10654-010-9434-8

Wetzels, W., Schmeets, H., van den Brakel, J., & Feskens, R. (2008). Impact of prepaid incentives in face-to-face surveys: A large-scale experiment with postage stamps. *International Journal of Public Opinion Research, 20*(4), 507–516. doi:10.1093/ijpor/edn050

Willimack, D.K., Schuman, H., Pennell, B.E., & Lepkowski, J.M. (1995). Effects of a prepaid nonmonetary incentive on response rates and response quality in a face-to-face survey. *Public Opinion Quarterly, 59*(1), 78–92. doi:10.1086/269459

Wotruba, T.R. (1966). Monetary inducements and mail questionnaire response. *Journal of Marketing Research, 3*(4), 398–400. doi:10.2307/3149858

Yammarino, F.J., Skinner, S.J., & Childers, T.L. (1991). Understanding mail survey response behavior: A meta-analysis. *Public Opinion Quarterly, 55*(4), 613–639. doi:10.1086/269284

Yu, J., & Cooper, H. (1983). A quantitative review of research design effects on response rates to questionnaires. *Journal of Marketing Research, 20*(1), 36–44. doi:10.2307/3151410

Section 7.5: Could privacy concerns prevent individuals from self-reporting?

Definition of terms – What are privacy concerns?

According to Merriam-Webster (2019), privacy is "freedom from unauthorized intrusion" (par. 1). By the very nature of self-report measures, when respondents agree to participate in a survey, they are, to some extent, giving up a certain level of privacy to provide the researcher with information. This section will discuss what a researcher can do to alleviate privacy concerns among their potential study participants.

It is important to note that most of the research discussed in this section does not explicitly evaluate the effects of privacy concerns on respondents' motivation. Most studies assess the impact of privacy concerns on response or cooperation rates. For our purposes, a nonresponse to a set of questions signifies a lack of motivation to answer them. We will equate higher or low response or cooperation rates with corresponding high or low levels of effectiveness in increasing respondent motivation.

In brief

Privacy is a prevalent concern among respondents, especially in the digital age, with researchers increasingly requesting study participants disclose personal information. Overall, there seems to be a consensus that privacy concerns negatively influence respondent motivation (Singer, 1978; Singer, 1984; Singer, 1993; Singer, 2003; Singer, Van Hoewyk, & Neugebauer, 2003; Martin, 2006; and Han, Albaum, Wiley, & Thirkell, 2009).

Privacy becomes a very prevalent concern when researchers need to request potentially sensitive information, such as about a person's finances or sexual behavior. Several studies found that in such contexts, problems can be alleviated with the promise of confidentiality (Singer, 1984; Dillman, Sinclair, & Clark, 1993; Singer, Von Thurn, & Miller, 1993; O'Neil & Penrod, 2001; Couper, Singer, Conrad, and Groves, 2008). However, some researchers did not find promises of anonymity or confidentiality assurances made a difference in respondent motivation to self-report (Fuller, 1974; Wildman, 1977; Reamer, 1979; Frey, 1986; and Bates, Dahlhamer, & Singer, 2008).

Demographic characteristics can also play a role, with higher levels of income and education correlating with higher levels of privacy concerns (Jones, 1979) and white respondents being more likely to be concerned about privacy than black respondents (Singer et al., 1993). Lastly, respondents feel that their privacy is less guaranteed when completing a survey via the web than by traditional pencil and paper (Denniston et al., 2010).

Expectations

- In general, privacy concerns appear to affect respondent motivation (Singer, 1978; Singer, 1984; Singer, 1993; Singer, 2003; Singer et al., 2003; Martin, 2006; and Han et al., 2009), although some researchers present evidence to the contrary (Fuller, 1974; Wildman, 1977; Reamer, 1979; Frey, 1986; and Bates et al., 2008).
- Requests for sensitive information such as finances or sexual behavior tend to yield higher levels of concern for privacy than less sensitive topics (Singer, 1984; Dillman et al., 1993; Singer et al., 1993; O'Neil & Penrod, 2001; Couper et al., 2008).
- Additionally, demographic characteristics may vary in privacy concerns, such as race, income, and population size (Jones, 1979; Singer et al., 1993).
- Respondents may perceive less privacy when completing surveys online than traditional pen-and-paper surveys (Denniston et al., 2010).

Principles

- Offer assurances of confidentiality and data privacy from the first point of contact with a potential study participant, re-emphasize these in all contacts, and include these assurances as part of the survey introduction.
- Repeatedly reassure populations with higher incomes and higher levels of education of the confidentiality of their responses. Clearly describe the steps you have taken to prevent the identity of individuals from being associated with specific answers.

Commentary

While no approach can guarantee 100% effectiveness, a researcher should take clear and effective steps to ensure privacy and confidentiality and then communicate these steps repeatedly to lower the worry and uncertainty of potential self-report study participants.

References and additional readings

Bates, N., Dahlhamer, J., & Singer, E. (2008). Privacy concerns, too busy, or just not interested: Using doorstep concerns to predict survey nonresponse. *Journal of Official Statistics, 24*(4), 591. No doi available.

Campbell, M.J., & Waters, W.E. (1990). Does anonymity increase response rate in postal questionnaire surveys about sensitive subjects? A randomised trial. *Journal of Epidemiology and Community Health, 44*(1), 75–76. doi:10.1136/jech.44.1.75

Couper, M.P., Singer, E., Conrad, F.G., & Groves, R.M. (2008). Risk of disclosure, perceptions of risk, and concerns about privacy and confidentiality as factors in survey participation. *Journal of Official Statistics, 24*(2), 255–275. No doi available.

Denniston, M.M., Brener, N.D., Kann, L., Eaton, D.K., McManus, T., Kyle, T.M., Roberts, A.M., Flint, K.H., & Ross, J.G. (2010). Comparison of paper-and-pencil versus Web administration of the Youth Risk Behavior Survey (YRBS): Participation, data quality, and perceived privacy and anonymity. *Computers in Human Behavior, 26*(5), 1054–1060. doi:10.1016/j.chb.2010.03.006

Dillman, D.A., Sinclair, M.D., & Clark, J.R. (1993). Effects of questionnaire length, respondent-friendly design, and a difficult question on response rates for occupant-addressed census mail surveys. *Public Opinion Quarterly, 57*(3), 289–304. doi:10.1086/269376

Dillman, D.A., Singer, E., Clark, J.R., & Treat, J.B. (1996). Effects of benefits appeals, mandatory appeals, and variations in statements of confidentiality on completion rates for census questionnaires. *Public Opinion Quarterly, 60*(3), 376–389. doi:10.1086/297759

Frey, J.H. (1986). An experiment with a confidentiality reminder in a telephone survey. *Public Opinion Quarterly, 50*(2), 267–269. doi:10.1086/268980

Fuller, C. (1974). Effect of anonymity on return rate and response bias in a mail survey. *Journal of Applied Psychology, 59*(3), 292–296. doi:10.1037/h0036630

Han, V., Albaum, G., Wiley, J.B. & Thirkell, P. (2009). Applying theory to structure respondents' stated motivations for participating in web surveys. *Qualitative Market Research: An International Journal, 12*(4), 428–442. doi:10.1108/13522750910993338

Jones, W.H. (1979). Generalizing mail survey inducement methods: Population interactions with anonymity and sponsorship. *Public Opinion Quarterly, 43*(1), 102–111. doi:10.1086/268495

Martin, E. (2006). Privacy concerns and the census long form: Some evidence from census 2000. *Survey Methodology, 10.* No doi available.

Mason, W.S., Dressel, R.J., & Bain, R.K. (1961). Living research: An experimental study of factors affecting response to a mail survey of beginning teachers. *Public Opinion Quarterly, 25*(2), 296–299. doi:10.1086/267022

O'Neil, K.M., & Penrod, S.D. (2001). Methodological variables in Web-based research that may affect results: Sample type, monetary incentives, and personal information. *Behavior Research Methods, Instruments, & Computers, 33*(2), 226–233. doi:10.3758/bf03195369

Privacy [Def. 1b]. (2019). In *Merriam-Webster Online*. Retrieved June 22, 2019, from https://www.merriam-webster.com/dictionary/privacy.

Reamer, F.G. (1979). Protecting research subjects and unintended consequences: The effect of guarantees of confidentiality. *Public Opinion Quarterly, 43*(4), 497–506. doi:10.1086/268546

Singer, E. (1978). Informed consent: Consequences for response rate and response quality in social surveys. *American Sociological Review, 43*(2), 144–162. doi:10.2307/2094696

Singer, E. (1984). Public reactions to some ethical issues of social research: Attitudes and behavior. *Journal of Consumer Research, 11*(1), 501–509. doi:10.1086/208986

Singer, E. (1993). Informed consent and survey response: A summary of the empirical literature. *Journal of Official Statistics - Stockholm, 9,* 361–361. No doi available.

Singer, E. (2003). Exploring the meaning of consent: participation in research and beliefs about risks and benefits. *Journal of Official Statistics, 19*(3), 273–286. No doi available.

Singer, E., Mathiowetz, N.A., & Couper, M.P. (1993). The impact of privacy and confidentiality concerns on survey participation: The case of the 1990 US census. *Public Opinion Quarterly, 57*(4), 465–482. doi:10.1086/269391

Singer, E., Van Hoewyk, J., & Neugebauer, R.J. (2003). Attitudes and behavior: The impact of privacy and confidentiality concerns on participation in the 2000 Census. *Public Opinion Quarterly, 67*(3), 368–384. doi:10.1086/377465

Singer, E., Von Thurn, D.R., & Miller, E.R. (1995). Confidentiality assurances and response a quantitative review of the experimental literature. *Public Opinion Quarterly, 59*(1), 66–77. doi:10.1086/269458

Wildman, R.C. (1977). Effects of anonymity and social setting on survey responses. *Public Opinion Quarterly, 41*(1), 74–79. doi:10.1086/268354

Section 7.6: Does the amount of interest a respondent has in the topic of the measures make a difference?

Definition of terms – What is personal interest in topic of measures?

According to Merriam-Webster (2019), an interest is "a feeling that accompanies or causes special attention to someone or something" (par. 1). In the context of surveys, the concept of 'interest' stems from the relevance of the topics and content of the questions to the respondents who are expected to react to them. In the research discussed in this section, interest is sometimes referred to as salience, which encapsulates personal interest in topics and relevance to the respondent's life.

It is important to note that most of the research discussed in this section does not explicitly evaluate the effects of personal interest in the topic being measured on respondents' motivation. Most studies assess the impact of personal interest in a topic on response or cooperation rates. We will equate higher or lower levels of response or cooperation rates with corresponding high or low levels of effectiveness in increasing respondent motivation.

In brief

Many researchers have shown that the level of interest respondents have in a topic being studied will affect their willingness to begin the survey and/or complete it (Blumberg, Fuller, & Hare, 1974; Heberlein & Baumgartner, 1978; Greer, Chuchinprakarn, & Seshadri, 2000; Crawford et al. 2001; Edwards et al., 2002; Roberts et al., 2002; Van Kenhove, Wijnen, & De Wulf, 2002; Groves, Presser, & Dipko, 2004; Galesic, 2006; Han et al., 2009; Fan & Yan, 2010; and Barrios et al. 2011). In addition to personal interest, topic salience due to timely events increases respondents' willingness to begin and/or complete a survey (Cook, Heath, & Thompson, 2000). Baker et al. (2010) also found that those who lacked a personal interest in the surveyed topic were less likely to participate in online surveys. In addition to confirming the importance of 'interest,' researchers also provide advice on measuring a respondent's interest in a topic and mitigating a lack of interest. For example, Van Kenhove et al. (2002) directly asked respondents to evaluate their involvement in the topics of their two experimental surveys, while Galesic (2006) conducted a survey broken up into distinct question blocks, in which respondents were asked "to evaluate how interesting they found the questions in that block" (p. 316). Roose et al. (2007) conducted a survey about arts performances with a sample specifically of audience members and measured interest by asking for respondents' frequency of attending such performances.

Expectations

- If a survey's topic is of interest to respondents or relevant to an aspect of their lives, they will be more likely to participate in surveys (Blumberg et al., 1974; Heberlein & Baumgartner, 1978; Cook et al., 2000; Greer et al., 2000; Crawford et al., 2001; Edwards et al., 2002; Van Kenhove et al., 2002; Groves et al., 2004; Galesic, 2006; Han et al., 2009; Baker et al., 2010; Fan & Yan, 2010; and Barrios et al., 2011).

Commentary

This is good to know for planning purposes. Suppose the researcher knows that the topic interests the study's intended participants or can find an angle of the topic that would make it interesting. In that case, the researcher can amplify the topic in their initial contact with the participants, and in subsequent communication, to increase their willingness to self-report.

References and additional readings

Baker, R., Blumberg, S.J., Beck, J.M., Couper, M.P., Courtright, M., Dennis, J.M., Dillman, D., Frankel, M.R., Garland, P., Groves, R.M., Kennedy, C., Krosnick, J., Lavrakas, P.J., Lee, S., Link, M., Piekarski, L., Rao, K., Thomas, R.K., & Zahs, D. (2010). Research synthesis: AAPOR report on online panels. *Public Opinion Quarterly 74*(4), 711–781. doi:10.1093/poq/nfq048

Barrios, M., Villarroya, A., Borrego. A., & Olle, C. (2011). Response rates and data quality in web and mail surveys administered to PhD holders. *Social Science Computer Review, 29*(2), 208–220. doi:10.1177/0894439310368031

Blumberg, H.H., Fuller, C., & Hare, A.P. (1974). Response rates in postal surveys. *Public Opinion Quarterly, 38*(1), 113. doi:10.1086/268140

Cook, C., Heath, F., & Thompson, R. L. (2000). A meta-analysis of response rates in web- or internet-based surveys. *Educational and Psychological Measurement, 60*(6), 821–836. doi:10.1177/00131640021970934

Crawford, S., McCabe, S., Couper, M. & Boyd, C. (2001) From mail to web: improving response rates and data collection efficiencies. Paper presented at the International Conference on Improving Surveys, Copenhagen, Denmark.

Edwards, P., Roberts, I., Clarke, M., DiGuiseppi, C., Pratap, S., Wentz, R., & Kwan, I. (2002). Increasing response rates to postal questionnaires: Systematic review. *BMJ, 324*(7347), 1183. doi:10.1136/bmj.324.7347.1183

Evangelista, F., Poon, P., & Albaum, G. (2008). Enhancing survey response rates: Lessons from a field experiment. Proceedings, Australia and New Zealand Marketing Academy Conference, Sydney, Australia.

Fan, W., & Yan, Z. (2010). Factors affecting response rates of the web survey: A systematic review. *Computers in Human Behavior, 26*(2), 132–139. doi:10.1016/j.chb.2009.10.015

Galesic, M. (2006). Dropouts on the web: Effects of interest and burden experienced during an online survey. *Journal of Official Statistics, 22*(2), 313. No doi available.

Greer, T. V., Chuchinprakarn, N., & Seshadri, S. (2000). Likelihood of participating in mail survey research: Business respondents' perspectives. *Industrial Marketing Management, 29*(2), 97–109. doi:10.1016/s0019-8501(98)00038-8

Groves, R.M., Presser, S., & Dipko, S. (2004). The role of topic interest in survey participation decisions. *Public Opinion Quarterly, 68*(1), 2–31. doi:10.1093/poq/nfh002

Han, V., Albaum, G., Wiley, J.B. & Thirkell, P. (2009). Applying theory to structure respondents' stated motivations for participating in web surveys. *Qualitative Market Research: An International Journal, 12*(4), 428–442. doi:10.1108/13522750910993338

Heberlein, T.A., & Baumgartner, R. (1978). Factors affecting response rates to mailed questionnaires: A quantitative analysis of the published literature. *American Sociological Review, 43*(4), 447–462. doi:10.2307/2094771

Interest [Def. 1a]. (2019). In *Merriam-Webster Online*. Retrieved June 12, 2019, from https://www.merriam-webster.com/dictionary/interest.

Marcus, B., Bosnjak, M., Lindner, S., Pilischenko, S., & Schütz, A. (2007). Compensating for low topic interest and long surveys: A field experiment on nonresponse in web surveys. *Social Science Computer Review, 25*(3), 372–383. doi:10.1177/0894439307297606

Roose, H., Lievens, J., & Waege, H. (2007). The joint effect of topic interest and follow-up procedures on the response in a mail questionnaire: An empirical test of the leverage-saliency theory in audience research. *Sociological Methods & Research, 35*(3), 410–428. doi:10.1177/0049124106290447

Van Kenhove, P., Wijnen, K., & De Wulf, K. (2002). The influence of topic involvement on mail-survey response behavior. *Psychology & Marketing, 19*(3), 293–301. doi:10.1002/mar.1053

Chapter 8
Principles and expectations: Respondent abilities

Objectives of Chapter 8: You will need to take many precautions to prevent errors associated with study participants' abilities. Factors that you need to take into account include whether you can assume participant knowledge levels regarding the topic about which you're trying to get their reactions, whether some participants will agree with statements regardless of what they say, whether some participants will react to statements based on how they believe their social circles would respond to them, whether you can assume that respondents can remember past events, and whether some participants will react to measures without reading their contents. While there are undoubtedly other precautions you will need to consider regarding the characteristics of study participants, this chapter addresses the aspects aligned in a sizeable proportion of the corresponding literature.

Which assumptions are addressed in this chapter?

Table 8.1: Assumptions made about respondents for self-report measures to achieve their intended purpose.

When reacting to a measure or answering a question, the respondent....	
Assumption A	Is willing to disclose information about themselves
Assumption B	Is truthful and not deliberately lying
Assumption C	Interprets each measure/question the way the researcher intended and in the same way that others who are also being measured are interpreting them
Assumption D	**Can correctly recall needed information from memory to react to each measure/question**
Assumption E	Can easily move from one measure/question to another when multiple measures/questions are included
Assumption F	Is self-aware
Assumption G	**Is not influenced by one or more aspects of the questions/measures to which they are asked to react**

The assumptions bolded in Tables 8.1 and 8.2 are affected by violations of the principles provided in the sections of this chapter. The less you consider the limitations of study participants, the more their reactions will be influenced by something other than what the researcher set out to measure. As a result, the researcher is more likely to measure something different from what they intended.

https://doi.org/10.1515/9783111590998-009

Table 8.2: Assumptions made about the measures so that they can achieve their intended purpose.

Each measure developed by the researcher should . . .	
Assumption H	Fully capture the concept or an aspect of the concept that it is intended to capture
Assumption I	Precisely capture the aspect of the concept that it is intended to capture
Assumption J	Capture a single concept and no other
Assumption K	Be consistent in its capturing of the concept that it was designed to capture

Section 8.1: Should I worry about what my respondents know about the topic that I am measuring?

Definition of terms – What is assumed knowledge?

When we discuss assumed knowledge in the context of surveys, we are generally referring to knowledge of the topic(s) addressed within the survey, which Diamantopoulos, Reynolds, and Schlegelmilch (1994) call subject knowledge, and specifically define as respondents' "familiarity with the topic of the survey" (p. 296).

In brief

When the topic or topics of self-report measures require familiarity that may not apply to all respondents, drastic measurement errors are introduced. All studies discussed in this section have pointed out that variation in knowledge regarding the measured topic will lead to data inconsistencies. Some evidence suggests that people who have obtained higher levels of education tend to be more knowledgeable about issues than those who are less educated. However, knowledge of a topic will most likely be related to the topic's relevance to one or more aspects of a respondent's life (Campanelli, Rothgeb, & Martin, 2005; Ferber, 1956; Lounsbury, Sundstrom, & DeVault, 1979).

Schuman and Presser (1980) explored the tendency of people to give opinions even when unfamiliar with a topic. They found that simply providing survey participants with a "don't know" response option would prevent them from feeling pressured to express an opinion when they didn't have enough information to express an opinion.

Techniques for checking on subject knowledge among respondents include:
1. Provide an open-ended measure that asks respondents to express what a technical term means to them in their own words. In this case, the technical term is central to the reaction the researcher is seeking from the respondent Ferber (1956). The researcher would then evaluate the respondent's own words to deter-

mine if their understanding of the technical term is the same as that of the researcher and only use the responses of those whose understanding is similar.
2. Include in the survey a battery of objective measures concerning the topic, e.g., knowledge about a nuclear power plant. For Lounsbury et al. (1979), "[k]nowledge about the nuclear plant was operationalized as the number of correct answers to seven multiple-choice items that were scored as either correct or incorrect" (p. 560). The knowledge score would be the total across all correctly answered measures.
3. Assess a respondent's subjective knowledge of the topic by providing a scale of subjective knowledge. Jung, Park, and Ahn (2019) used multiple scale items to evaluate respondents' subjective understanding of "sustainable design and construction" (p. 7). Examples include "What is your level of knowledge in sustainable design and construction" (p. 7). The latter technique provides a general self-assessment that assumes the individual is self-aware. As such, this subjective knowledge approach is more likely to be effective on non-technical and non-complex topics.

Expectations

- The extent of respondents' knowledge of topics addressed within a survey significantly influences their responses and causes concern regarding data quality. Ensuring that those who pretest the survey know about the topic can help detect and fix specific issues early in the process (Diamantopoulos et al., 1994).
- When variations in respondents' knowledge of a topic can be quantitatively assessed, researchers can increase the validity of their data (Ferber, 1956).
- In the case of telephone interviews, survey data will be significantly affected by the extent to which interviewers are trained on the subject and their ability to homogenously clarify the meaning of terms used in survey measures when requested by the respondent. If the respondent's knowledge of the topic is low and the interviewer is unable to clarify when asked, then data quality will be negatively affected (Campanelli et al., 2005).
- Including a "don't know" response option mitigates the effects of insincerely captured attitudes (Schuman & Presser, 1980).

Principles

- When budget and time allow, determine the extent of topic knowledge by pretesting the self-report measures with a small group of your intended study participants.

- For self-report measures on topics that likely vary widely across the sample, include measures that assess a respondent's knowledge regarding the topic.
- For self-report measures that address fact-based knowledge, include an "I don't know enough about this topic to answer this question" response option so that respondents are not forced to give an opinion when they do not have any opinion due to lack of familiarity with the topic being measure (see Chapter 6 Section 1 for a discussion).

Commentary

I remember watching an instructional video in the early 1990s where a supposed survey interviewer was on-location in the Boston Common (a public garden in the center of Boston) and asked nearby pedestrians if they supported or opposed U.S. aid to the rebels in Alpha Centauri. Not surprisingly, many of those asked seriously expressed an opinion about such aid. Even though Alpha Centauri is a star, and no U.S. aid is going to rebels located on stars. The point of the video was to show that people will often express opinions about topics they know nothing about. The burden is on the researcher to ensure the study participants are reacting to measures about a topic with which they are familiar. Otherwise, the data collected by the researcher would be useless. If a researcher can conduct a pretest of the self-report measures with a probability sample of the population they wish to study, a straightforward technique for detecting familiarity with a topic is to add a measure that asks the participants how much they know about this topic. How familiar a respondent needs to be will depend on how in-depth the measures regarding the specific topic are and how much they rely on a respondent's knowledge of objective facts. If the measures ask for a general impression, then a low level of familiarity will suffice. If the measures assume knowledge of facts, then a high level of understanding will be required before their reactions can be counted. A pretest of the self-report measures is always a good idea when time and budget permit doing so.

References and additional readings

Campanelli, P.C., Rothgeb, J.M., & Martin, E.A. (2005). The role of respondent comprehension and interviewer knowledge in CPS labor force classification. Washington, D.C.: Statistical Research Division, U.S. Bureau of the Census.

Diamantopoulos, A., Reynolds, N., & Schlegelmilch, B. (1994). Pretesting in questionnaire design: The impact of respondent characteristics on error detection. *Journal of the Market Research Society, 36*(4), 295–311. doi:10.1177/147078539403600402

Ferber, R. (1956). The effect of respondent ignorance on survey results. *Journal of the American Statistical Association, 51*(276), 576–586. doi:10.1080/01621459.1956.10501347

Jung, Y., Park, K, & Ahn, J. (2019). Sustainability in higher education: perceptions of social responsibility among university students. *Social Sciences, 8*(90), 1–14.

Lounsbury, J.W., Sundstrom, E., & DeVault, R.C. (1979). Moderating effects of respondent knowledge in public opinion research. Journal of Applied Psychology, 64(5), 558–563. doi:10.1037/0021-9010.64.5.558

Schuman, H., & Presser, S. (1980). Public opinion and public ignorance: The fine line between attitudes and nonattitudes. *American Journal of Sociology, 85*(5), 1214–1225. doi:10.1086/227131

Section 8.2: Is it possible that my respondents are consistently agreeing to measures because they are the type of people who always agree?

Definition of terms – What is acquiescence?

In survey research, acquiescence refers to "the tendency to agree with test items, regardless of their content," which negatively influences data quality (McGee, 1962, p. 229). Fortunately, the tendency to agree with a statement regardless of content is not ubiquitous. It occurs more frequently among certain socioeconomic and cultural groups, and the conditions under which acquiescence is more frequently found will be detailed below.

In brief

Research is generally divided on the causes of acquiescence. Yet, there have been enough findings that allow us to make some generalizations so that we know what to look for when conducting research. Several researchers have found that respondent characteristics, including race, age, education level, and socioeconomic status, can all influence a respondent's likelihood to acquiesce. Respondents with lower levels of education and lower socioeconomic status may be more likely to acquiesce, in addition to older respondents and respondents from minority groups (Bachman & O'Malley, 1984; Baron-Epel et al., 2010; Bass, 1956; Carr, 1971; Johnson et al., 2005; Marin et al., 1992; Ross et al., 1995; Ross & Mirowsky, 1984). Additionally, when an interviewer is involved, if the respondent feels a socioeconomic distance between the interviewer and themselves, then acquiescence is more likely (Lenski & Legett, 1960). Studies have also shown respondents from collectivist cultures or countries (e.g., East Asian countries), as compared to individualistic cultures countries (e.g., Western European countries), are hesitant to disagree and more likely to acquiesce (Baron-Epel et al., 2010; Johnson et al., 2005; Marin et al., 1992; Smith, 2004).

Some researchers believe acquiescence is a stable personality trait that remains consistent across time and cannot be avoided in research (Couch & Keniston, 1960; Knowles & Nathan, 1997; Weijters et al., 2010; Wetzel et al., 2016). However, other researchers have found certain survey elements, such as ensuring the balance of all scales and utilizing item-specific measures rather than agree-disagree measures, can help prevent acquiescence (Baumgartner & Steenkamp, 2001; Cloud & Vaughan, 1970; Ferrando et al., 2004; Kuru & Pasek, 2016; McGee, 1962; Saris et al., 2010; Toner, 1987; Winkler et al., 1980).

Researchers have three strategies for preempting or detecting acquiescence (see Chun Seng Kam, 2016; Saris et al., 2010). To preempt acquiescence, they can use item-specific or balanced scales. Item-specific scales are sometimes called forced-choice response scales

Saris et al. (2010) provide examples of agreement-based and item-specific scales to contrast them from one another.

Using health as the focus of the measure, the agreement scale would be:

> "To what extent do you agree strongly or disagree strongly that your health is excellent?" The respondent would be given the following response options: "agree completely, agree somewhat, neither agree nor disagree, disagree somewhat, disagree completely" (p. 62).

The alternative, which avoids acquiescence, according to Saris et al. (2010), would be an item-specific measure:

> How you would rate your health overall: excellent, very good, good, fair, bad, very bad? (p. 62).

Saris et al. (2010) point to the 14-item stress scale by Cohen, Kamarck, and Mermelstein (1983) as a balanced scale. Here are four items taken from that scale:

> "In the last month, how often have you felt confident about your ability to handle your personal problems?"; "In the last month, how often have you felt that things were going your way?"; "In the last month, how often have you found that you could not cope with all the things that you had to do?"; "In the last month, how often have you been able to control irritations in your life?". And the respondents were given the following scale: "never, almost never, sometimes, fairly often, very often" (Cohen, Kamarck & Mermelstein, 1983, p. 394).

Expectations

- Respondents with lower levels of education and lower socioeconomic status are more likely to acquiesce, in addition to older respondents and respondents from minority groups (Bachman & O'Malley, 1984; Baron-Epel et al., 2010; Bass, 1956; Carr, 1971; Johnson et al., 2005; Marin et al., 1992; Ross & Mirowsky, 1984; Ross et al., 1995).
- Acquiescence is more common among respondents from collectivist cultures than individualistic cultures (Baron-Epel et al., 2010; Johnson et al., 2005; Marin et al., 1992; Smith, 2004).

- More significant socioeconomic status differences between interviewer and respondent may produce acquiescence (Lenski & Legett, 1960).
- Preemptive strategies, such as ensuring the balance of all scales and utilizing item-specific measures rather than agree-disagree measures can help minimize the effects of acquiescence (Baumgartner & Steenkamp, 2001; Cloud & Vaughan, 1970; Ferrando et al., 2004; Kuru & Pasek, 2016; McGee, 1962; Saris et al., 2010; Toner, 1987; Winkler et al., 1980).
- Techniques can be used to detect whether acquiescence is present in the data after the completion of data collection and before analysis.

Principle

- Utilize item-specific or balanced scales (e.g., forced-choice measures) instead of agree-disagree scales when conducting surveys among groups susceptible to acquiescence.

Commentary

Please refer to Chapter 9 in this book for a comprehensive approach to quantifying errors due to measurement (EDM) when using multiple-item measures. The approach described in Chapter 9 can detect many sources of error, including those due to acquiescence.

References and additional readings

Bachman, J.G. & O'Malley, P.M. (1984). Yea-saying, nay-saying, and going to extremes: Black-white differences in response styles. *The Public Opinion Quarterly, 48*(2), 491–509. doi:10.1086/268845

Baron-Epel, O., Kaplan, G., Weinstein, R., Green, M.S. (2010). Extreme and acquiescence bias in a bi-ethnic population. *European Journal of Public Health, 20*(5), 543–548. doi:10.1093/eurpub/ckq05

Bass, B. (1956). Development and evaluation of a scale for measuring social acquiescence. *Journal of Abnormal Psychology, 53*(3), 296–299. doi:10.1037/h0047161

Baumgartner, H. & Steenkamp, J. (2001). Response styles in marketing research: A cross-national investigation. *Journal of Marketing Research, 38*(2), 143–156. doi:10.1509/jmkr.38.2.143.18840

Carr, L. (1971). The Srole items and acquiescence. *American Sociological Review, 36*(2), 287–293. doi:10.2307/2094045

Chun Seng Kam, C. (2016). Further considerations in using items with diverse content to measure acquiescence. *Educational and Psychological Measurement, 76*(1), 164–174. doi:10.1177/0013164415586831

Cohen, S, Kamarck, T. & Mermelstein, R. (1983). A global measure of perceived stress. *Journal of Health and Social Behavior, 24*, 385–396.

Cloud, J., & Vaughan, G. (1970). Using balanced scales to control acquiescence. *Sociometry, 33*(2), 193–202. doi:10.2307/2786329

Couch, A. & Keniston, K. (1960). Yeasayers and naysayers: Agreeing response set as a personality variable. *Journal of Abnormal Psychology, 60*(2), 151–174. doi:10.1037/h0040372

Ferrando, P.J., Condon, L., & Chico, E. (2004). The convergent validity of acquiescence: an empirical study relating balanced scales and separate acquiescence scales. *Personality and Individual Differences, 37*(7), 1331–1340. doi:10.1016/j.paid.2004.01.003

Johnson, T., Kulesa, P., Cho, Y., & Shavitt, S. (2005). The relation between culture and response styles: Evidence from 19 countries. *Journal of Cross-Cultural Psychology, 36*(2), 264–277. doi: 10.1177/0022022104272905

Knowles, E.S., & Nathan, K.T. (1997). Acquiescent responding in self-reports: cognitive style or social concern? *Journal of Research in Personality, 31*(2), 293–301. doi:10.1006/jrpe.1997.2180

Kuru, O. & Pasek, J. (2016). Improving social media measurement in surveys: Avoiding acquiescence bias in Facebook research. *Computers in Human Behavior, 57*(I), 82–92. doi:10.1016/j.chb.2015.12.008

Lenski, G., & Leggett, J. (1960). Caste, class, and deference in the research interview. *American Journal of Sociology, 65*(5), 463–467. doi:10.1086/222750

Marin, G., Gamba, R.J., & Marin, B.V. (1992). Extreme response style and acquiescence among Hispanics. *Journal of Cross-Cultural Psychology, 23*(4), 498–509. doi:10.1177/0022022192234006

McGee, R.K. (1962). The relationship between response style and personality variables: I. The measurement of response acquiescence. *Journal of Abnormal and Social Psychology, 64*(3), 229–233. doi:10.1037/h0043076

Ross, C.E. & Mirowsky, J. (1984). Socially-desirable response and acquiescence in a cross-cultural survey of mental health. *Journal of Health and Social Behavior, 25*(2), 189–197. doi:10.2307/2136668

Ross, C., Steward, C., & Sinacore, J. (1995). A comparative study of seven measures of patient satisfaction. *Medical Care, 33*(4), 392–406. doi:10.1097/00005650-19954000-00006

Saris, W.E., Revilla, M., Krosnick, J.A., & Schaeffer, E.M. (2010). Comparing questions with agree/disagree response options to questions with item-specific response options. *Survey Research Methods, 4*(1), 61–79. doi: 10.18148/srm/2010.v4i1.2682

Smith, P. (2004). Acquiescent response bias as an aspect of cultural communication style. *Journal of Cross-Cultural Psychology, 35*(1), 50–61. doi:10.1177/0022022103260380

Toner, B. (1987). The impact of agreement bias on the ranking of questionnaire response. *The Journal of Social Psychology, 127*(2), 221–222. doi:10.1080/00224545.1987.9713684

Weijters, B., Geuens, M., & Schilewaert, N. (2010). The stability of individual response styles. *Psychological Methods, 15*(1), 96–110. doi:10.1037/a0018721

Wetzel, E., Lüdtke, O., Zettler, I., & Böhnke, J.R. (2016). The stability of extreme response style and acquiescence over 8 years. *Assessment, 23*(3), 279–291. doi:10.1177/1073191115583714

Winkler, J., Kanouse, D., & Ware, J. (1982). Controlling for acquiescence response set in scale development. *Journal of Applied Psychology, 67*(5), 555–561. doi:10.1037/0021-9010.67.5.555

Section 8.3: Should I worry that respondents' reactions to measures are influenced by what they think others believe is the right way to react?

Definition of terms – What is social desirability?

According to Kreuter, Presser, and Tourangeau (2008), "The concept of social desirability rests on the notions that there are social norms governing some behaviors and attitudes and that people may misrepresent themselves to appear to comply with these norms" (p. 848).

In brief

Social desirability is very closely tied to the issue of sensitive survey topics. However, researchers have explicitly examined the role of the pressure respondents may feel to provide socially desirable answers when taking a survey. For example, several studies have shown respondents are much more comfortable providing honest (and potentially socially undesirable) responses in self-administered formats, particularly Web surveys, rather than in face-to-face or telephone interviews, in which they must provide answers to another person (Crawford et al., 2001; Kreuter et al., 2008; Tourangeau & Smith, 1996).

Baker et al. (2010) express concerns that many studies on this issue "simply demonstrate differences in rates of reporting socially desirable or undesirable attributes, without providing any direct tests of the notion that the differences were due to intentional misreporting inspired by social desirability pressures" (p. 735). The ultimate evidence would be a respondent admitting they lied because telling the truth would have been socially undesirable, and they do not want to come across as complying with what is socially desirable. However, being able to obtain such evidence is very challenging.

It is worth noting social desirability effects have most often been detected when measures deal with topics about which societal norms exist, such as sexual behaviors and substance use. Some researchers find it helpful to include measures that try to predict whether a respondent is susceptible to wanting to conform to social norms. Two of the leading instruments are the Marlowe-Crowne Social Desirability Scale (Crowne & Marlowe, 1964) and the Balanced Inventory of Desirable Responding (BIDR) (Paulhus, 1984). Once a researcher scores respondents in terms of how susceptible they are to conform to social norms, they can then use these scores to determine if those who were susceptible responded differently to the measures that embody the main goals of the survey. By doing so, the researcher can determine whether a social desirability bias influenced the reactions of those coded as highly susceptible. Many studies cited here utilize one or more of these social desirability bias scales. It is worth noting that studies that add social desirability detection instruments tend to be academic.

In addition to the above, there is also evidence a social desirability effect can occur when interviewers are involved. For example, if a survey's questions are about topics such as race or gender and the race or gender of the interviewer is identifiable in some way, respondents are likely to provide answers that will be socially desirable to the race or gender of the interviewer (Cotter et al., 1982; Huddy et al., 1997; Kane & Macaulay, 1993).

Expectations

- When social desirability bias is a concern, two main instruments can be used to quantify a respondent's susceptibility to be influenced by social norms: the Marlowe-Crowne Social Desirability Scale MCSD (Crowne & Marlowe, 1964) and the Balanced Inventory of Desirable Responding (BIDR).
- These scales are supplemental to the core measures of a survey and are more commonly used in academic studies rather than industry studies.
- Short forms of the MCSD scale or the BIDR scale can be helpful when there are time restrictions, and there is some evidence to suggest that the short forms may even be more valid (Asgeirsdottir et al., 2016; Hart et al., 2016; Loo & Thorpe, 2000; Reynolds, 1982; Strahan & Gerbasi, 1972).
- There is preliminary research to suggest that popular measures of social desirability bias, particularly the BIDR as it is currently written, may not be effective in non-western research settings (Li & Li, 2008; Li & Reb, 2009).
- Respondents tend to answer sensitive questions in socially desirable ways when in the presence of an actual interviewer but are more honest in solitary administration modes, such as a Web survey (Crawford et al., 2001; Kreuter et al., 2008; Tourangeau & Smith, 1996).
- If a survey's questions are about topics such as race or gender and the race or gender of the interviewer is identifiable in some way, respondents are likely to provide answers that will be socially desirable to that race or gender (Cotter et al., 1982; Huddy et al., 1997; Kane & Macaulay, 1993).

Principles

- Consider using short forms of the MCSD scale or the BIDR when possible and appropriate.
- When researching personal topics to which respondents may feel embarrassed to speak honestly (examples include sexual behavior or illicit drug use), select a

mode that allows them to feel their answers are as private as possible (ideally Web, but traditional mail may work as well).
- Similarly, when using an interviewer and conducting research on socially charged topics such as race or gender, be sure that the race or gender of the interviewer cannot be identified so that respondents do not feel obligated to respond in ways that will be favorable to the interviewer based on their perceived characteristics. In this case, the Web or mail are the ideal modes of data collection.

Commentary

A social desirability effect is one of many other sources of errors due to measurement (EDM). We should do all we can to eliminate as many of these sources of error as possible. Otherwise, the data we collect will not be helpful.

References and additional readings

Armacost, R., Hosseini, J., Morris, S., & Rehbein, K. (1991). An empirical comparison of direct questioning, scenario, and randomized response methods for obtaining sensitive business information*. *Decision Sciences, 22*(5), 1073–1090. doi:10.1111/j.1540-5915.1991.tb01907.x

Arnold, H. J., & Feldman, D. C. (1981). Social desirability response bias in self-report choice situations. *Academy of Management Journal, 24*(2), 377–385. doi:10.5465/255848

Asgeirsdottir, R., Vésteinsdóttir, V., & Thorsdottir, F. (2016). Short form development of the balanced inventory of desirable responding: Applying confirmatory factor analysis, item response theory, and cognitive interviews to scale reduction. *Personality and Individual Differences, 96*, 212–221. doi:10.1016/j.paid.2016.02.083

Baker, R., Blumberg, S.J., Beck, J.M., Couper, M.P., Courtright, M., Dennis, J.M., Dillman, D., Frankel, M.R., Garland, P., Groves, R.M., Kennedy, C., Krosnick, J., Lavrakas, P.J., Lee, S., Link, M., Piekarski, L., Rao, K., Thomas, R.K., & Zahs, D. (2010). Research synthesis: AAPOR report on online panels. *Public Opinion Quarterly 74*(4), 711–781. No doi available.

Ballard, R. (1992). Short forms of the Marlowe-Crowne social desirability scale. *Psychological Reports, 71*(3f), 1155–1160. doi:10.2466/pr0.71.8.1155-1160

Ballard, R., Crino, M.D., & Rubenfeld, S. (1988). Social desirability response bias and the Marlowe-Crowne social desirability scale. *Psychological Reports, 63*(1), 227–237. doi:10.2466/pr0.1988.63.1.227

Barger, S.D. (2002). The Marlowe-Crowne affair: Short forms, psychometric structure, and social desirability. *Journal of Personality Assessment, 79*(2), 286–305. doi:10.1207/S15327752JPA7902_11

Becker, W.M. (1976). Biasing effect of respondents' identification on responses to a social desirability scale: A warning to researchers. *Psychological Reports, 39*(3), 756–758. doi:10.2466/pr0.1976.39.3.756

Beebe, T.J., Harrison, P.A., Mcrae, J A., Anderson, R.E., & Fulkerson, J. A. (1998). An evaluation of computer-assisted self-interviews in a school setting. *Public Opinion Quarterly, 62*(4), 623–632. doi:10.1086/297863

Bernardi, R. (2006). Associations between Hofstede's cultural constructs and social desirability response bias. *Journal of Business Ethics, 65*(1), 43–53. doi:10.1007/s10551-005-5353-0

Bernardi, R., & Guptill, S. (2008). Social desirability response bias, gender, and factors influencing organizational commitment: An international study. *Journal of Business Ethics, 81*(4), 797–809. doi:10.1007/s10551-007-9548-4

Booth-Kewley, S., Edwards, J.E., & Rosenfeld, P. (1992). Impression management, social desirability, and computer administration of attitude questionnaires: Does the computer make a difference? *Journal of Applied Psychology, 77*(4), 562–566. doi:10.1037/0021-9010.77.4.562

Booth-Kewley, S., Larson, G.E., & Miyoshi, D.K. (2007). Social desirability effects on computerized and paper-and-pencil questionnaires. *Computers in Human Behavior, 23*(1), 463–477. doi:10.1016/j.chb.2004.10.020

Cotter, P.R., Cohen J., & Coulter, P.B. (1982). Race-of-interviewer effects in telephone interviews. *Public Opinion Quarterly, 46*(2), 278–284. doi:10.1086/268719

Crawford, S., McCabe, S., Couper, M. & Boyd, C. (2001) From mail to web: Improving Response rates and data collection efficiencies. Paper presented at the International Conference on Improving Surveys, Copenhagen, Denmark.

Crowne, D.P., & Marlowe, D. (1960). A new scale of social desirability independent of psychopathology. *Journal of Consulting Psychology, 24*(4), 349–354. doi:10.1037/h0047358

Dodou, D., & de Winter, J. C. F. (2014). Social desirability is the same in offline, online, and paper surveys: A meta-analysis. *Computers in Human Behavior, 36*, 487–495. doi:10.1016/j.chb.2014.04.005

Dwight, S.A., & Feigelson, M.E. (2000). A quantitative review of the effect of computerized testing on the measurement of social desirability. *Educational and Psychological Measurement, 60*(3), 340–360. doi:10.1177/00131640021970583

Edwards, A.L. (1953). The relationship between the judged desirability of a trait and the probability that the trait will be endorsed. *Journal of Applied Psychology, 37*(2), 90–93. doi:10.1037/h0058073

Edwards, A.L., & Edwards, L.K. (1992). Social desirability and Wiggins's MMPI content scales. *Journal of Personality and Social Psychology, 62*(1), 147–153. doi:10.1037/0022-3514.62.1.147

Ellingson, J.E., Sackett, P.R., & Hough, L.M. (1999). Social desirability corrections in personality measurement: Issues of applicant comparison and construct validity. *Journal of Applied Psychology, 84*(2), 155–166. doi:10.1037/0021-9010.84.2.155

Fang, J., Wen, C., & Prybutok, V. (2014). An assessment of equivalence between paper and social media surveys: The role of social desirability and satisficing. *Computers in Human Behavior, 30*, 335–343. doi: doi:10.1016/j.chb.2013.09.019

Fastame, M. C., & Penna, M. P. (2012). Does social desirability confound the assessment of self-reported measures of well-being and metacognitive efficiency in young and older adults? *Clinical Gerontologist, 35*(3), 239–256. doi:10.1080/07317115.2012.660411

Feigelson, M.E., & Dwight, S.A. (2000). Can asking questions by computer improve the candidness of responding? A meta-analytic perspective. *Consulting Psychology Journal: Practice and Research, 52*(4), 248–255. doi:10.1037/1061-4087.52.4.248

Finegan, J.E., & Allen, N.J. (1994). Computerized and written questionnaires: Are they equivalent? *Computers in Human Behavior, 10*(4), 483–496. doi:10.1016/0747-5632(94)90042-6

Fisher, R. J. (1993). Social desirability bias and the validity of indirect questioning. *Journal of Consumer Research, 20*(2), 303–315. doi:10.1086/209351

Fisher, R. J., & Katz, J. E. (2000). Social-desirability bias and the validity of self-reported values. *Psychology & Marketing, 17*(2), 105–120. doi:10.1002/(SICI)1520-6793(200002)17:2<105::AID-MAR3>3.0.CO;2-9

Fox, S., & Schwartz, D. (2002). Social desirability and controllability in computerized and paper-and-pencil personality questionnaires. *Computers in Human Behavior, 18*(4), 389–410. doi:10.1016/S0747-5632(01)00057-7

Fraboni, M., & Cooper, D. (1989). Further validation of three short forms of the Marlowe-Crowne scale of social desirability. *Psychological Reports, 65*(2), 595–600. doi:10.2466/pr0.1989.65.2.595

Futrell, C.M., & Swan, J.E. (1977). Anonymity and response by salespeople to a mail questionnaire. *Journal of Marketing Research, 14*(4), 611–616. doi:10.2307/3151211

Ganster, D. C., Hennessey, H. W., & Luthans, F. (1983). Social desirability response effects: Three alternative models. *Academy of Management Journal, 26*(2), 321–331. doi:10.2307/255979

Hancock, D.R., & Flowers, C.P. (2001). Comparing social desirability responding on world wide web and paper-administered surveys. *Educational Technology Research and Development, 49*(1), 5–13. doi:10.1007/bf02504503

Hart, C.M., Ritchie, T.D., Hepper, E.G., & Gebauer, J.E. (2015). The balanced inventory of desirable responding short form (BIDR-16). *SAGE Open, 5*(4), 1–9. doi:10.1177/2158244015621113

Heerwegh, D. (2005). Effects of personal salutations in e-mail invitations to participate in a web survey. *Public Opinion Quarterly, 69*(4), 588–598. doi:10.1093/poq/nfi053

Hofstee, W.K.B. (2003). Structures of personality traits. In I.B. Weiner, T. Millon, & M. Lerner (Eds.), *Handbook of Psychology: Personality and Social Psychology* (Vol. 5, pp. 231–254). Hoboken, NJ: Wiley.

Holtgraves, T. (2004). Social desirability and self-reports: Testing models of socially desirable responding. *Personality and Social Psychology Bulletin, 30*(2), 161–172. doi:10.1177/0146167203259930

Huddy, L., Billig, J., Bracciodieta, J., Hoeffler, L., Moynihan, J., & Pugliani, P. (1997). The effect of interviewer gender on the survey response. Political Behavior, 19(3), 197–220. doi:10.1023/a:1024882714254

Joinson, A. (1999). Social desirability, anonymity, and Internet-based questionnaires. *Behavior Research Methods, Instruments, & Computers, 31*(3), 433–438. doi:10.3758/bf03200723

Kam, C. (2013). Probing item social desirability by correlating personality items with balanced inventory of desirable responding (BIDR): A validity examination. *Personality and Individual Differences 54*(4), 513–518. doi:10.1016/j.paid.2012.10.017

Kane, E.W., & Macaulay, L.J. (1993). Interviewer gender and gender attitudes. *Public Opinion Quarterly, 57*(1), 1–28. doi:10.1086/269352

Kiesler, S., & Sproull, L.S. (1986). Response effects in the electronic survey. *Public Opinion Quarterly, 50*(3), 402–413. doi:10.1086/268992

Konstabel, K., Aavik, T., & Allik, J. (2006). Social desirability and consensual validity of personality traits. *European Journal of Personality, 20*(7), 549–566. doi:10.1002/per.593

Kreuter, F., Presser, S., & Tourangeau, R. (2008). Social desirability bias in CATI, IVR, and Web surveys. *Public Opinion Quarterly, 72*(5), 847–865. doi:10.1093/poq/nfn063

Kroner, D.G., & Weekes, J.R. (1996). Balanced inventory of desirable responding: Factor structure, reliability, and validity with an offender sample. *Personality and Individual Differences, 21*(3), 323–333. doi:10.1016/0191-8869(96)00079-7

Lambert, C., Arbuckle, S., & Holden, R. (2016). The Marlowe–Crowne Social Desirability Scale outperforms the BIDR impression management scale for identifying fakers. *Journal of Research in Personality, 61*, 80–86. doi:10.1016/j.jrp.2016.02.004

Lautenschlager, G.J., & Flaherty, V.L. (1990). Computer administration of questions: More desirable or more social desirability? *Journal of Applied Psychology, 75*(3), 310–314. doi:10.1037/0021-9010.75.3.310

Leite, W.L., & Beretvas, S.N. (2005). Validation of scores on the Marlowe-Crowne social desirability scale and the balanced inventory of desirable responding. *Educational and Psychological Measurement, 65*(1), 140–154. doi:10.1177/0013164404267285

Li, F., & Li, Y. (2008). The balanced inventory of desirable responding (BIDR): A factor analysis. *Psychological Reports, 103*(3), 727–731. doi:10.2466/pr0.103.3.727-731

Li, A., & Reb, J. (2009). A cross-nations, cross-cultures, and cross-conditions analysis on the equivalence of the balanced inventory of desirable responding. *Journal of Cross-Cultural Psychology, 40*(2), 214–233. doi:10.1177/0022022108328819

Link, M.W., & Mokdad, A. H. (2005). Effects of survey mode on self-reports of adult alcohol consumption: A comparison of mail, web and telephone approaches. *Journal of Studies on Alcohol and Drugs, 66*(2), 239–245. doi:10.15288/jsa.2005.66.239

Loo, R., & Thorpe, K. (2000). Confirmatory factor analyses of the full and short versions of the Marlowe-Crowne social desirability scale. *Journal of Social Psychology, 140*(5), 628–635. doi:10.1111/j.1559-1816.2004.tb01980.x

Martin, C.L., & Nagao, D.H. (1989). Some effects of computerized interviewing on job applicant responses. *Journal of Applied Psychology, 74*(1), 72–80. doi:10.1037/0021-9010.74.1.72

McCrae, R.R., & Costa, P.T. (1983). Social desirability scales: more substance than style. *Journal of Consulting and Clinical Psychology, 51*(6), 882–888. doi:10.1037/0022-006X.51.6.882

Meston, C.M., Heiman, J.R., Trapnell, P.D., & Paulhus, D.L. (1998). Socially desirable responding and sexuality self-reports. *The Journal of Sex Research, 35*(2), 148–157. doi:10.1080/00224499809551928

Moorman, R. H., & Podsakoff, P. M. (1992). A meta-analytic review and empirical test of the potential confounding effects of social desirability response sets in organizational behaviour research. *Journal of Occupational and Organizational Psychology, 65*(2), 131–149. doi:10.1111/j.2044-8325.1992.tb00490.x

Ones, D.S., Viswesvaran, C., & Reiss, A.D. (1996). Role of social desirability in personality testing for personnel selection: The red herring. *Journal of Applied Psychology, 81*(6), 660–679. doi:10.1037/0021-9010.81.6.660

Paulhus, D.L. (1984). Two-component models of socially desirable responding. *Journal of Personality and Social Psychology, 46*, 598–609. doi:10.1037/0022-3514.46.3.598

Pauls, C.A., & Stemmler, G. (2003). Substance and bias in social desirability responding. *Personality and Individual Differences, 35*(2), 263–275. doi:10.1016/S0191-8869(02)00187-3

Ramanaiah, N.V., & Martin, H.J. (1980). On the two-dimensional nature of the Marlowe-Crowne social desirability scale. *Journal of Personality Assessment, 44*(5), 507–514. doi:10.1207/s15327752jpa4405_11

Reynolds, W.M. (1982). Development of reliable and valid short forms of the Marlowe-Crowne social desirability scale. *Journal of Clinical Psychology, 38*(1), 119–125. doi:10.1002/1097-4679(198201)38:1<119::AID-JCLP2270380118>3.0.CO;2-I

Richman, W.L., Kiesler, S., Weisband, S., & Drasgow, F. (1999). A meta-analytic study of social desirability distortion in computer-administered questionnaires, traditional questionnaires, and interviews. *Journal of Applied Psychology, 84*(5), 754–775. doi:10.1037/0021-9010.84.5.754

Risko, E.F., Quilty, L.C., & Oakman, J.M. (2006). Socially desirable responding on the web: Investigating the candor hypothesis. *Journal of Personality Assessment, 87*(3), 269–276. doi:10.1207/s15327752jpa8703_08

Rosenfeld, P., Booth-Kewley, S., Edwards, J.E., & Thomas, M.D. (1996). Responses on computer surveys: Impression management, social desirability, and the big brother syndrome. *Computers in Human Behavior, 12*(2), 263–274. doi:10.1016/0747-5632(96)00006-4

Skinner, H.A., & Allen, B.A. (1983). Does the computer make a difference? Computerized versus face-to-face versus self-report assessment of alcohol, drug, and tobacco use. *Journal of Consulting and Clinical Psychology, 51*(2), 267–275. doi:10.1037/0022-006x.51.2.267

Strahan, R., & Gerbasi, K.C. (1972). Short, homogeneous versions of the Marlowe-Crowne social desirability scale. *Journal of Clinical Psychology, 28*(2), 191–193. doi:10.1002/1097-4679(197204)28:2<191::AID-JCLP2270280220>3.0.CO;2-G

Tourangeau, R., & Smith, T.W. (1996). Asking sensitive questions the impact of data collection mode, question format, and question context. *Public Opinion Quarterly, 60*(2), 275–304. doi:10.1086/297751

Turner, C.F., Ku, L., Rogers, S.M., Lindberg, L.D., Pleck, J.H., & Sonenstein, F.L. (1998). Adolescent sexual behavior, drug use, and violence: Increased reporting with computer survey technology. *Science, 280*(5365), 867–873. doi: 10.1126/science.280.5365.867

Whitener, E.M., & Klein, H.J. (1995). Equivalence of computerized and traditional research methods: The roles of scanning, social environment, and social desirability. *Computers in Human Behavior, 11*(1), 65–75. doi:10.1016/0747-5632(94)00023-b

Wilkerson, J.M., Nagao, D.H., & Martin, C.L. (2002). Socially Desirable Responding in Computerized Questionnaires: When Questionnaire Purpose Matters More Than the Model. *Journal of Applied Social Psychology, 32*(3), 544–559. doi:10.1111/j.1559-1816.2002.tb00229.x

Zanes, A., & Matsoukas, E. (1979). Different settings, different results? A comparison of school and home responses. *Public Opinion Quarterly, 43*(4), 550–557. doi:10.1086/268553

Section 8.4: Should I worry respondents cannot recall the information I am asking them about?

Definition of terms – What is the accuracy of recall?

In surveys, "Recall refers to the reproduction of a target item experienced earlier" (Leigh, Zinkhan, & Swaminathan, 2006, p. 106). Even more specifically, "The product of retrieval (what is found in memory) is the basis for inferences that combine the recalled information into a single-valued response" (Bradburn, Rips, & Shevell, 1987, p. 157).

In brief

The recall is influenced by many factors, which can reasonably be divided into two categories: (1) The context of the question (the events researchers are asking respondents to recall) and (2) How the question is delivered (the measurement techniques implemented by researchers to aid in respondent recall).

The timing of the recall period is part of the context of the question being asked. In general, the longer the time since an event happened, the more recall errors are present and the fewer the events that will be recalled (Neter & Waksberg, 1964; Klemetti & Saxen, 1967; Collins et al., 1984; Blair & Burton, 1987; Mathiowetz & Duncan, 1988; Peters, 1988; Winkielman et al., 1998; Pierret, 2001; and Igou et al., 2002). Another part of the context of the question being asked is its saliency: the more critical the event being recalled is to a person, the less recall error is present (Loftus & Marburger, 1983). Researchers frequently consider saliency more influential in event recall than the time since the event occurred.

Researchers can use specific techniques to aid participants in recalling specific information. One such strategy is to provide "landmarks" as a point of reference before asking someone to remember a particular event that they experienced. Landmark events are those deemed necessary enough in a person's life that the person can effortlessly recall and use as a relative basis when asked to remember other less memorable events (e.g., for U.S. residents who are old enough to remember the 9/11 attack on the U.S. would be a landmark). Researchers can ask participants first to draw a personal history calendar of important landmarks in their life, then ask them to recall less worthy events situated in between the landmarks (Freedman et al., 1988; Auriat, 1993; Belli et al., 2001; Yu et al., 2003; Belli et al., 2007; Van der Vaart & Glasner, 2007; Morris & Slocum, 2010; and Sayles et al., 2010).

Another technique used is the Decomposition Strategy (Jobe & Mingay, 1989; Belli et al., 2000). Belli et al. (2000) define "Decomposition [a]s a questionnaire design strategy, often advocated in survey research, in which behavioral frequency reports for a category are broken down by asking about the behavioral frequencies for subcategories" (Belli et al., 2000, p. 295). As an example of decomposition, Belli et al. (2000) provided the following: "instead of asking respondents how often they have eaten at a restaurant during a specified reference period, this question may be 'decomposed' into several more specific ones, about how often respondents have eaten at a fast-food restaurant; an Italian restaurant; a Chinese restaurant; and so on" (Belli et al., 2000, p. 295).

The scale provided to the respondent can also inadvertently influence recall accuracy. For example, suppose a researcher is trying to determine the amount of time respondents spend watching TV and provides a range of values to the respondent. In that case, the respondent might compare themselves to the low and high ends of the range and might not be comfortable being on either end. As a result, a respondent might choose the middle even though the middle does not represent their TV viewing frequency. This type of error is known as "Frame of Reference Bias" (Schwarz & Bienias, 1990, p. 61). Researchers should consider the preceding and provide unbiased response scales to avoid this source of error. Studies have shown the frequency of event occurrence from the point of view of a respondent can change according to the frequency options given to the respondent. Respondents will tend to overestimate the occurrence of an event in their lives when all high-frequency options are presented and underestimate its frequency when all low-frequency options are given (Schwarz et al., 1985; Schwarz et al., 1988; Schwarz & Bienias, 1990; Schwarz et al., 1991; and Wright et al., 1994).

Researchers can also use an ordered sequence of information to help the respondents better recall the occurrence of certain events in their lives. This would increase the size of the question being asked, which generally would not be desirable but, in this case, would result in "a greater number of relevant items of information" (p. 300). An example of this appears in an article by Laurent (1972). The shorter measure is "Have you ever had trouble hearing" (p. 299), followed by a "yes" or "no" response. The longer measure is "Trouble hearing is the last item of this list. We are looking for some information about it. Have you ever had any trouble hearing?" (p. 299), which was also followed by a "yes" or "no" response.

Another example is found in Cannell et al. (1981). The shorter measure is "What health problems have you had in the past year" (p. 405). The longer measure is "The next question asks about health problems during the last year. This is something we are asking everyone in the survey. What health problems have you had in the past year" (p. 406). In both contexts, the presentation of sequenced information in the longer measure is used to prime memory and help the respondent more easily retrieve information by progressive introduction of the required information the researcher needs.

Expectations

- The longer the period of time since an event occurred, the more you can expect errors in its recall. The longer the period of time since events have occurred, the fewer will be the events that are remembered, with only the most extreme events

standing out (Collins et al., 1984; Klemetti & Saxen, 1967; Mathiowetz & Duncan, 1988; Neter & Waksberg, 1964; Pierret, 2001).
- The less salient the event is to a respondent, the more errors are expected in the recall (Auriat, 1993; Loftus & Marburger, 1983).
- The frequency of response options given to respondents in closed-format questions can influence their perception of what they consider normal behavior and, therefore, also affect their responses (Schwarz et al., 1985; Schwarz et al., 1988; Schwarz & Bienias, 1990; Schwarz et al., 1991; Wright et al., 1994).

Principles

- Use life event history calendars and personal or major event landmarks to reduce recall errors when time and budget allow.
- Break up into smaller pieces and ask individuals to recall the smaller portions one at a time in a sequence to reduce the errors associated with recall.
- Using open-ended answer formats that ask respondents to report on the frequency of behavior eliminates the potential bias of providing them with a preset range of frequencies. It reduces the errors associated with the recall.

Commentary

Recall-related errors are hard to quantify unless a researcher can compare two data sources for the same variable: the self-report of behavior frequency versus a logged frequency of that behavior. However, having access to data that allows such comparisons is scarce. So, a researcher must adopt as many recall-enabling strategies as possible to reduce recall errors in self-report measures.

References and additional readings

Auriat, N. (1993). "My wife knows best": A comparison of event dating accuracy between the wife, the husband, the couple, and the Belgium population register. *The Public Opinion Quarterly, 57*(2), 165–190. doi:10.1086/269364

Belli, R., Schwarz, N., Singer, E., & Talarico, J. (2000). Decomposition can harm the accuracy of behavioral frequency reports. *Applied Cognitive Psychology, 14*, 295–308. doi:10.1002/1099-0720(200007/08)14:4<295::AID-ACP646>3.0.CO;2-1

Belli, R., Shay, W., & Stafford, F. (2001). Event history calendars and question list surveys: a direct comparison of interviewing methods. *The Public Opinion Quarterly, 65*(1), 45–74. doi:10.1086/320037

Belli, R., Smith, L., Andreski, P., & Agrawal, S. (2007). Methodological comparisons between CATI event history calendar and standardized conventional questionnaire instruments. *Public Opinion Quarterly, 71*(4), 603–622. doi:10.1093/poq/nfm045

Blair, E., & Burton, S. (1987). Cognitive processes used by survey respondents to answer behavioral frequency questions. *Journal of Consumer Research, 14*(2), 280-288. doi:10.1086/209112

Bradburn, N., Rips, L., & Shevell, S. (1987). Answering autobiographical questions: The impact of memory and inference on surveys. *Science, 236*(4798), 157-161. doi:10.1126/science.3563494

Cannell, C.F., Miller, Peter, V. & Oskenberg, L. (1981). Research on interviewing techniques *Sociological Methodology 12*, 389-437

Collins, L., Graham, J., Hansen, W., & Johnson, C. (1985). Agreement between retrospective accounts of substance use and earlier reported substance use. *Applied Psychological Measurement, 9*(3), 301-309. doi: 10.1177/014662168500900308

Freedman, D., Thornton, A., Camburn, D., Alwin, D., & Young-DeMarco, L. (1988). The life history calendar: A technique for collecting retrospective data. *Sociological Methodology, 18*, 37-68. doi:10.2307/27044

Gaskell, G., O'Muircheartaigh, C., & Wright, D. (1994). Survey questions about the frequency of vaguely defined events: the effects of response alternative. *The Public Opinion Quarterly, 58*(2), 241-254. doi:10.1086/269420

Igou, E., Bless, H., Schwarz, N. (2002). Making sense of standardized survey questions: The influence of reference periods and their repetitions. *Communication Monographs, 69*(2), 179-187. doi:10.1080/714041712

Jobe, J. & Mingay, D. (1989). Cognitive research improves questionnaires. *American Journal of Public Health, 79*(8), 1053-1055. doi:10.2105/AJPH.79.8.1053

Klemetti, A., & Saxen, L. (1967). Prospective versus retrospective approach in the search for environmental causes of malformations. *American Journal of Public Health, 57*(1), 2071-2075. doi: 10.2105/AJPH.57.12.2071

Laurent, Andre (1972) Effects of Question Length on Reporting Behavior in the Survey Interview *Journal of the American Statistical Association, 67*, 338, 298-305.

Leigh, J.H., Zinkhan, G.M., & Swaminathan, V. (2006). Dimensional relationships of recall and recognition measures with selected cognitive and affective aspects of print ads. *Journal of Advertising, 35*(1), 105-122. doi:10.2753/JOA0091-3367350107

Loftus, E., & Marburger, W. (1983). Since the eruption of Mt. St. Helens, has anyone beaten you up? Improving the accuracy of retrospective reports with landmark events. *Memory & Cognition, 11*(2), 114-120. doi:10.3758/BF03213465

Mathiowetz, N., & Duncan, G. (1988). Out of work, out of mind: response errors in retrospective reports of unemployment. *Journal of Business & Economic Statistics, 6*(2), 221-229. doi:10.2307/1391559

Menon, G., Raghubir, P., & Schwarz, N. (1995). Behavioral frequency judgments: an accessibility-diagnosticity framework. *Journal of Consumer Research, 22*(2), 212-228. doi:10.1086/209446

Morris, N., & Slocum, L. (2010). The validity of self-reported prevalence, frequency, and timing of arrest: an evaluation of data collected using a life event calendar. *Journal of Research in Crime and Delinquency, 47*(2), 210-240. doi:10.1177/0022427809357719

Neter, J., & Waksberg, J. (1964). A study of response errors in expenditures data from household interviews. *Journal of the American Statistical Association, 59*(305), 18-55. doi:10.2307/2282857

Peters, H.E. (1988). Retrospective versus panel data in analyzing lifecycle events. *The Journal of Human Resources, 23*(4), 488-513. doi:10.2307/145810

Pierret, C.R. (2001). Event history data and survey recall: An analysis of the national longitudinal survey of youth 1979 recall experiment. *The Journal of Human Resources, 36*(3), 439-466. doi:10.2307/3069626

Rothman, A., Haddock, G., & Schwarz, N. (2001). "How many partners is too many?" Shaping perceptions of personal vulnerability. *Journal of Applied Social Psychology, 31*(10), 2195-2214. doi:10.1111/j.1559-1816.2001.tb00171.x

Sayles, H., Belli, R.F., & Serrano, E. (2010). Interviewer variance between event history calendar and conventional questionnaire interviews. *Public Opinion Quarterly, 74*(1), 140-153. doi:10.1093/poq/nfp089

Schober, M., & Conrad, F. (2002). A collaborative view of standardized survey interviews. In D. Maynard, H. Houtkoop-Steenstra, N.C. Schaeffer, & J. van der Zouwen (Eds.), *Standardization and Tacit Knowledge: Interaction and Practice in the Survey Interview* (pp. 67–94). Hoboken, NJ: John Wiley & Sons.

Schwarz, N. & Bienias, J. (1990). What mediates the impact of response alternatives on frequency reports of mundane behaviors? *Applied Cognitive Psychology, 4*, 61–72. doi:10.1002/acp.2350040106

Schwarz, N., Bless, H., Bohner, G., Harlacher, U., & Kellenbenz, M. (1991). Response scales as frames of reference: the impact of frequency range on diagnostic judgements. *Applied Cognitive Psychology, 5*, 37–49. doi:10.1002/acp.2350050104

Schwarz, N., Hippler, H., Deutsch, B., & Strack, F. (1985). Response scales: effects of category range on reported behavior and comparative judgments. *The Public Opinion Quarterly, 49*(3), 388–395. doi:10.1086/268936

Schwarz, N., Strack, F., Muller, G., & Chassein, B. (1988). The range of response alternatives may determine the meaning of the question. *Social Cognition, 6*, 107–117. doi:10.1521/soco.1988.6.2.107

Strack, F., Schwarz, N., & Gschneidinger, E. (1985). Happiness and reminiscing: the role of time perspective, affect, and mode of thinking. *Journal of Personality and Social Psychology, 49*(6), 1460–1469. doi:10.1037/0022-3514.49.6.1460

Van Der Vaart, W., & Glasner, T. (2007). Applying a timeline as a recall aid in a telephone Survey: A record check study. *Applied Cognitive Psychology, 21*(2), 227–238. doi:10.1002/acp.1338

Whitten, W., & Leonard, J. (1981). Directed search through autobiographical memory. *Memory & Cognition, 9*(6), 566–579. doi:10.3758/BF03202351

Winkielman, P., Knauper, B., & Schwarz, N. (1998). Looking back at anger: Reference periods change the interpretation of emotional frequency questions. *Journal of Personality and Social Psychology, 75*(3), 719–728. doi:10.1037/0022-3514.75.3.719

Wright, D., Gaskell, G., & O'Muircheartaigh, C. (1994). How much is 'Quite a bit'? Mapping between numerical values and vague quantifiers. *Applied Cognitive Psychology, 8*, 479–496. doi:10.1002/acp.2350080506

Yu, M., Cheng, F., Callegaro, M., Chang, M.Y., & Belli, R.F. (2003, November). Comparison of computerized event history calendar and question-list interviewing methods: A two-year health history study. Paper presented at the Annual Conference of the Midwest Association for Public Opinion Research (MAPOR), Chicago (pp. 1–28).

Section 8.5: Should I worry that my respondents are reacting mindlessly to my measures?

Definition of terms – What is satisficing?

When a researcher asks for a respondent's reaction to a measure, the respondent needs to read the measure, understand its contents and then provide a reaction. This involves a considerable amount of cognitive effort. Satisficing is the label given when a respondent does not invest the cognitive effort needed when reacting to measures, and applies "insufficient effort responding (IER)" (Krosnick, 1991, p. 213).

In brief

The theory of satisficing was proposed by Herbert Simon in the 1950s (Hamby & Taylor, 2016, p. 913). It was popularized by Jon Krosnick in the context of survey measurement in the 1990s (Krosnick, 1991). Under ideal circumstances, respondents will undergo four cognitive processes before reacting to self-report measures: comprehension, information retrieval to formulate an answer, and answer selection based on the options given (Callegaro et al., 2009). "Weak satisficing occurs when respondents perform all four processes but not thoroughly". Strong satisficing occurs when respondents fail to perform all four processes and quickly select an answer (Callegaro et al., 2009, p. 7).

The most common forms of satisficing are: (1) speeding (responding too quickly) (Conrad et al., 2017, p. 45) and (2) item non-differentiation (giving the same answer repeatedly across different measures, sometimes called "straightlining") (Hamby & Taylor, 2016, p. 916). Speeding when reacting to measures is the most common outcome of satisficing. Other outcomes can also be overusing "don't know" and "neutral" response categories (Barge & Gehlbach, 2012, p. 203; Lindhjem & Navrud, 2011; Hamby & Taylor, 2016; Zhang & Conrad, 2016). Completion time is a good predictor of satisficing behavior, but it shouldn't be the only predictor used when screening for this behavior (Meade & Craig 2012, p. 16). Acquiescence (the tendency to agree to a question without considering the content) and item nonresponse (choosing not to respond to a measure before going to the next) are also associated with satisficing (Krosnick, Narayan, & Smith, 1996). As the survey progresses, the frequency of satisficing behaviors increases (Barge, Gehlbach, 2012, p. 203). About 10–12% of respondents will display satisficing behaviors (Meade & Craig, 2012, p. 16).

Some respondent characteristics have been associated with satisficing behavior. Non-demographic predictors include past satisficing behavior (Hamby & Taylor, 2016, p. 925). Other predictors include a respondent's cognitive ability, motivation, and perceived difficulty of the measurement task (Hamby & Taylor, 2016, p. 925; Krosnick, Narayan, & Smith, 1996, p. 42). In terms of demographics, respondents with lower education levels seem to exhibit higher levels of satisficing (Krosnick & Alwin, 1987; Narayan & Krosnick, 1996; Zhang & Conrad, 2013). Younger (Conrad, Tourangeau, Couper & Zhang, 2017, p. 49), minority (African Americans, Native Americans, Asian/ Pacific Islanders, Hispanic, and foreign-born students), first-generation college students, and male respondents seem to exhibit higher satisficing tendencies (Chen, 2011, p. 667, 669).

Progress has been made in finding strategies to detect the prevalence of satisfaction in surveys. In general, prompted intervention strategies have proven most useful in reducing satisficing behaviors (Kapelner & Chandler, 2010; Oppenheimer, Meyvis & Davidenko, 2009; Zhang & Conrad, 2016). This prompting can take the form of an IMC test (Instructional Manipulation Check) to measure whether a participant reads the instructions and eliminate respondents who do not pass (Oppenheimer, Meyvis & Davidenko, 2009). Examples of IMC include instructing a respondent to select a specific response category on a measure that the researcher adds to test the respondent's attention level, asking the respondent to click on a specific color button, etc. Another form of IMC is CAPTCHA, which can also help detect if bots are reacting to the measures.

Lastly, prompted intervention immediately after speeding or non-differentiating behaviors reduces both forms of satisficing and increases desirable respondent behavior throughout the rest of the survey (Kapelner & Chandler, 2010, p. 8). For example, after a respondent displays speeding behavior, a researcher presents them with a pop-up message reminding them of the purpose of the survey and asks if they'd still like to continue. These prompts should be phrased in a way that encourages good behavior (ex., including a smiley face) as opposed to discouraging bad behavior (ex., Including an error symbol) to avoid triggering a social desirability bias (Zhang & Conrad, 2016, p. 19). Anonymous web surveys are most likely to experience satisficing behaviors (Heerwegh & Loosveldt, 2008, p. 844), followed by paper and pencil, then telephone interviews, and finally, face-to-face interviews (Chen, 2011, p. 671; Holbrook, Green, Krosnick, 2003, p. 109–110).

Expectations

- Satisficing will most often take the form of speeding (going very fast through the survey) and non-differentiation (answering different measures in the same way), and sometimes result in an increase in "no-opinion" or "don't know" responses in the data (Barge & Gehlbach, 2012; Grezski et al., 2015; Krosnick et al., 2002; Lindhjem & Navrud, 2011; Zhang & Conrad, 2013).
- As the survey progresses, the tendency to display satisficing behaviors increases (Callegaro et al., 2009).
- Respondents' cognitive abilities, education levels, motivations, personality traits, experience levels with surveys, and how difficult they find the measures to be are strong predictors of satisficing behavior (Bowling et al., 2016; Chen, 2011; Kaminska et al., 2010; Krosnick et al., 1996; Narayan & Krosnick, 1996; Schwarz et al., 2002; Toepoel et al., 2008).
- Face-to-face interviews might be less susceptible to satisficing behaviors than telephone surveys or web surveys (Holbrook et al., 2003; Heerwegh & Loosveldt, 2008), although there is some contradictory evidence (Chang & Krosnick, 2010).
- Anonymous web surveys most likely elicit satisficing behaviors (Lelkes et al., 2012; Meade & Craig, 2012).
- Prompted intervention strategies are most likely to reduce satisficing behaviors among respondents (Conrad et al., 2017; Huang et al., 2012; Kapelner & Chandler, 2010; Oppenheimer et al., 2009; Zhang & Conrad, 2012).

Principles

- Simplify the wording and complexity of your measures to reduce the cognitive effort required to understand them and react to them
- Use prompted intervention strategies to reduce satisficing behaviors such as speeding and non-differentiation in web surveys.
- Use response speed to detect satisficing behavior but do not rely on speed as the only predictor when screening data.
- Do not include survey measures that require deep self-reflection or self-analysis since these are difficult and might encourage satisficing
- Consider including "Instructional Manipulation Checks" to detect satisficing behavior in your measurement task

Commentary

There will always be some respondents who will not take the measurement task seriously, not read the measures, skip over measures, and react similarly to very different measures. These types of respondents need to be detected and their responses removed from the data set. Other respondents, however, will be triggered to satisfice because of the cognitive effort required by the measures. Satisficing is yet another reason for us to ensure that the measures a researcher uses require the least amount of cognitive effort. This means that the measures need to be as simple as possible in terms of word choice and sentence structure. The measures need to rely only on basic information readily available to the respondents and do not require them to engage in deep self-reflection or self-analysis. Suppose the construct that the researcher is seeking to capture is complex. In that case, it is the researcher's responsibility to find a way to break it up into indicators that a respondent would find simple, basic, and easily accessible. After measuring each of these indicators, the researcher can assemble them into a complex construct.

The preceding is only possible if the researcher uses an approach that relies on multiple indicators (see Chapters 1 and 3). Using simple, basic, and easily accessible information will reduce the possibility that the complexity of the measures will trigger satisficing and address the assumption of self-awareness, noted in Table 8.1. We cannot assume that respondents are highly self-aware. If the information being measured is simple, basic, and easily accessible, a high level of self-awareness would not be required for respondents to react to our measures.

References and additional readings

Appeal [Def. 3]. (n.d.). In Merriam-Webster Online. Retrieved February 24, 2019, from https://www.merriam-webster.com/dictionary/appeal.

Barge, S., & Gehlbach, H. (2012). Using the theory of satisficing to evaluate the quality of survey data. *Research in Higher Education, 53*(2), 182–200. doi:10.1007/s11162-011-9251-2

Bowling, N., Huang, J., Bragg, C., Khazon, S., Liu, M., & Blackmore, C. (2016). Who cares and who is careless? Insufficient effort responding as a reflection of respondent personality. *Journal of Personality and Social Psychology, 111*(2), 218–229. doi:10.1037/pspp0000085

Callegaro, M., Yang, Y., Bhola, D., Dillman, D., & Chin, T. (2009). Response latency as an indicator of optimizing in online questionnaires. *BMS: Bulletin of Sociological Methodology, 103*(1), 5–25. doi:10.1177/075910630910300103

Chang, L., & Krosnick, J. (2010). Comparing oral interviewing with self-administered computerized questionnaires an experiment. *Public Opinion Quarterly, 74*(1), 154–167. doi:10.1093/poq/nfp090

Chen, D. (2011). Finding quality responses: The problem of low-quality survey responses and its impact on accountability measures. *Research in Higher Education, 52*(7), 659–674. doi:10.1007/s11162-011-9217-4

Conrad, F., Tourangeau, R., Couper, M., & Zhang, C. (2017). Reducing speeding in web surveys by providing immediate feedback. *Survey Research Methods, 11*(1), 45–61. doi:10.18148/srm/2017.v11i1.6304

Greszki, R., Meyer, M., & Schoen, H. (2015). Exploring the effects of removing "too fast" responses and respondents from web surveys. *Public Opinion Quarterly, 79*(2), 471–503. doi:10.1093/poq/nfu058

Hamby, T., & Taylor, W. (2016). Survey satisficing inflates reliability and validity measures: An experimental comparison of college and amazon mechanical turk samples. *Educational and Psychological Measurement, 76*(6) 912–932. doi:10.1177/0013164415627349

Heerwegh, D., & Loosveldt, G. (2008). Face-to-face versus web surveying in a high-internet-coverage population. *Public Opinion Quarterly, 72*(5), 836–846. doi:10.1093/poq/nfn045

Holbrook, A., Green, M. & Krosnick, J. (2003). Telephone versus face-to-face interviewing of national probability samples with long questionnaires: Comparisons of respondent satisficing and social desirability response bias. *Public Opinion Quarterly, 67*(1), 79–125. doi:10.1086/346010

Huang, J., Curran, P., Keeney, J., Poposki, E., & DeShon, R. (2012). Detecting and deterring insufficient effort responding to surveys. *Journal of Business and Psychology, 27*(1), 99–114. doi:10.1007/s10869-011-9231-8

Kaminska, O., McCutcheon, A., & Billiet, J. (2010). Satisficing among reluctant respondents in a cross-national context. *Public Opinion Quarterly, 74*(5), 956–984. doi:10.1093/poq/nfq062

Kapelner, A., & Chandler, D. (2010). Preventing satisficing in online surveys: A "Kapcha" to ensure higher quality data. *Information Systems Journal*, 1–10. No doi available.

Krosnick, J.A. (1991). Response strategies for coping with the cognitive demands of attitude measures in surveys. *Applied Cognitive Psychology, 5*(3), 213–236. doi:10.1002/acp.2350050305

Krosnick, J., & Alwin, D. (1988). A test of the form-resistant correlation hypothesis: Rating, rankings, and the measurement of values. *Public Opinion Quarterly, 52*(4). 526–538. doi:10.1086/269128

Krosnick, J., Holbrook, A., Berent, M., Carson, R., Hanemann, W., Kopp, R., Mitchell, R., Presser, S., Ruud, P., Smith, V., Moody, W., Green, M., & Conaway, M. (2002). The impact of "no opinion" response options on data quality: Non-attitude reduction or an invitation to satisfice? *Public Opinion Quarterly, 66*, 371–403. doi:10.1086/341394

Krosnick, J. A., Narayan, S., & Smith, W.R. (1996). Satisficing in surveys: Initial evidence. *New Directions for Evaluation, 70*, 29–44. doi:10.1002/ev.1033

Lelkes, Y., Krosnick, J., Marx, D., Judd, C., & Park, B. (2012). Complete anonymity compromises the accuracy of self-reports. *Journal of Experimental Social Psychology, 48*, 1291–1299. doi:10.1016/j.jesp.2012.07.002

Lindhjem, H., & Navrud, S. (2011). Are internet surveys an alternative to face-to-face interview in contingent valuation? *Ecological Economics, 70*(9), 1628–1637. doi:10.1016/j.ecolecon.2011.04.002

Meade, A., & Craig, S. (2012). Identifying careless responses in survey data. *Psychological Methods, 17*(3) 437–455. doi: 10.1037/a0028085

Muhlbock, M., Steiber, N., & Kittel, B. (2017). Less supervision, more satisficing? Comparing completely self-administered web-surveys and interviews under controlled conditions. *Statistics, Politics, and Policy, 8*(1). doi:10.1515/spp-2017-0005

Narayan, S. & Krosnick, J. (1996). Education moderates some response effects in attitude measurement. *Public Opinion Quarterly, 60,* 58–88. doi:10.1086/297739

Oppenheimer, D., Meyvis, T., & Davidenko, N. (2009). Instructional manipulation checks: Detecting satisficing to increase statistical power. *Journal of Experimental Social Psychology, 45,* 867–872. doi:10.1016/j.jesp.2009.03.009

Schwartz, B., Ward, A., Monterosso, J., Lyubomirsky, S., White, K., & Lehman, D.R. (2002). Maximizing versus satisficing: happiness is a matter of choice. *Journal of Personality And Social Psychology, 83,* 1178–1197. doi:10.1037/0022-3514.83.5.1178

Toepoel, V., Das, M., Soest, A. (2008). Effects of design in web surveys: Comparing trained and fresh respondents. *Public Opinion Quarterly, 72*(5), 985–1007. doi:10.1093/poq/nfn060

Zhang, C., & Conrad, F. (2013). Speeding in web surveys: The tendency to answer very fast and its association with straightlining. *Survey Research Methods, 8*(2), 127–135. doi:10.18148/srm/2014.v8i2.5453

Zhang, C. & Conrad, F. (2016). Intervening to reduce satisficing behaviors in web surveys: Evidence from two experiments on how it works. *Social Science Computer Review, 1*(25), 1–25. doi:10.1177/0894439316683923

Chapter 9
A roadmap for quantifying the errors stemming from violations of the principles of self-report measurement: The Red Flags Approach (RFA)

Objectives of Chapter 9: This chapter provides academic and industry researchers with a roadmap for quantifying the errors due to measurement (EDM) in their self-report measures. These errors determine whether the data they collected through self-report measures can be used in statistical analyses designed to uncover relationships among the variables measured. Over a century of solid self-report measurement science has shown that there is no such thing as self-report measurement without error. Having a large amount of error due to measurement (EDM) will devastate the relationships subsequently tested with the data and the resulting conclusions and recommendations stemming from such testing.

Can I find out how much error is present in my measures?

What happens if the self-report measurement principles are violated even with the best intentions? Errors due to measurement (EDM) begin plaguing the study. In Chapters 1 and 3, I explained that I would be using the term "errors due to measurement" (EDM) instead of measurement error since the latter has been traditionally confined to random errors as captured by a reliability coefficient. In contrast, EDM refers to the combination of both systematic and random errors attributed to measurement. EDM is the sum of all violations of the principles of self-report measurement and the violations of the Golden Assumption of self-report measurement (GA) in each study that uses these types of measures (see Chapter 3).

If a researcher has a large amount of EDM in their study and they don't know it, these errors will prevent them from seeing the true patterns in their data, will prevent them from finding relationships among variables, and might even lead them to arrive at erroneous relationships among variables. These outcomes would, in turn, influence any conclusions and recommendations this researcher draws from their analysis. In essence, errors due to measurement (EDM) can destroy a study that uses data extracted from self-report measures (see McNabb, 2014 discussion within the context of measurement error). It is helpful to remember that studies using self-report measures always have some level of EDM (see Carmines & Zeller, 1979 mentions within the context of measurement error). EDM is inevitable given the variation among human respondents' interpretation of the wording of each measure, attention level when reacting to measures, etc. The question is not whether errors due to measurement (EDM) are present but the extent to which they are present. It is often the case that researchers simply assume no errors due to measurement (EDM) and proceed with their data analyses. This is not advisable, given the detrimental effects of EDM noted above. Prudent researchers insist on determining how much EDM is present. The good news is if a researcher plans ahead, then EDM can be quantified. Quantifying EDM tells the researcher how much of it is present for each construct they measured and can even pinpoint specific indicators introducing more error than others.

A note on what is needed to understand the contents of this chapter

Previous chapters in this book have provided you with a way to conceptualize self-report measurement using the invisible-to-visible framework (ITVF) and with principles and expectations that would help you preempt measurement-related errors when preparing self-report measures for use in a research project. Previous chapters did not require technical knowledge to understand the information they presented. This current chapter will be better understood if the reader has prior SPSS experience, can run frequency distributions, Pearson's correlations, factor analysis, and Cronbach's alpha, and is familiar with research terminology. While this chapter does not invent new techniques, it organizes existing techniques into an intertwined and sequenced process that, if followed, will allow a researcher to quantify the errors stemming from the violation of the principles of self-report measurement.

This chapter will present a case study that:
1. Illustrates the use of a theoretical framework that contextualizes the variables needed and serves as a basis for understanding the specific role of self-report measurement in the grand plan for the research project. The theoretical framework is also an example of a proposed thought-process that would be tested if the self-report measures used for each of its building blocks have an acceptable level of EDM.
2. Describes the preparations needed for the measures used in the research project to meet the requirements necessary for quantifying the errors associated with them
3. Presents and walks you through a road map that quantifies, through demonstration, the errors associated with a sample of measures used in the research project.

Contextualizing the case study

This case study is part of a larger research project I started in 2011. It focuses on the predictors that drive people to use social media and the effects stemming from their usage (see Elasmar, 2012). The specific angle this chapter's case study focuses on is

Facebook usage. We know that not everyone uses Facebook and, among Facebook users, not everyone uses it at the same frequency. We also know that not everyone who uses Facebook equally intends to continue using it. This case study's dependent variable (DV) is a student's intention to continue using Facebook.

Contextualizing the DV

The research question for the case study is: What influences a student's intention to continue using Facebook in the future? As a starting point, I began by asking: what type of dependent variable is this project trying to explain? The dependent variable here is an intention to engage in a specific behavior in the future, and that behavior is "using Facebook." The intention approximates a student's future behavior. Since the dependent variable involves a behavior, and before I could begin thinking about measurement, I first needed to find two essential and complementary sources of information related to this behavior:
1. An established theoretical framework that I can adopt to organize various building blocks about a student's intention to use Facebook in the future.
2. The results of studies have already been conducted about people's usage or intention to use social media.

The theoretical framework

In brief, the theoretical framework I adopted is Ajzen's Theory of Planned Behavior (TPB) since it is very well established across numerous fields of study and can accommodate a wide variety of explanations for the DV (see Ajzen, 1985; Bosnjak, Ajzen, & Schmidt, 2020; Fishbein & Ajzen, 1972, 1975; https://people.umass.edu/aizen/tpb.html).

The literature review

I conducted a literature review to identify studies that have already been published about people's usage or intention to use social media. I searched for articles on databases such as PsychInfo, Communication and Mass Media Complete, Google Scholar, and others and located articles focused on a similar DV. Then, I used the results of these studies to identify building blocks that could explain the variation in students' intention to continue using Facebook in the future.

The components of the TPB were used in two ways:
a. As additional likely explanations for the dependent variable; and
b. As a way of organizing the various potential explanations found through the literature review.

Visualizing the big picture

Integrating the results of studies found in the literature review into the TPB reveals a proposed thought-process model for students' intention to use Facebook in the future. Figure 9.1 shows the various components of the TPB model, selected variables found during the literature review, and how the TPB model helped organize these variables.

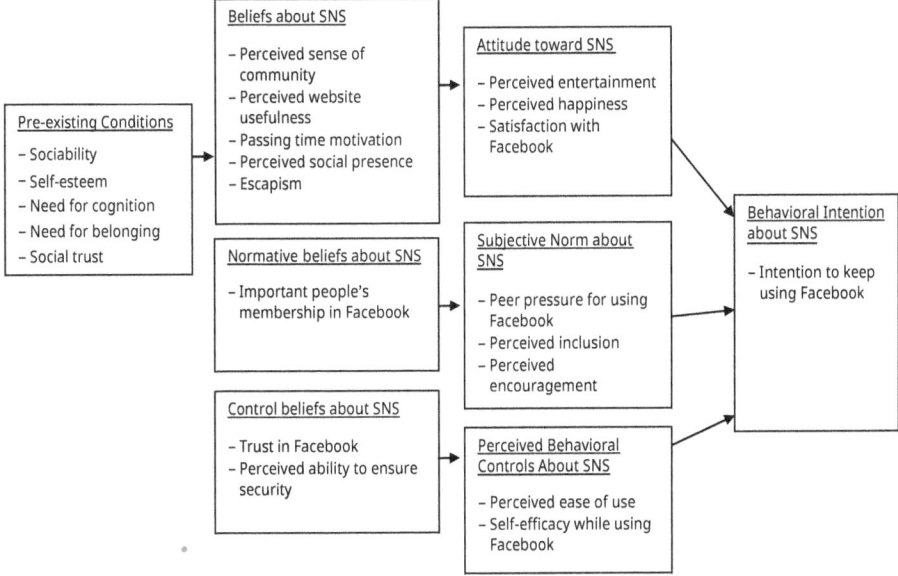

Figure 9.1: Adopting the TPB as a theoretical framework for understanding students' intention to continue using Facebook in the future – selected variables. Source: Author.

The diagram in Figure 9.1 is read from left to right, with the last component to the right being the study's dependent variable (DV). The diagram helps contextualize the measurement testing tasks I will be carrying out. It shows the big picture inside of which self-report measurement will reside. For each component of this diagram, each variable listed will need to be captured with self-report measures, and the measures used will need to be tested to determine if they successfully captured their corresponding building block. We test them by computing the errors due to measurement (EDM) present in the measures, and this testing will be demonstrated later in this chapter. The diagram in Figure 9.1 helps generate hypotheses regarding how each building block of the diagram is related to others. The diagram illustrates a hypothesized thought-process related to students' intention to continue using Facebook.

An arrow pointing from one component to another in the diagram signifies evidence from prior studies that can lead me to hypothesize a relationship between the two components. For example, one of the hypotheses in the model states that the more a person believes using Facebook allows them to escape their everyday life, the more likely they are to have a positive attitude toward using Facebook. Since the relationships shown in Figure 9.1 are hypothesized, we don't know for certain whether the results of our research will support them until we conduct such analyses. And, of course, we can't perform any analyses to test the hypotheses shown in Figure 9.1 unless we have data. We don't have data unless we have developed measures for each building block shown in Figure 9.1, administered these measures to a sample of students, and captured the students' reactions to the measures. So, the next and immediate task was to find or develop measures for each building block shown in Figure 9.1. It is important to note the testing of the hypotheses shown in the diagram occurs at step 10 of the research process given in Table 2.1 of Chapter 2 and falls outside the objectives of this book. The diagram showing the hypotheses among the components of the TPB is presented here solely to contextualize the role of self-report measurement in the big picture of a research project.

How were the measures developed?

The diagram in Figure 9.1 identified the variables for which we needed to develop measures. My approach to developing measures is first to find out if such measures already exist in the literature. Two primary resources are used to locate existing measures:
a. The articles found in the literature review and from which the potential predictors of the DV were extracted.
b. Published compilations of measures used by others (see, for example, the Marketing Scales Handbook by Bruner & Hensel, 1994).

In either case, once existing measures are located, they are immediately evaluated qualitatively along the lines of the principles of measurement given earlier in Chapters 5 through 8. Existing measures that do not fully conform to the principles of self-report measurement are edited or modified to become more compatible with these principles. The measures are then organized in a document by construct. Table 9.1 shows an example of measures found for selected constructs.

After measures for all constructs were found and either adopted or adapted, these measures were organized in a self-report instrument commonly known as a questionnaire. In the questionnaire, the constructs are ordered from general to specific relative to the investigated topic, with the dependent variable being the most specific, placed toward the end. To preempt errors due to order effects, measures of constructs are randomized with those of other constructs that share the same degree of specificity (e.g., measures of general constructs are randomized along with measures of other general constructs, non-network specific social media-focused questions are randomized together, Facebook-specific questions are randomized together, etc.).

Table 9.1: Constructs used in this case study and their corresponding measures.

Construct and definition	Measures
Perceived social trust: Slightly modified from the measures used by Valenzuela, Park, and Kee, 2009, p. 885. Definition: The degree to which a respondent believes that other people will not "knowingly or unknowingly harm" them (p. 878).	– Generally speaking, I would say that people can be trusted – People try to take advantage of me if they got the chance (r) – People try to be fair
Perceived sense of community: The first two items are taken from Park, Kee, & Valenzuela, 2009, p. 730 in what they labeled as "socializing." The third item is adapted and modified from a measure from the same source. Definition: The degree to which a person attributes their use of Facebook to a sense of belonging to a community.	– I use Facebook to get peer support from others – When I use Facebook, I feel like I belong to a community – I use Facebook to talk to others who have the same interests as me
Perceived Encouragement The concept came from Kwon and Wen (2010). The measures used here were inspired by their description of the concept. Definition: The degree to which a respondent believes that their Facebook friends positively value what this respondent posts on Facebook.	– My friends on Facebook think that what I have to say is worth reading – My friends give me feedback that what I share on Facebook in interesting – My friends on Facebook don't pay much attention to what I post (r)
Escapism Motivation: The first three items were adapted from those used by Mathwick in 1997 and appear on p. 136. The last item was inspired by these. Definition: The degree to which the respondent believes using Facebook allows them to get away from their daily lives mentally.	– Being on Facebook "gets me away" from it all – Using Facebook makes me feel like I am in a different world – I get so involved when I am on Facebook that I forget everything else

Once the questionnaire was administered to a sample of respondents and a data file containing all their reactions was saved, we were ready to determine the extent of errors due to measurement (EDM) present in the reactions we captured. The data for this case study was administered to a sample of students via Qualtrics, and an SPSS data file was exported when the data collection step was completed.

A Red Flags Approach for quantifying errors due to measurement (EDM)

Now that we had a data file containing the respondents' reactions to the measures we used, we needed a road map to determine the amount of error in the measures. The Red Flags Approach (RFA) constitutes such a road map. Following the road map offered by the RFA helps researchers anticipate and preempt the common procedural mistakes that prevent them from successfully using available tools to quantify errors due to measurement. Although the RFA doesn't invent any new techniques or tools of analysis, it provides a specific sequence and approach for using existing techniques. If the sequence is followed – exactly as specified – then the user will maximize their chances of quantifying the errors due to measurement (EDM) present in the measures they used. The RFA is presented in Figure 9.2.

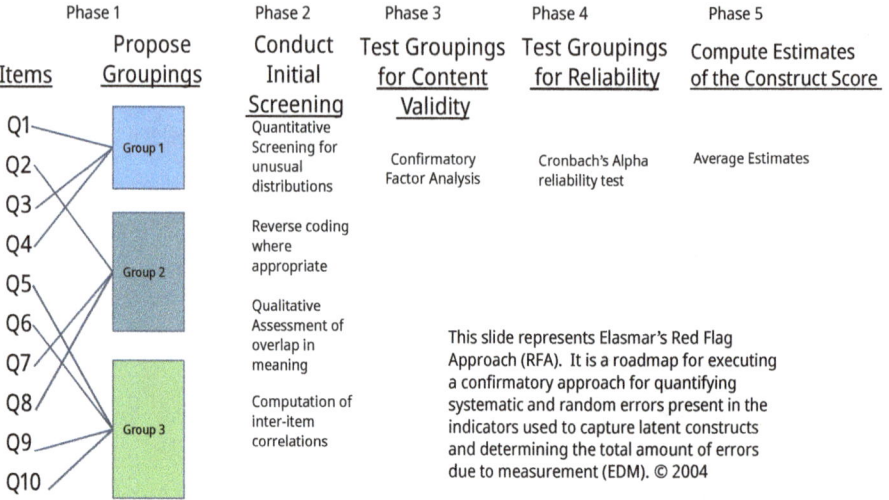

Figure 9.2: The Red Flags Approach (RFA).

An overview of the Red Flags Approach (RFA)

The general mindset of the RFA is to proceed very cautiously, stop at every task undertaken, evaluate the outcome of the task, and, depending on such an evaluation, determine whether we should stop and act or continue to the next task. What you observe while carrying out a particular task can lead you to do one of three things:
a. See nothing unusual and move to the next task.
b. See something unusual, raise a red flag to keep an eye on the measure associated with what you saw and observe how this measure will behave during the next task.
c. See a definite violation and remove the measure associated with the violation to prevent it from being included in further analyses.

Here is a description of what happens in each of the five phases of the RFA.

Phase 1 – Propose item groupings
The first task of the RFA consists of proposing the grouping of measures organized by the constructs these measures are supposed to capture. Two scenarios influence how these groupings will come about. Scenario 1 involves a situation where you developed the measures yourself. In this case, you would have identified the concepts and constructs through a literature review, defined each construct, adopted, adapted, or created measures for each construct, and ensured they are as consistent as possible with the principles of self-report measurement provided earlier in this book. In this scenario, the measures' grouping will already be done by the time you get to this point in your project. Scenario 2 involves a situation where someone else developed measures, and you're asked to analyze them. In this scenario, the person who created the measures is no longer reachable, and you don't know what constructs these measures are supposed to capture. However, you notice that many of the measures address an identical theme. In this less-than-ideal scenario, you need to reverse engineer the intentions of the original researcher when organizing the measures into groupings. When reverse engineering, the rule is that a grouping of measures should reflect a common theme across items and have a unique theme relative to other groupings. The theme for each grouping needs to be very specific. This second scenario occurs if you join an organization after the data has been collected and are tasked to analyze the data of an ongoing project. However, the team that collected the data is no longer affiliated with the organization and has not documented how they developed the measures. Luckily, scenario 1 is most likely to occur, but scenario 2 is possible.

Whichever of the two preceding scenarios leads you to group the measures, by grouping them, you are hypothesizing that the same invisible construct is driving the measures within the same group. By grouping the measures, you won't know if the hypotheses that an invisible construct underlies each group will be supported until the end of Phase 4 of the RFA.

Phase 2 – Initial screening
Four important tasks need to be carried out here. It is critical not to cut corners and skip any of these tasks as they are all designed to provide observations to determine if you can move forward to the next task or need to stop.
1. Run frequency distributions for all measures. For each measure, carefully look at the patterns in the frequency distributions. Be sure that you have:
   a. No constants: a constant is a distribution with only a single value. For example, everyone reacted to a measure by choosing "strongly agree" on a response scale. Measures that are constants need to be removed and cannot be included in subsequent analyses.

b. No outliers: Outliers are numerals very distant from the other numerals in a distribution. In the case of response scales on a 1 to 5 or on a 1 to 7, outliers rarely occur. What might occur are patterns of responses that indicate that a respondent is "satisficing" or "straight-lining" or choosing the same reaction to all measures regardless of content. This possibility is usually detected and managed at the point of data cleaning and should no longer be an issue once you reach this point. Outliers are more detectable in variables captured at the ratio level, such as the number of times respondents engage in a specific behavior. Any outlier situation needs to be resolved before moving forward.

c. No heavily skewed distributions: Here, we should be worried about a situation where nearly everyone reacted similarly, for example, by choosing "strongly agree" except for only 2 respondents who chose "strongly disagree." This kind of distribution is very problematic, and measures with such frequency distribution patterns need to be removed and cannot be included in subsequent analyses. The tools we will use in subsequent RFA phases are robust. Robust means they can still be functional despite some violations of their assumptions. So, while a perfectly normal distribution of reactions is unnecessary, heavily skewed distributions will be problematic, and measures associated with such distributions should be removed and not be analyzed in subsequent phases.

d. No significantly smaller sample size: Here, we need to keep an eye on the sample size of respondents who reacted to each measure relative to the overall sample size of the study. Measures with a sample size much smaller than the overall sample size of the study need to be removed and cannot be included in subsequent analyses. The problem with sample size differences becomes tangible if measures with a small number of respondents are combined with other measures that have larger samples. When this happens, the overall sample size of all subsequent analyses will drop to match the sample size of the measures with the smallest sample. And this will be problematic for numerous reasons.

2. Check that reverse coding of measures was done where needed
   a. Review the wording of the measures you used
   b. Review the definition of the construct to which they belong
   c. Double-check you recoded the scores on any negatively worded measures relative to the other measures used for the same construct.

3. Check on the overlap in meaning
   a. This qualitative assessment serves as a basic screening for consistency between the meaning conveyed by a definition of a construct and the meaning conveyed by a measure used to capture this construct. This task falls under what Allen (2017) calls face validity.
   b. For each measure proposed as capturing the same construct, be sure there is a substantial overlap in meaning between the expression conveyed in the definition and the expression communicated in the measure.

c. For measures proposed as belonging to the same grouping, be sure that there is also substantial overlap in meaning between the expression conveyed in one measure, and the expression communicated in another measure of the same grouping. When you do the above and find some inconsistencies in meaning-overlap, raise a red flag on the measures that did not overlap very well in meaning and keep an eye on them as you move forward.
4. Run inter-item correlations among all measures
   a. In this context, correlation coefficients are seen as an early screening tool for the overlap in meaning between two measures designed to capture a same concept. The idea is this: if two measures are really capturing the same construct, then we should expect to find a sizeable positive correlation between them. We certainly cannot have a zero-sized correlation between them. This is a preliminary check on whether the qualitative assessment of overlap in meaning done earlier is consistent with what the data is showing (see Campbell & Fiske, 1959).
   b. Correlations among measures believed to capture the same construct and are therefore hypothesized to belong to the same grouping, should be positive and relatively sizeable (see below for tips on how to evaluate the size of correlations in this context).
   c. The best approach is to move sequentially: begin by running a correlation matrix among items that belong to the same grouping and observe the patterns that you are getting. Look for problem correlations (see below for how to spot them). If you don't see any problems, add the items that belong to the second grouping to your correlation matrix, and repeat the above process. Do the preceding for all measures in all groupings. Correlations should be run by specifying "listwise deletion" of missing data. Doing so will instruct the software to use a single sample size when computing all correlations. This will enable you to compare correlations since they would all have been computed based on the same sample of respondents.
   d. When trying to detect patterns in the correlation matrix, look only at the size and direction of the correlation coefficients. Here, you are not interested in statistical significance since you are not trying to generalize. You are using the size of the correlation coefficient to screen whether it is quantitatively reasonable to have included the measures in the groupings that you proposed.
   e. The size of a correlation coefficient between two measures proposed to belong to a same grouping should not be zero or close to zero. If a correlation is zero in size, it is very problematic, and the associated measure should be removed and cannot be included in subsequent analyses.
   f. Evaluate correlation coefficient sizes other than zero relative to the highest correlation size present in the same matrix to determine whether to raise a red flag for specific measures. For example, if the highest correlation in the

matrix is .60, finding a correlation of .20 between a specific measure and another measure belonging to the same grouping should prompt you to raise a red flag and you would need to keep an eye on how this item will behave in the next phase of the RFA. This is so since a .20 in this context suggests that the item with which it is associated shares a lot less meaning with one or more items from its grouping, and this pattern will become more pronounced when looking at the results in the next phase of RFA.

g. Correlations among items in the same grouping cannot be negative. If you obtain a negative correlation, you need to stop and investigate why it is so. The most common error in this context is that you forgot to reverse the coding for that measure. Suppose you find out that you are still getting a negative correlation even after correcting any reverse coding issues. In that case, the item resulting in the negative correlation should be removed and cannot be used in subsequent analyses.

Phase 3 – Test the groupings for content validity

You can use many tools to run a confirmatory factor analysis (see Hoyle & Duvall, 2011).). For reasons outlined by Anderson and Gerbing (1988), a confirmatory factor analysis here is being run as a standalone technique in contrast to doing it simultaneously as part of structural equation modeling. You should also know that there are many techniques to test multiple aspects of construct validity (see Nunnally, 1978; Frey, 2018). To keep it simple, streamlined, and accessible, the tool I will be using here is the factor analysis function built into SPSS to test the internal structure of a set of multiple indicators, test unidimensionality, and partially address the content (see Allan, 2017) and discriminant aspects of construct validity (see Pedhazur and Pedhazur Shmelkin, 1991; Frey, 2018). It is beyond the scope of this book to discuss how to do a factor analysis, but there are many useful books that explain how to do so (Dunteman, 1989; Kim & Mueller, 1978; Long, 1983). Although the SPSS factor analysis function was initially designed to perform exploratory analyses, I will use it in a confirmatory way by specifying the number of factors (invisible constructs) I am proposing underly the measures I am testing. While I won't tell SPSS which measures I am hypothesizing as belonging to a same group, I will tell it how many groupings (factors) I believe underlie the measures I am testing and see whether the quantitative analysis is consistent with my thinking – the confirmatory approach.

1. Run a principle components factor analysis with varimax rotation by specifying the number of groupings you proposed in Phase 1 as the number of factors that you are testing.
2. In the output of the factor analysis, look for the total percentage of variance explained in your data by the number of factors that you specified. This is a preliminary look at how adequate your analysis is for the data you collected. A total percentage of variance explained of 50% or greater indicates the number of factors

you specified reasonably explain the variation in the data you collected. This number, by itself, is a good start but is not sufficient to evaluate a factor analysis solution.
3. In the output of this analysis, look at the table labeled "Rotated Component Matrix." The terms factor and component will be used interchangeably in the paragraphs below. This table organizes the measures you tested into components (or factors). Since the algorithms used do not know what you're measuring and cannot read the wording of the measures you used, they carry out their advanced computations and derivations on the numerals corresponding to the respondent's reactions to the measures. Essentially, a factor can be thought of as an invisible construct that drives the variation in respondents' reactions to specific measures. The "Rotated Component Matrix" quantifies the relationships between the invisible construct and the specific measures you are testing. The numbers in this table are fractions between 0 and 1.0. These are known as factor loadings. A factor loading can be thought of as the strength of association between a factor and a self-report measure i.e., the strength of influence of an invisible construct onto an indicator. There is a factor loading for each of the measures you are testing on each factor extracted by the algorithms.
4. A measure belongs to the factor on which it has its largest loading.
5. A measure should only have a large loading on a single factor. Ideally, it should have zero loadings or close to zero on all other factors (a way of confirming discriminant validity).
6. A factor loading quantifies the arrows coming from on top in the Invisible to Visible Framework (ITVF). As such, it tells us how valid a specific measure is relative to the invisible construct it is designed to capture.
7. Among measures designed to capture the same construct, the size of the factor loading of one measure relative to the sizes of the factor loadings of other measures tells us about the quality of that measure relative to the quality of the other measures. When making such relative comparisons, the higher the factor loading, the higher the quality of its corresponding measure.
8. A measure's factor loading on the component to which it belongs cannot be negative. If it is negative, then a procedural error is present. The error is most likely due to recoding, and you would need to go back to the previous RFA phase to investigate this error and solve it before moving forward.
9. If all measures you proposed as belonging to one factor have their highest factor loading on another factor, then you should stop and consider whether the number of factors you proposed was incorrect. You should have anticipated a problem when screening the measures with the correlation matrix, as their inter-item correlations must have been substantial. It could be that the two factors are the same, that the two factors are two dimensions of the same (known as a second-order factor), or that the two factors are separate though theoretically related. The latter possibility is less likely than the former. By scrutinizing the meaning

behind the wording of the measures, you can evaluate which of the preceding possibilities is more likely. If, for example, you find that measures proposed to capture two different constructs but show up under the same factor in the analysis are indeed capturing the same construct, consider re-proposing the number of factors by reducing the number of factors by one and repeating the analysis.

10. If a measure has substantial factor loadings on more than one factor and was raised with a red flag when you screened its correlations with other measures, then this measure most likely has validity issues. For example, let's say item X has a factor loading of .53 on the same factor that the other items within its own proposed grouping have their largest factor loadings. However, item X also has a factor loading of .35 on another factor. Item X has validity problems, and this is so since a valid measure can be an indicator of a single construct and nothing else. If this is the only item in the output exhibiting this problem, then this item needs to be removed and not included in subsequent phases of the RFA.

11. If you find two or more measures you proposed as belonging to a single grouping are showing up under more than one factor, then these measures have validity issues, and you must act on them. A prudent approach is to first deal with the measure with the most significant problem and see if removing this measure will resolve the issue with the other measures. For example, in addition to the observation about item X made earlier, item Y also has a factor loading of .53 on the same factor that the other items within its proposed grouping have their largest factor loading. However, Item Y also has a factor loading of .50 on another factor. Between items X and Y, the one with the bigger problem is item Y, which should be removed first, and the analysis should be re-run without it. By eliminating item Y and re-running the analysis, the problem with item X might disappear. If, after removing item Y, the problem with item X disappears, then you can move forward. If the problem with item X remains, then item X should also be removed, and the analysis should be re-run without it.

12. A measure with validity issues should be removed and not be used in subsequent analyses, and the analysis should be re-run after removing it. The factor loadings obtained after re-running the analysis should be re-evaluated to determine if any additional problems are present.

13. Once the analyses of the measures corresponding to the groupings you are analyzing show an output free of errors, then the measures belonging to an additional grouping should be added and the analysis should be repeated. This procedure should be done again until the measures of all groupings are analyzed and a clean overall output is obtained. A clean output is one where the measures have their largest factor loading on a given factor share an unidentifiable meaning and have factors loadings of near zero on all other factors.

14. Compare the measures found under each factor in your clean final solution with the measures you had initially proposed as part of the same grouping. If the measures proposed in one of your groupings were found under the same factor

in the rotated factor matrix, these measures capture the same construct. This is also true if the same pattern of outcome occurs for each additional grouping you proposed. It is important to reiterate that the algorithms used in this phase cannot read the wording of the measures. They simply rely on numerals representing the respondents' reactions to the measures. So, only you would know the linguistic meaning shared among a set of measures under the same factor. The algorithm is simply telling you that, through mathematical derivation, these measures share something in common that is different from what other measures under different factors have in common.

15. After all measures are analyzed, you arrive at a factor analysis solution that assigns each measure to a single factor and no other. Each factor is qualitatively interpretable and reasonable relative to the item groupings you started with. Once this is achieved, you can move forward to the next phase of the RFA.

Phase 4 – Test the groupings for reliability

Here, you only include the measures found to be valid based on the analyses of Phase 3. It is crucial to note that testing for reliability should only occur after testing for validity and only for the measures found to be valid.

1. We compute a reliability coefficient for each grouping of valid measures. When we do so, the reliability coefficient is essentially the reverse of random error (1-random error). By looking at the reliability coefficient, we also look at the random error present in a grouping (the label "measurement error" is often used to signify random error). In other words, we are looking at the influence of the errors coming from the bottom in the Invisible to Visible Framework (ITVF). The reliability coefficient we will use is Cronbach's Alpha (see Spector, 1992).
2. There is a tendency among social scientists and statisticians to shy away from recommending how to evaluate the size of Cronbach's Alpha (see, for example, Pedhazur and Pedhazur Shmelkin, 1991). Here is a rule of thumb for interpreting the size of Cronbach's Alpha that has worked well for me and my students over 30+ years. It is based on the idea that although random errors due to measurement are always present, we should always have more information than error to conclude that the measures are usable. Here is a rule of thumb for interpreting Cronbach's Alpha: if less than .50, then the reliability is unacceptable; between .50 and .59, then it is mediocre; between .60 and .69, then it is good; between .70 and .79, then it is very good; and if it is equal to or greater than .80, then it is excellent.
3. To pinpoint specific measures in a grouping that are introducing more random errors than others, we will use the following logic:
    a. Each grouping of measures will be analyzed separately.
    b. First, we will compute an overall reliability coefficient for all the measures in a specific grouping. Then, we will ask SPSS to remove a measure from that grouping and recompute the reliability coefficient.

c. Suppose the size of the reliability coefficient goes up substantially after removing the measure. In that case, we will conclude that the measure we removed introduces more random error than others in its grouping and will stop using it in subsequent analyses. Suppose the size of the reliability coefficient goes down after removing a specific measure. In that case, we will conclude this measure does not introduce more errors than others in the same grouping and, therefore, should be kept as part of the grouping.
d. We will repeat this process for all measures that are part of the same grouping, one grouping at a time. This analysis can only be done if we have more than two measures per grouping. If we only have two measures, then we can only rely on the overall reliability coefficient and cannot pinpoint whether one measure introduces more random error than the other.
4. After you run the reliability analysis for the items found to be valid for each of your constructs, you can move forward to the next phase of the RFA for the measures that were found to be valid and reliable.

Phase 5 – Compute your estimates of a construct's score

Only the measures confirmed to be valid and reliable are used in this phase. Once validity and reliability are quantified and found to be acceptable for a set of measures designed to capture a specific construct, we can use these measures to compute a score on that construct for every respondent in our data set. This score becomes the best available estimate for a person on that construct. This is typically done by computing everyone's mean scores on all the measures that passed Phases 3 and 4 for a given construct. This is the simplest and most common approach. However, many adjustments to computing a simple mean can be made with advantages and disadvantages associated with each method – see Nunnally (1978). In SPSS, this is typically done using the "compute" command. For each construct, you would create a new variable, which is the mean of all scores for the measures found to be valid and reliable for that construct. These scores will then be used when testing the relationships among building blocks hypothesized at the start of a study, such as those in Figure 9.1. A reminder: the testing of relationships among building blocks of a thought-process model is beyond the scope of this book.

Applying the RFA to selected measures used in the case study

Case study phase 1 – Propose item groupings

The proposed groupings already existed for the case study since I had assembled them by adapting or adopting measures used in past studies. Table 9.1 from earlier shows the grouped measures by construct.

Case study phase 2 – Initial screening

1. Run frequency distributions for all measures: Frequency distributions were computed. A sample of these distributions is presented in Figure 9.3. A close inspection of the patterns in these distributions confirmed there are no constants, outliers, heavily skewed distributions, or differences in the sample size across distributions.

Please tell us whether you agree or disagree with the following statements about Facebook.
I use Facebook to talk to others who have the same interests as me.

		Frequency	Percent	Valid Percent	Cumulative Percent
Valid	Strongly Disagree	30	5.8	5.9	5.9
	Disagree	109	21.1	21.3	27.2
	Neither Agree nor Disagree	122	23.6	23.9	51.1
	Agree	211	40.9	41.3	92.4
	Strongly Agree	39	7.6	7.6	100.0
	Total	511	99.0	100.0	
Missing	System	5	1.0		
Total		516	100.0		

Figure 9.3: A sample frequency distribution of a measure. Source: Author.

2. Check that all reverse coding was done where needed: All measures were checked, and those that needed to be recoded were indeed recoded, and these were denoted with an "r" in Table 9.1.
3. Check on the overlap in meaning: All measures designed to capture the same construct were checked against the definitions of the constructs they are supposed to measure and against one another. Overall, the measures were found to reasonably overlap in meaning with one another and reasonably overlap with their corresponding construct's definition.
4. Run inter-item correlations among all measures: Figure 9.4 shows the correlation matrix computed for all 13 measures. The correlations highlighted in yellow are those belonging to the same grouping. Correlations highlighted in red show the red flags I raised at this point. Here are a few observations from the matrix:
    a. The highest correlation in the matrix is .69. This becomes the relative size against which all other correlations within groupings are evaluated. As such, many of the correlations within groupings are much lower. For example, those for "social trust" are between .22 and .30. This suggests we might find quite a bit of errors due to measurement (EDM) associated with social trust in later phases of the RFA, so I raise a red flag on these. I also raised a red flag for a measure that was part of the "perceived sense of community" grouping since it has a correlation of .19 with another measure of this same construct.
    b. Aside from the size of the correlations within a grouping, it is also important to look at the correlations between measures of different groupings. There

are many reasons why these correlations might exist. If they exist, then it is important to determine if the correlations are among all measures of two different groupings or one or two measures. Suppose we find sizeable correlations among all measures of two different groupings. In that case, it is helpful to consider whether the two groupings possibly reflect a common theme or whether the two constructs are simply associated. Some correlations occurring outside the groupings indicate a problem. In contrast, others simply reflect that two constructs might be correlated, and the correlation among the constructs would explain why their measures are also correlated. When figuring out why measures not proposed to belong to the same grouping and do not seem to share a common theme are correlated, look at the interrelationships among constructs depicted by the theoretical framework you use for your study to see if the constructs are linked. That's another reason why a clear theoretical framework should organize the variables that you found in your literature review.

c. By looking at the pattern in Figure 9.4, I noticed the same measure of "perceived sense of community," for which I raised a red flag earlier, has equal size correlations with other measures outside the construct it was designed to capture. This further confirms the need to keep an eye on this measure as I move to the subsequent phases of the RFA.

d. I also noticed several other correlations between an item for a specific grouping and items from other groupings. Although these correlations are much smaller than the items within the groupings, I still raised a red flag to signal that I am conscious they exist and might indicate trouble ahead in subsequent phases of the RFA.

e. No zero or near zero correlations among items belonging to the same grouping exist. As a result, no actions, aside from raising red flags, needed to be taken at this point.

Case study phase 3 – Test the groupings for content validity

Here, we are testing the strength of the arrows coming from on top in the Invisible to Visible Framework (ITVF).

1. A confirmatory factor analysis was carried out, which resulted in a solution that explains 54% of the variance in the measures being analyzed. (The progressive testing approach described earlier was not followed here to save space but is highly recommended for beginning researchers). The factor loadings corresponding to this solution are in Figure 9.5.

Figure 9.4: Inter-item correlations for the measures in the case study.

Rotated Component Matrix[a]

	Component			
	1	2	3	4
Please tell us how much you agree or disagree with each of the following statements-Generally speaking, I would say that people can be trusted	0.044	0.015	0.732	0.116
Please tell us how much you agree or disagree with each of the following statements-People try to be fair	0.098	0.020	0.721	-0.021
Please tell us how much you agree or disagree with each of the following statements-People try to take advantage of me if they got the chance	-0.191	0.064	0.655	-0.072
Please tell us whether you agree or disagree with the following statements about Facebook.-I use Facebook to get peer support from others	0.304	0.130	0.066	0.703
Please tell us whether you agree or disagree with the following statements about Facebook.-I use Facebook to talk to others who have the same interests as me	-0.053	0.005	-0.104	0.817
Please tell us whether you agree or disagree with the following statements about Facebook.-When I use Facebook I feel like I belong to a community	0.385	0.207	0.149	0.526
Think about how often the following takes place on Facebook-My friends on Facebook think that what I have to say is worth reading	0.094	0.850	0.040	0.069
Think about how often the following takes place on Facebook-My friends give me feedback that what I share on Facebook is interesting	0.046	0.867	-0.048	0.106
Think about how often the following takes place on Facebook-My friends on Facebook don't pay much attention to what I post	-0.141	0.622	0.099	0.048
Please tell us how much you agree or disagree with the following statements-I get so involved when I am on Facebook that I forget everything else	0.669	0.106	-0.069	0.132
Please tell us how much you agree or disagree with the following statements-Using Facebook makes me feel like I am in a different world	0.800	-0.074	-0.043	0.121
Please tell us how much you agree or disagree with the following statements-Being on Facebook "gets me away" from it all	0.735	0.016	0.073	0.129
Please tell us how much you agree or disagree with the following statements-Being on Facebook makes me feel like I am in a separate world	0.842	-0.111	-0.020	0.004

Extraction Method: Principal Component Analysis.
Rotation Method: Varimax with Kaiser Normalization.
a. Rotation converged in 5 iterations.

Figure 9.5: Rotated factor (component) matrix for the measures in the case study. Source: Author.

1. A glance at the values of the factor loadings in Figure 9.5 shows that two measures of "perceived sense of community" have substantial loadings on two factors. This is unacceptable since a measure is supposed to capture what it is supposed to capture and nothing else. When looking at the two problematic measures, I first removed "When I use Facebook, I feel like I belong to a community" because it has the lowest factor loading on its factor and re-run the analysis without it.

2. The re-run confirmatory factor analysis resulted in a solution explaining 59% of the variance in the analyzed measures. This is a slight improvement over the previous solution, reflecting a slight reduction in error when removing a problematic measure. However, a glance at the pattern of loadings shows the other measure previously identified as problematic is still loading up on two factors. I decided to remove this measure, too. By removing it, however, only one measure remains in this grouping, and a single measure cannot be analyzed for validity, so I decided to remove both measures of "perceived sense of community." By doing so, I acknowledge that I failed to capture a "perceived sense of community".
3. After removing the two items noted above and losing one of the constructs I was testing, I am left with three groupings. I re-ran the confirmatory factor analysis by testing for three factors, and the resulting solution explains 59% of the variance in the analyzed measures. The rotated component matrix is in Figure 9.6. By looking at the pattern of loadings, I found all measures that are loading on one factor are not loading on any other factor, which was a good sign. However, I also noticed differences in the size of the factor loadings within each factor. As I stated earlier, a measure with a lower factor loading relative to others within the same factor is an item of lower quality. The items with the lowest relative factor loadings are: "My friends on Facebook don't pay much attention to what I post" and "I get so involved when I am on Facebook that I forget everything else." I raised a red flag on both and kept an eye on them as I moved to the next phase of the RFA.

Case study phase 4 – Test the groupings for reliability

Now that we have confirmed the validity of the measures in the previous phase, we can test the amount of random error within each grouping and figure out if a specific measure within a grouping is introducing more errors than the other measures. Here, we are testing the strength of the arrows coming from the bottom in the Invisible to Visible Framework (ITVF).

Starting with the "social trust" measures, I computed an overall Cronbach's alpha and asked that the measures be removed one at a time and each time Cronbach's alpha be recomputed. The results reported in Figure 9.7 show that the overall Cronbach's alpha is .50, and none of the three measures, when removed, result in an improvement of over .50. This means that none of the measures introduce more errors than others. However, Cronbach's overall alpha for "Need for belonging" is mediocre. I captured the students' variation in terms of social trust, but the information captured had quite a bit of errors due to measurement. The information is usable but barely passes the minimum threshold.

1. A Cronbach's alpha was also computed for the measures of "Perceived Encouragement." Figure 9.8 shows the overall Cronbach's alpha is .71. When looking at what happens to this value when items are removed, I noticed the overall alpha goes up to .80 when "My friends on Facebook don't pay much attention to what I post"

Rotated Component Matrix [a]

	Component		
	1	2	3
Please tell us how much you agree or disagree with each of the following statements-Generally speaking, I would say that people can be trusted	0.076	0.043	0.741
Please tell us how much you agree or disagree with each of the following statements-People try to be fair	0.090	0.015	0.724
Please tell us how much you agree or disagree with each of the following statements-People try to take advantage of me if they got the chance	−0.210	0.049	0.654
Think about how often the following takes place on Facebook- My friends on Facebook think that what I have to say is worth reading	0.099	0.853	0.045
Think about how often the following takes place on Facebook- My friends give me feedback that what I share on Facebook is interesting	0.062	0.878	−0.040
Think about how often the following takes place on Facebook- My friends on Facebook don't pay much attention to what I post	−0.140	0.625	0.097
Please tell us how much you agree or disagree with the following statements-I get so involved when I am on Facebook that I forget everything else	0.684	0.120	−0.066
Please tell us how much you agree or disagree with the following statements-Using Facebook makes me feel like I am in a different world	0.816	−0.063	−0.032
Please tell us how much you agree or disagree with the following statements-Being on Facebook "gets me away"from it all	0.750	0.028	0.079
Please tell us how much you agree or disagree with the following statements-Being on Facebook makes me feel like I am in a separate world	0.844	−0.112	−0.005

Extraction Method: Principal Component Analysis.
Rotation Method: Varimax with Kaiser Normalization.
a. Rotation converged in 4 iterations.

Figure 9.6: Rotated factor (component) matrix when testing three factors for the measures in the case study. Source: Author.

is removed. This is one of the measures for which I had raised a red flag in the validity phase of RFA. I removed this measure since it introduces more errors than the others within its grouping. I re-ran the analysis to obtain an overall reliability of .80, which is excellent. I successfully captured the variation of a student's "perceived encouragement when using Facebook" with very little error.

2. A Cronbach's alpha was also computed to measure "Escapism motivation." Figure 9.9 shows that Cronbach's overall alpha is .78, which is very good and cannot be improved by removing any of the four measures that are part of this grouping. I successfully captured the variation of a student's escapism motivation with very little error.

Reliability Statistics

Cronbach's Alpha	N of Items				
0.501	3				
Item-Total Statistics					
	Scale Mean if Item Deleted	Scale Variance if Item Deleted		Corrected Item-Total Correlation	Cronbach's Alpha if Item Deleted
Please tell us how much you agree or disagree with each of the following statements-Generally speaking, I would say that people can be trusted	6.10	2.066		0.346	0.353
Please tell us how much you agree or disagree with each of the following statements-People try to be fair	6.36	2.327		0.327	0.393
Please tell us how much you agree or disagree with each of the following statements-People try to take advantage of me if they got the chance	6.32	1.980		0.289	0.462

Figure 9.7: Reliability analysis for the measures of "social trust".

Reliability Statistics

Cronbach's Alpha	N of Items				
0.706	3				
Item-Total Statistics					
	Scale Mean if Item Deleted	Scale Variance if Item Deleted		Corrected Item-Total Correlation	Cronbach's Alpha if Item Deleted
Think about how often the following takes place on Facebook-My friends on Facebook think that what I have to say is worth reading	7.24	1.793		0.600	0.519
Think about how often the following takes place on Facebook-My friends give me feedback that what I share on Facebook is interesting	7.17	1.595		0.631	0.467
Think about how often the following takes place on Facebook-My friends on Facebook don't pay much attention to what I post	7.07	2.245		0.361	0.797

Figure 9.8: Reliability analysis for the measures of "perceived encouragement".

Reliability Statistics				
Cronbach's Alpha		N of Items		
0.780		4		
Item-Total Statistics				
	Scale Mean if Item Deleted	Scale Variance if Item Deleted	Corrected Item-Total Correlation	Cronbach's Alpha if Item Deleted
Please tell us how much you agree or disagree with the following statements-I get so involved when I am on Facebook that I forget everything else	6.35	5.871	0.488	0.780
Please tell us how much you agree or disagree with the following statements-Using Facebook makes me feel like I am in a different world	6.47	5.607	0.639	0.699
Please tell us how much you agree or disagree with the following statements-Being on Facebook "gets me away" from it all	6.65	5.892	0.553	0.743
Please tell us how much you agree or disagree with the following statements-Being on Facebook makes me feel like I am in a separate world	6.67	5.570	0.675	0.682

Figure 9.9: Reliability analysis for the measures of "escapism motivation".

Placing the results in the Invisible to Visible Framework (ITVF)

Figure 9.10 shows the factor analysis results in the Invisible to Visible Framework (ITVF) context. Note that "Escapism Motivation" is the construct I needed to capture, and it is invisible. The four measures I adopted from prior studies and to which I asked the respondents to react are visible. These visible measures were analyzed to determine their validity and reliability in capturing the same construct. The quantification of the arrows coming from on top are the factor loadings. You might recall from Chapter 3 that, ideally, the arrows coming from on top should be very strong. The size of the factor loadings placed next to each of the measures in Figure 9.10 reveals all four measures seem to be driven by the same invisible construct, and all four are relatively strong. However, the differences among the sizes of the factor loadings reveal differences in quality among the measures: two of the measures are higher in quality than the others, and one is relatively lower in quality. The two of the highest quality are "Using Facebook makes me feel like I am in a different world" and "Being on Facebook makes me feel like I am in a separate world." The one with the relatively lowest quality is "I get so involved when I am on Facebook that I forget everything else."

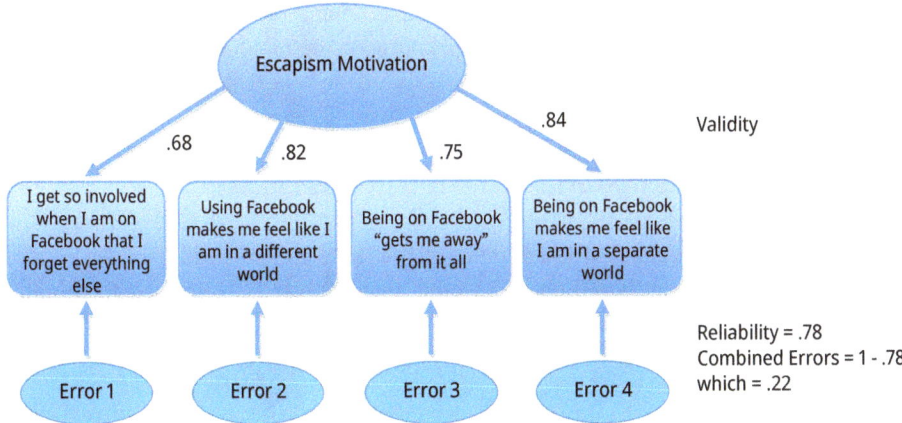

Figure 9.10: Validity and reliability results for "Escapism Motivation" within the ITVF. Source: Author.

Remember, the factor analysis algorithms do not read the wording of the measures but derive their findings by analyzing the numerals reflected in the study participants' reactions to these measures. It is interesting to note that the two measures with the highest factor loadings are closest in meaning. The measure with the relatively lowest factor loading is the furthest in meaning from the others. What we are witnessing here is the transformation of the study participants' reactions to these measures into numerals which have preserved the meaning embedded in the wording of these measures. Even though these differences in quality exist, all four measures are unidimensional, driven by the same invisible construct, which is an important determinant of content validity.

Figure 9.10 also shows the combined influence of the errors coming from the bottom is .22. This was achieved by taking the reliability coefficient of .78 and subtracting it from 1 (1 − .78 = .22). You might recall that, ideally, the influence of the arrows coming from the bottom should be minimal. In this case, the combined errors are relatively small.

Now that we have confirmed the validity and reliability of the measures for the three constructs, we can move forward to the next phase of the RFA.

Case study phase 5 – Compute estimates of the construct scores

As stated earlier, this is typically done using the "compute" command in SPSS. For each of the constructs confirmed for validity and reliability, a new variable that contains everyone's scores on each of the three constructs is created. This new construct score is the mean of all the measures used to capture that construct. Doing so makes a score on each construct for each respondent in the data set. This score can then be used when conducting a wide array of statistical analyses and mathematical modeling since it is based on measures confirmed to be valid and reliable. Data analysis techniques in testing hypothesized relationships among thought-process building blocks are carried out as part of Step 10 of the research process in Table 2.1 of Chapter 2. They are beyond the scope of this book.

Reflections on the materials covered in this chapter

What would have happened if I had assumed that all the measures I used were valid and reliable and had not tested them? I would have analyzed one construct I couldn't successfully capture and another with a measure that introduced quite a bit of error into my ability to represent that construct. Both situations would have been unacceptable.

As I noted at the start of this chapter, it is often the case that researchers don't stop and evaluate their self-report measures for validity and reliability. By not conducting this evaluation, researchers assume no errors due to measurement.

If researchers wrongly assume valid and reliable measures and base their tests of relationships among constructs on defective measures, then the results of these models will be fraught with errors. As a result, the researchers' predictions based on these models will be worthless, and the decisions made based on their predictions will be misguided. Depending on the nature of the project, any actions based on flawed predictions will lead to revenue losses and/or negative impacts on human lives. In research projects that rely on self-report measurement, it is essential to plan on using multiple indicators for the less visible concepts to quantify validity and reliability before moving forward with any tests of relationships among the captured constructs.

References

Ajzen, I. (1985). From Intentions to Actions: A Theory of Planned Behavior. In: Kuhl, J., Beckmann, J. (eds) *Action Control*. SSSP Springer Series in Social Psychology. Springer, Berlin, Heidelberg.

Allen, M. (2017). *The SAGE Encyclopedia of Communication Research Methods* (Vols. 1–4). Thousand Oaks, CA: SAGE Publications, Inc doi: 10.4135/9781483381411

Anderson, J.C. & Gerbing, D. W. (1988). Structural Equation Modeling in Practice: A Review and Recommended Two-Step Approach. *Psychological Bulletin, 103* (3), 411–423.

Bosnjak M, Ajzen I, Schmidt P. (2020) The Theory of Planned Behavior: Selected Recent Advances and Applications. *European Journal of Psychology, 16*(3):352–356. doi: 10.5964/ejop.v16i3.3107. PMID: 33680187; PMCID: PMC7909498.

Bruner, G.C. & Hensel, P.J. (1994). *Marketing Scales Handbook: A Compilation of Multi-Item Measures*. Chicago, IL: American Marketing Association.

Carmine, E.G. & Zeller, R.A. (1979). *Validity and Reliability Assessment*. Thousand Oaks, CA: Sage.

Campbell, D.T. & Fiske, D.W. (1959). Convergent and discriminant validation by the multitrait-multimethod matrix. *Psychological Bulletin, 56*(2), 81–105.

Elasmar, M.G. (2012). *The Impact of Facebook Usage on Young Adults' International Cognitive Maps*. Paper presented during the Global Fusion conference, October 2012, Athens, Ohio.

Fishbein, M., & Ajzen, I. (1972). Attitudes and opinions. *Annual Review of Psychology*, 487–544.

Fishbein, M., & Ajzen, I. (1975). *Belief, Attitude, Intention and Behavior: An Introduction to Theory and Research.* Reading, MA: Addison Wesley Publishers.

Frey, B. (2018). *The SAGE Encyclopedia of Educational Research, Measurement, and Evaluation* (Vols. 1–4). Thousand Oaks, CA: SAGE Publications, Inc. doi: 10.4135/9781506326139

Hoyle, R. H. & Duvall, J. L. (2004). Determining the number of factors in exploratory and confirmatory factor analysis. In *The SAGE handbook of quantitative methodology for the social sciences* (pp. 302–317). SAGE Publications, Inc., https://www.doi.org/10.4135/9781412986311

Dunteman, G.H. (1989). *Principle Components Analysis.* Thousand Oaks, CA: Sage.

Kim, JO, & Mueller, C.W. (1978). *Factor Analysis: Statistical Methods and Practical Issues.* Thousand Oaks, CA: Sage.

Kwon, O. and Wen, Y. (2010). An empirical study affecting social network service use. *Computers in Human Behavior, 26,* 254–263.

Long, J.S. (1983). *Confirmatory Factor Analysis.* Thousand Oaks, CA: Sage.

Mathwick, C. (1997). *Model of Contextual Antecedents and Exchange Outcomes of Customer Value: An Empirical Investigation into the Catalog and Internet Shopping Context.* Unpublished Dissertation, Georgia Institute of Technology.

McNabb, D. E. (2014). Measurement error. In *Nonsampling error in social surveys* (pp. 97–113). SAGE Publications, Inc., https://www.doi.org/10.4135/9781483352923

Park, N. Kee, K., & Valenzuela, S. (2009). Being Immersed in Social Networking Environment: Facebook Groups, Uses and Gratifications, and Social Outcomes. *Cyberspsychology & Behavior, 12 (*6), 729–733. doi: 10.1089=cpb.2009.0003

Pedhazur, E. & Pedhazur Schmelkin, L. (1991). *Measurement, Design and Analysis.* Hillsdale, NJ: Erlbaum.

Spector, P.E. (1992). *Summated Rating Scale Construction.* Thousand Oaks, CA: Sage.

Valenzuela, S., Park, K. and Kee, K. (2009). Is There Social Capital in a Social Network Site?: Facebook Use and College Students' Life Satisfaction, Trust, and Participation. *Journal of Computer-Mediated Communication, 14,* 875–901. doi:10.1111/j.1083-6101.2009.01474.x

Chapter 10
Implications for extracting self-report measurement from social media text content – What role can Artificial Intelligence (AI) play?

Objectives of Chapter 10: Can social media text be transformed into building blocks of a shared thought-process about a topic? This chapter proposes that when individuals express themselves by posting text on social media, they self-report. The information they reveal on social media is volunteered without being asked. As such, to differentiate it from the traditional contexts of information collected from individuals through surveys and experiments, information revealed through social media text is labeled here as unsolicited self-reports. This chapter briefly overviews thought-processes and then demonstrates a methodology for extracting thought-process building blocks from social media text. Quantifying thought-process building blocks is equally relevant to academic and industry researchers. The methods proposed and demonstrated in this chapter also allow the researcher to quantify the errors due to measurement (EDM) associated with the indicators of each building block. If these errors are deemed reasonably low, scores can be computed for each extracted thought-process building block and then used to test a shared thought-process about specific topics.

Self-report measurement science and opinion-extraction

In this chapter, I attempt to bridge the established science of self-report measurement, traditionally applied in the context of surveys and experiments, with the emerging science of opinion-extraction, which focuses on social media text content. I am using the label "opinion-extraction" to include all efforts that involve analyzing social media text to arrive at conclusions about what people on social media think, know, and feel, what they intend to do, what they do, and other similar variables. I know that not everyone who conducts such research labels their work as opinion-extraction. However, given that this label has been used for a sizeable body of literature coming out of the field of computer science (e.g., Cai, Xia, & Yu, 2021; Gao et al., 2021), I thought that it would be a unifying rubric for all similar work including computational linguistics, computational communication, and related fields.

The information from the previous chapters in this book has shown that efforts towards a science of self-report measurement have been made for more than a century. As a result, a solid body of knowledge already exists and is mainly applied in the context of surveys and experiments. However, opinion-extraction is relatively new and resides under the broad umbrella of big data mining. It's important to note that while the field of big data is vast, this chapter focuses narrowly on the type of opinion-extraction involving social media text content as expressed by individuals. This type of written content is found in online reviews, Tweets, Facebook posts, etc...

A broad brushstroke of current practice within the field of opinion-extraction

Researchers interested in opinion-extraction from social media text typically analyze what individuals write, whether a whole tweet, a whole product review, a whole post on Facebook, or others (see Amangeldi, Usmanova, & Shamoi, 2024). The typically analyzed corpus comprises the aggregation of patterns across whole text posts (e.g., Valarmathi et al., 2024). Over the past decade, opinion-extraction researchers have mostly focused on the sentiment in social media texts (see Xu, Chang & Jayne, 2022). The conclusions of such efforts are about the sentiment trends in the text analyzed and very indirectly about the group of humans expressing this content.

A shift to conceptualizing social media content as a type of self-report

Opinion-extraction researchers need to recognize that what they are trying to achieve is consistent with the goals of those who have traditionally used self-report measurement in the context of surveys and experiments. While they might not all be aware they are doing so, both groups of researchers are trying to externalize invisible aspects of the thought-process of humans about specific topics. Figure 10.1 repeats Figure 3.1, which illustrates the difference between the visible and invisible regarding human expressions. Here, we have multiple humans looking at the same tree. By observing their behavior, a researcher would conclude that they are looking at the same tree and thus are homogeneous in what they do.

What the researcher does not see is symbolically illustrated by the thought bubbles in Figure 10.2, which are typically invisible. The invisible is critically important to capture since knowing it would shatter the assumption of homogeneity based on the same observed behavior.

It might be difficult for someone looking at social media posts with evident text to conceive that these visible posts are potential indicators of an invisible (i.e., latent) concept. However, when it is confirmed that the source generating the text content on social media is an individual and not a bot, this content can reflect this individual's inner state of mind, including thoughts and feelings. And these inner states of mind, if captured correctly, can be used to understand a shared or collective thought-process about specific topics.

Figure 10.1: Visible behavior regarding a tree.

What is in a shared thought-process?

In a nutshell, for this book, the human thought-process about a specific topic consists of relationships among multiple building blocks that include knowledge, beliefs, attitudes, emotions, intentions, and behaviors related to the topic, in addition to background factors (see Fishbein & Ajzen, 1972, 1975; Ajzen, 1985; Bosnjak, Ajzen, & Schmidt, 2020; and https://people.umass.edu/aizen/tpb.html.) A more elaborate taxonomy of thought-process building blocks by Strapparava (2004) lists the following: "Emotion, mood, trait, cognitive state, physical state, hedonic signal, emotion-eliciting situation, emotional response, behavior, attitude, and sensation" (p. 2086). For over 100 years, researchers interested in understanding thought-processes related to specific topics have utilized self-report measurement techniques to capture one or more thought-process building blocks (e.g., a belief, an attitude, an intention, etc.). Those who use self-report measurement in the context of surveys and experiments analyze a human's expressed reaction to statements developed by a researcher. Those using the emerging techniques of opinion-extraction analyze free-style text expressions voluntarily disclosed by humans on social media. In both cases, researchers are focused on extracting information from human expressions to arrive at invisible constructs (e.g., a belief, an attitude, etc.). To differentiate between the two approaches, in Chapter 3, I used the term "unsolicited ex-

Figure 10.2: Visible behavior versus invisible thoughts regarding a tree.

pressions" for the type of social media content analyzed by opinion-extraction researchers and "solicited expressions" for the kind studied by researchers using traditional self-report measurement techniques in the context of surveys and experiments.

Although it is beyond the scope of this book to delve in-depth into the notion of human thought-processes, a convenient way to visualize the anatomy of a thought-process is shown in Figure 10.3 (see Elasmar, 2007 for an elaboration).

Human thought-processes and the role of self-report

The diagram in Figure 10.3 adapts the social cognition approach from within the field of cognitive psychology (see Fiske & Taylor, 1984) to the context of self-report measurement. The idea is simple: when a human being expresses themselves about a topic, their expression is a function of their understanding of the topic, which, in turn, is a function of the building blocks of their thought-process related to this topic. This is true regardless of whether a question in a survey prompted such expression or it was simply volunteered in a social media post. The term "schema" is often used to label the interrelated building blocks associated with specific topics within the human

182 — Chapter 10 Implications for extracting self-report measurement from social media

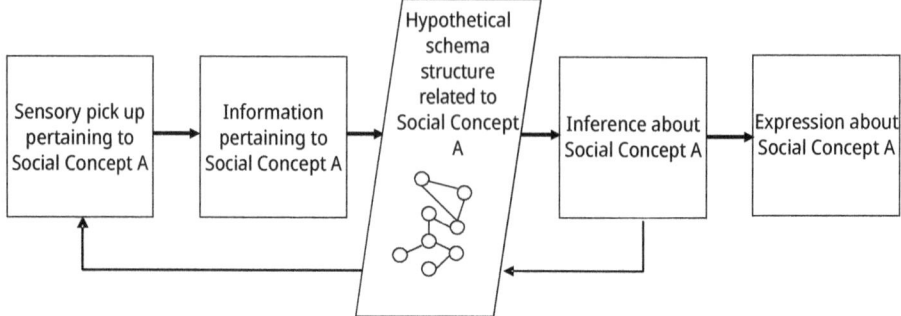

Figure 10.3: Social Cognition as a Conceptual Framework for Understanding Human Expressions.
Source: Elasmar, 2007 "Basic Process of Social Cognition Highlighting Opinion as an Outcome" (p. 48).

brain. Figure 10.4 illustrates what a schema might look like for a person about to purchase an item of clothing. We usually see the purchase behavior, and we don't see the intricate schema associated with the behavior. The building blocks within a schema and the interrelationships among these blocks should be the mystery that each researcher interested in self-report measurement must strive to understand.

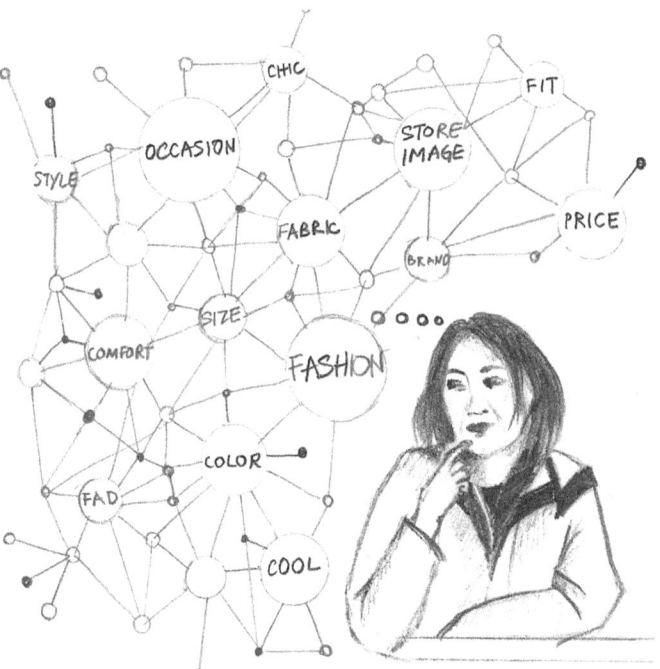

Figure 10.4: Hypothetical schema components related to evaluating an item of clothing.

It is important to remember that researchers interested in capturing the building blocks of a thought-process are not particularly interested in those that might be present in the mind of a single individual. Researchers are interested in the building blocks shared across individuals and in the relationships that exist among these building blocks. Altogether, these relationships illustrate the shared thought-process of a specific topic among a group of individuals.

Example of a shared thought-process

An example of a shared thought-process is the outcome of the analysis I conducted for my 2007 book, which detailed the factors that predicted support for the U.S.-led war on terror among people of the Muslim faith across seven countries with substantial Muslim populations (Elasmar, 2007). Countries were first analyzed individually, resulting in country-specific models of a shared thought-process. I then looked at the building blocks shared across all seven countries. Figure 10.5 shows the shared thought-process that predicted the level of support for the U.S.-led war on terror across the respondents of all seven countries.

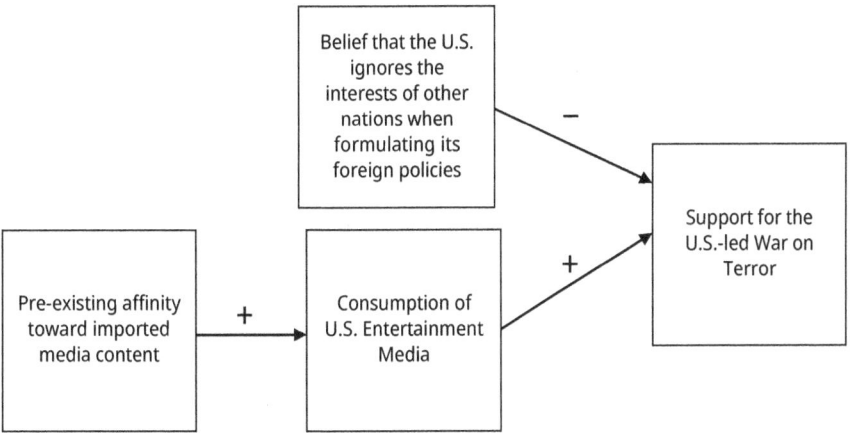

Figure 10.5: An Overall Model of International Public Opinion about the U.S.-Led War on Terror in 7 countries. Source: Elasmar (2007).

The benefits of understanding a shared thought-process become apparent when the model that is quantitatively tested has practical implications. Here, the model shows that across all seven countries, there are two competing sources of influence on a person's level of support for the U.S.-led war on terror. The more a person believes this U.S. policy is solely self-serving and ignores the interests of other countries, the less likely this person will support this U.S. foreign policy. However, this influence is offset among those with a pre-existing affinity toward imported media content and consume U.S. entertainment media. The more they have a pre-existing affinity toward consuming imported media content, the more they consume U.S. entertainment media, and, in turn, the more they support this U.S. foreign policy. Since this shared thought-process pertains to U.S. foreign policy, the relationships uncovered in the abovementioned model would be relevant to U.S. policymakers. One takeaway would be that, to increase support for the U.S.-led war on terror, public diplomacy efforts need to demonstrate this foreign policy is not solely self-serving to the U.S. and does not ignore the interests of other countries.

As you can imagine, a health-related shared thought-process would have implications for health policies, a brand-related shared thought-process would impact specific brand strategies, etc. The knowledge gained by arriving at a shared thought-process is unequaled.

Thought-processes can be simple relationships between two or three variables. Over the last three decades, many researchers in communication science, psychology, public health, and related areas have tested complex thought-processes that depict elaborate relationships among many variables. While it is outside the scope of this book to discuss thought-process model testing procedures, it's important to recognize that once the relevant building blocks of a shared thought-process have been measured and validated, there are established quantitative methods that can help a researcher test and visualize the structure of their corresponding shared thought-process.

Proposed shifts for a better understanding of human thought-processes through opinion-extraction from social media text

As a starting point, it would be constructive for opinion-extraction researchers to use the thought-process framework as the goal of their efforts. What will it take for opinion-extraction research to uncover the building blocks of a thought-process? Many obstacles must be overcome, some of which are listed in Chapter 3, Table 3.1. In the following paragraphs I try to harness the knowledge gained from more than a century of solicited self-report science and adapt it to the field of opinion-extraction. I propose the following shifts to focus everyone's efforts on using social media text to arrive at the shared building blocks of a thought-process concerning specific topics:

1. A shift to using unsolicited text expressions to arrive at the invisible
Once we begin thinking of social media text expressions as a form of self-report, the Invisible to Visible Framework (ITVF) model provided in Chapter 3 becomes a good way for visualizing what opinion-extraction researchers are trying to achieve. However, the traditional process of arriving at the invisible will need to be adapted to the context of unsolicited human expressions (more on this later in this chapter). At the heart of the Invisible to Visible Framework (ITVF) is having multiple indicators. In Chapters 1 and 3, the logic and power of having multiple indicators were explained.

Without multiple indicators, the validity and reliability of unsolicited human expressions cannot be computed (see Chapter 9).

2. A shift from analyzing a social media post as a whole to analyzing it in parts

One very definite principle from over a hundred years of science about solicited expressions is that a researcher cannot consider expressions that simultaneously reflect multiple concepts to be a single expression. Doing so would directly violate the principle given in Chapter 5 for double-barreled measures and substantially increase errors due to measurement (EDM). The current practice among opinion-extraction researchers to analyze the whole content of unsolicited expressions (such as entire Tweets or whole product reviews) is essentially making the same errors as those experimenting with solicited expressions many decades ago realized should not be made. The entire text might reflect multiple building blocks of a thought-process, each of which needs to have the sentiment embedded in it be separately quantified. In addition, if the goal is to understand human thought-processes concerning a topic (e.g., President Biden), then, in addition to coding sentiments, expressions about the topic need to be coded by the type of thought-process building blocks they represent (e.g., belief, attitude, intention, etc.) and the specific object about which the expression is being made (e.g., Biden foreign policy; Biden support for the arts, etc.). The reason for doing so is, for example, "attitude toward President Biden's policy on military support for Ukraine" would be different than "attitude toward President Biden's policy on alternative energy." In these examples, the "attitude" is the expression type for both, and "President Biden's policy on military support for Ukraine" is the object of one attitude, while "President Biden's policy on alternative energy" is the object for another attitude. Combinations of expression types by objects (e.g., attitude toward President Biden's policy on alternative energy versus attitude toward President Biden's policy on military support for Ukraine) capture different building blocks of a thought-process and need to be differentiated quantitatively from one another (e.g., each needs to have its own sentiment score).

3. A shift from considering social media text as the unit of analysis to making the human expressing the social media text be the unit of analysis

Given the critical importance of obtaining multiple indicators for each concept we aim to measure (see Chapters 1 and 3), one methodological change will require making the human communicator be the unit of analysis. If the big picture goal is to understand thought-processes, the unit of analysis needs to become the individual making the expression along with the expressions that this individual is making. A reader might raise privacy concerns when linking multiple expressions to the same individual. It's important to remember here that the individual's identity is not as important as linking multiple expressions to the same individual so that they can be considered multiple indicators of the same building block. Safeguards would need to be implemented to anonymize the individual's identity while linking expressions to them.

A process of derivation or "reverse engineering" will be necessary when adapting the visible/invisible mindset to the context of unsolicited social media expressions.

This means that once a series of expressions tied to the same author are found, the contents present within each expression need to be examined to determine if two or more expressions reflect a common meaning. If two or more expressions reflect a common meaning, then they will be considered to embody multiple indicators of the same building block. The meaning that overlaps between/among them will be the invisible concept that the researcher was able to extract (see Chapters 3 and 9). For example, if two or more expressions by the same individual are deemed to reflect an "attitude about President Biden's policies about unemployment compensation during the post-pandemic period," then these would count as multiple indicators of this individual's invisible attitude toward President Biden's policies about unemployment compensation during the post-pandemic period. Essentially, while we can't directly look inside someone's brain to see first-hand what they think, how they feel, what they intend to do, what they know or what they did, we are using the contents of their text expressions as reflections of these thoughts, feelings, intentions, knowledge, and behaviors. The ultimate focus is thus on the human being authoring the social media text.

4. A shift in the precision of quantifying the sentiment embedded in each expression

The standard practice among many opinion-extraction researchers is to use a 3-point scale consisting of negative, neutral, and positive (e.g., Çeliktuğ, 2018; Qi & Shabrina, 2023). As I noted in my comments concerning the number of scale points in chapter 6, convincing evidence from over a century of solid science points out that a 5- to 7-point scale enables a researcher to fulfill the requirements of continuous data and, by doing so, allows them to run analyses that go beyond descriptives. Such analyses, as correlations and others, were shown to be instrumental in Chapter 9 for confirming the validity and reliability of solicited self-report measurement. So, a 3-point scoring system consisting of negative, neutral, and positive, is not sufficient. Some opinion-extraction researchers have already realized this scale is insufficient in capturing the variation of sentiments and have tried expanding it (e.g., Rosenthal, Farra, & Nakov, 2019). Expanding the scale to at least five points should be standard. It is important to note that Google NLP already uses a scale from -.9 to +.9, which works very well (see https://cloud.google.com/natural-language/docs/analyzing-sentiment). While humans are limited in their ability to differentiate among scale gradations that exceed 5 to 7 points when reacting to self-report measures, machines do not have the same limitation when coding social media text. So, the 19-point scale used by Google NLP to code sentiment in social media text is appropriate in this context.

5. A shift to quantifying errors associated with efforts to extract the invisible from social media text

The ability to link social media expressions to the same individual is a prerequisite for overcoming key obstacles that currently limit the science of opinion-extraction from social media. These obstacles include the current absence of methods for quantifying the validity and reliability of information extracted from social media texts (see Chapter 3,

Table 3.1). The concept of measurement error, or as labeled in Chapters 1 and 3: errors due to measurement (EDM), is absent from the field of opinion-extraction (Elasmar, 2019). This is so even though over a century of solid science related to solicited self-report measurement has shown that there is no such thing as measurement with no error. Errors due to measurement can be devastating to a research project. In solicited self-report measurement, the key has been to find the ratio of error to information in the data captured. If there is more information than error, the data is usable. However, the reverse means the data is unusable. Without knowing the extent to which errors due to measurement are present when extracting opinion from social media text, researchers are simply assuming no errors. Doing so is unrealistic and can devastate a researcher's ability to uncover one or more building blocks of a shared thought-process. Adapting the methods of quantifying errors due to measurement (EDM) from the solid science of analyzing solicited expressions could be the easiest way to solve this obstacle.

A catalyst has arrived: What can AI do to help?

Until 2022, proposing the five needed shifts above would have only been followed by a call to opinion-extraction researchers to prioritize developing solutions for these shifts to become possible. However, the advent and rapid evolution of AI assistants, such as ChatGPT, allows us to explore actual solutions. In the paragraphs below, I will describe the challenges of applying the approaches and techniques associated with the Invisible to Visible Framework (ITVF) to the context of extracting opinion from social media text. I will also outline a starting point for a methodology that might overcome these challenges.

From theory to coding social media text aided by AI: Can we break up whole social media content expressed by an individual into the thought-process building blocks of the individual who authored that social media content?
Let's take, for example, a whole text expressed by one individual and downloaded from a customer review database accessible through BrandWatch, a commercial service that provides access to consumer social media content. The identity of the store was replaced with "Department Store." Otherwise, the review was left intact:

> I hate this "Department Store" more and more each time I go here. These employees are disgustingly rude the crazy part is it is the customer service and management like fix your nasty attitudes. You people need to get a hand on your disrespected employees. I went in this store to the money center with my nephew to cash HIS CHECK "DEPARTMENT STORE" PAID HIM FOR WORKING the check wouldn't even clear, but the miserable employee/csm Alycia or Alicia or something like that red hair rude, disrespectful embarrassment. I was speaking to MY NEPHEW, not the redhead supervisor Alycia, and I said that's weird they wrote your check, but they won't cash it? This broad starts moving her head and neck, looking like a turtle, shaking it back and forth, saying it's not "Department Store" I the check place ok ma'am and wouldn't shut up I was never talking to her that's what's funny I said I was talking to my nephew she was really trying to

argue with me I was tired of hearing her talk and seeing her turtle neck shake so yes I told her shut up lady. This lady said get out of my money center pretty sure this isn't YOU'RE money center what the heck is your problem good grief are they that miserable working there? She made all that disrespectful scene and nobody was ever even speaking to her maybe if she shut up like I said because I was talking to my nephew instead of playing like a big bad I don't know what turtle I cannot stand this store it's always a bad integration with a miserable employee at the checkouts if they don't want to work then don't buy your definitely not about to disrespect customers who don't even acknowledge you try minding your business and you won't have to go turtle power with your neck.

During the summer of 2024, I asked the ChatGPT 3.5 AI assistant to break up this whole review into the thought building blocks present in it. I specified the thought building blocks I am interested in, which are: beliefs, attitudes, intentions of future behavior, behaviors, and emotions, and defined each for the assistant. I then asked ChatGPT to score the sentiment in each thought building block from negative to positive on a -.9 to a .9 scale. The results are reported in Table 10.1.

Table 10.1: ChatGPT's Analysis of Thought Building Blocks.

Expression	Building Block	Sentiment	ChatGPT's Analysis
I hate this "Department Store" more and more each time I go here.	Emotion	−0.80	The use of "hate" and the negative tone suggests a strong negative sentiment.
These employees are disgustingly rude.	Belief	−0.85	The use of "disgustingly" intensifies the negativity in the statement.
The crazy part is it is the customer service and management like fix your nasty attitudes.	Belief	−0.75	The tone is negative, expressing frustration with customer service and management.
You people need to get a hand on your disrespected employees.	Belief	−0.70	The tone is negative, expressing dissatisfaction with the management of employees.
I went in this store to the money center with my nephew to cash HIS CHECK "DEPARTMENT STORE" PAID HIM FOR WORKING.	Behavior	+0.10	This statement is more neutral, focusing on a specific action.
The check wouldn't even clear, but the miserable employee/csm Alycia or Alicia or something like that red hair rude disrespectful embarrassment.	Belief	−0.85	The negative descriptors and frustration contribute to a highly negative sentiment.

Table 10.1 (continued)

Expression	Building Block	Sentiment	ChatGPT's Analysis
I was speaking to MY NEPHEW not the red head supervisor Alycia, and I said that's weird they wrote your check but they won't cash it?	Belief	−0.30	The tone is less negative here, more neutral with a hint of confusion.
This broad starts moving her head and neck looking like a turtle shaking it back and forth saying it's not "Department Store" I the check place, okay ma'am and wouldn't shut up.	Behavior	−0.75	The description and frustration contribute to a negative sentiment.
I was never talking to her that's what's funny. I said I was talking to my nephew; she was really trying to argue with me.	Behavior	−0.40	The tone is less negative, expressing surprise and a bit of frustration.
I was tired of hearing her talk and seeing her turtle neck shake, so yes, I told her shut up lady.	Emotion	−0.70	The negative emotion and the directive contribute to a negative sentiment.
This lady said get out of my money center.	Behavior	−0.50	The directive contributes to a negative sentiment, but it's less intense.
Pretty sure this isn't YOUR money center. What the heck is your problem?	Belief	−0.40	The tone is more neutral with a hint of frustration.
Good grief, are they that miserable working there?	Emotion	−0.60	The negative emotion contributes to a negative sentiment.
She made all that disrespectful scene, and nobody was ever even speaking to her.	Behavior	−0.75	The negative descriptors contribute to a negative sentiment.
Maybe if she shut up like I said because I was talking to my nephew instead of playing like a big bad, I don't know what turtle.	Belief	−0.70	The frustration and negative descriptors contribute to a negative sentiment.
I cannot stand this store.	Belief	−0.80	The strong negative expression contributes to a highly negative sentiment.
It's always a bad integration with a miserable employee at the checkouts.	Belief	−0.75	The negative descriptors contribute to a negative sentiment.
If they don't want to work then don't, but you're definitely not about to disrespect customers who don't even acknowledge you.	Belief	−0.40	The tone is less negative, expressing a suggestion and frustration.
Try minding your business and you won't have to go turtle power with your neck.	Attitude	−0.30	The tone is more neutral with a hint of frustration.

Was the AI assistant able to help? During the summer of 2024, ChatGPT, an AI Assistant, was able to follow my instructions to break up the whole social media text content provided by one individual into the building blocks of this individual's thought-process reflected in that social media text content. Further, this same AI assistant also followed my instructions for scoring the sentiment associated with each building block. Looking over the results, it is reasonable to conclude that this AI assistant did a reasonable job of identifying expression types (e.g., attitude, belief, etc.) and scoring the sentiment embedded within them. This demonstration shows that through AI assistants, it is possible for opinion-extraction researchers to break up whole social media text content into building blocks of a thought-process and quantify each for further analysis. It is important to note that one whole social media text was broken up into 19 different building blocks, each with its own sentiment score. This shows that the current practice among opinion-extraction researchers to analyze the whole text misses the nuances present within the pieces of that text. Analyzing the text as a whole, despite its many distinct parts, violates the double-barreled principle given in Chapter 5.

Automating the coding of social media expression types and quantifying the valence or sentiment makes the five shifts noted earlier a lot more realistic and feasible. While being able to pinpoint the expression type and the sentiment present in the text is a great improvement over analyzing social media text as a whole, what is still missing is identifying the object of the content being expressed. The object here is the target of an expression. For example, in the expression "I like to eat pizza," the expression type is "attitude," and the object is "eat pizza." Pinpointing the object of each statement is critically important since, within the same general topic, the same expression types might have different objects and sentiment scores. In the next section of this chapter, I will demonstrate the possibility of identifying expression type, sentiment, and object in social media text content.

Foundations of a methodology for extracting thought-process building blocks from social media text

In May 2024, I decided to explore whether the five shifts I recommended earlier can be demonstrated in a methodological proof-of-concept comprising a sizeable body of social media text focusing on a single topic. I picked what I thought was a timely topic: the TikTok ban. I thought this topic might have generated lots of social media content. For my source of Tweets, I used BrandWatch (BrandWatch.com), a commercial service that gave me access to the Twitter firehose. Here is a chronology of my approach:

Step 1: A search for "TikTok ban" on X (previously known as Twitter) via BrandWatch and covering a period from January through May 2024 resulted in 53,806 Tweets. BrandWatch is a subscription-based service that provides access to consumer social media data posted on various platforms.

Tool used for Step 1: Brandwatch search and download feature

Step 2: After filtering and removing retweets from the data set, the new total became 3,664 Tweets. Retweets were removed for two reasons: (1) Keeping retweets and counting them as data would be akin to asking someone to fill out a survey and then asking others to fill out the survey only to be told by the others: "we respond to the survey in the exact same way as the first person did". In such a case, it wouldn't be reasonable to consider the repetition of responses as reflecting others' thoughts and feelings. (2) In later stages of this methodology, keeping the retweets would result in spurious reliability coefficients that are deceptively large, since the exact same content is being repeated by others who are simply forwarding the original author's contents.

Tool used for Step 2: Brandwatch filter option for removing retweets

Step 3: We removed authors who were organizations. After using R to remove authors that were organizations and not individuals, the new total became 3,493 Tweets. Organizations were removed since the ultimate objective of this effort is to arrive at the shared thoughts, feelings, intentions, knowledge, past behaviors, and emotions of individuals.

Tool used for Step 3: R

Step 4: We checked the data and found that some retweets were missed by Step 3. We used R to remove these missed retweets, and the new total became 3,477 Tweets.

Tool used for Step 4: R

Step 5: We rechecked the data and found some retweets were still in it. We manually removed the remaining retweets that were still in the data set, and the new total became 3,404 Tweets. The total number of authors for these Tweets was 3158.

Tool used for Step 5: Visual inspection

Step 6: We asked ChatGPT to identify and separate the following types of expressions embedded within each of the 3404 Tweets: belief, attitude, intention of future behavior, behavior and emotion and defined each. After ChatGPT identified these expression types, we asked it to find the object about which each expression was made. We specified that, when identifying the object, only a single object should be associated with each expression type. This resulted in a data set containing "expression types by objects." After identifying the expression types by objects, we asked ChatGPT to quantify the sentiment embedded within each "expression type by object" on a scale of -0.9 to +0.9. The analysis by ChatGPT resulted in 5847 "expression type by objects." Out of 5847 combinations, 4862 were unique combinations (non-repeating), reflecting the diversity of expressions made in the corpus of 3,404 whole Tweets.

Tools used for Step 6: ChatGPT 3.5 and 4.0. And R for the calculation of combinations and frequencies.

Step 7: We visually checked the results and noticed that some of the "expression type by object" combinations were still focusing on more than a single object.

For example, here is one that still had two objects:

"And sleepy joe is 81 years old not much of a difference while Donald Trump is 78."
Expression type: Belief; Object: Joe Biden, Donald Trump; Sentiment score: -0.2

We used R to split the "expression type by object" with a comma with more than one object so that a single object became associated with each expression type. A total of 2956 "expression types by objects" first identified by ChatGPT had to be split to arrive at expression types that had a single object associated with them. The number of "expression type by object" combinations grew from 5847 rows to 10056 rows with 5062 unique (i.e., non-repeating) "expression type by object" combinations.

Tools used for Step 7: Visual inspection and R

Step 8: We visually checked the results and noticed some of the combinations were the same but considered separate due to minor spelling errors of the object. Examples here include: Tik Tok, tik tok, tiktok, TikTok, Tik Tok Ban, Tik Tok ban.

We fixed the spelling errors so that combinations that were the same but spelled differently were now considered to be one. Out of 10056 total rows in our data file, 2170 were fixed for spelling errors. The total number of unique (i.e., non-repeated) "expression type by object" combinations across authors became 4589.

With the importance of finding multiple indicators in the back of our mind (see Chapters 1 and 3), we decided to focus on "expression type by object" combinations with frequencies of 10 or more because doing so would increase the chances of finding two or more same "expression by object" provided by the same author. This gave us 76 unique combinations of expression types by object with frequencies of 10 or more, attributed to 2081 distinct authors. A unique combination is a combination of an expression type (e.g., belief, attitude, intention, etc.) by object (e.g., Tik Tok Ban; Biden, Trump, United States Congress, etc.) that does not copy another "expression type by object" found in the data set – non-repeating (see Table 10.2).

Tools used for Step 8: Visual inspection and R

Table 10.2 shows the 76 unique combinations of "expression type by object" and their frequencies as found in the final analysis.

As a side note, it is important to observe how varied the "expression type by object" are under the same search term: Tik Tok Ban. This means a researcher should never assume that the Tweets found under the same search term are all expressions about the same concept.

Table 10.2: Frequency of "Expression Type by Object" Combinations.

Expression Type	Object	Frequency	Combined
Belief	Tik Tok Ban	1419	Belief Tik Tok Ban
Emotion	Tik Tok Ban	300	Emotion Tik Tok Ban
Belief	Tik Tok	201	Belief Tik Tok
Intention of future Behavior	Tik Tok Ban	141	Intention of future Behavior Tik Tok Ban
Belief	Biden	139	Belief Biden
Attitude	Tik Tok Ban	129	Attitude Tik Tok Ban
Behavior	Tik Tok Ban	115	Behavior Tik Tok Ban
Emotion	Speaker	96	Emotion Speaker
Belief	China	80	Belief China
Belief	Government	80	Belief Government
Belief	Us	67	Belief Us
Belief	Congress	61	Belief Congress
Belief	Israel	61	Belief Israel
Belief	Trump	55	Belief Trump
Belief	America	46	Belief America
Belief	Senate	46	Belief Senate
Behavior	Tik Tok	38	Behavior Tik Tok
Emotion	Tik Tok	38	Emotion Tik Tok
Belief	Joe Biden	34	Belief Joe Biden
Belief	Ukraine	34	Belief Ukraine
Belief	Ban	33	Belief Ban
Belief	Us Government	33	Belief Us Government
Behavior	Speaker	30	Behavior Speaker
Belief	Bill	29	Belief Bill
Belief	House	29	Belief House
Belief	Censorship	27	Belief Censorship
Belief	National Security	26	Belief National Security
Belief	People	26	Belief People
Belief	Usa	26	Belief Usa
Belief	Democrats	25	Belief Democrats
Belief	Americans	22	Belief Americans
Belief	Bytedance	22	Belief Bytedance
Belief	Facebook	22	Belief Facebook
Belief	Free Speech	21	Belief Free Speech
Belief	Meta	21	Belief Meta
Belief	Tik Tok Ban Bill	21	Belief Tik Tok Ban Bill
Emotion	User	21	Emotion User
Intention of future Behavior	Speaker	21	Intention of future Behavior Speaker
Belief	Republicans	20	Belief Republicans
Belief	Speaker	20	Belief Speaker
Belief	Politicians	18	Belief Politicians
Belief	Taiwan	18	Belief Taiwan
Belief	Instagram	17	Belief Instagram
Belief	Legislation	17	Belief Legislation

Table 10.2 (continued)

Expression Type	Object	Frequency	Combined
Belief	Twitter	17	Belief Twitter
Belief	Tik Tok Bill	16	Belief Tik Tok Bill
Belief	X	16	Belief X
Belief	Election	15	Belief Election
Belief	Foreign Aid	15	Belief Foreign Aid
Belief	Genocide	15	Belief Genocide
Belief	Reason For Tik Tok Ban	15	Belief Reason For Tik Tok Ban
Belief	Social Media	15	Belief Social Media
Belief	Freedom Of Speech	13	Belief Freedom Of Speech
Belief	President	13	Belief President
Belief	Foreign Aid Bill	12	Belief Foreign Aid Bill
Belief	Government Actions	12	Belief Government Actions
Belief	President Biden	12	Belief President Biden
Belief	Public Reaction	12	Belief Public Reaction
Belief	U.S.	12	Belief U.S.
Belief	YouTube	12	Belief YouTube
Emotion	Ban	12	Emotion Ban
Intention of future Behavior	Tik Tok	12	Intention of future Behavior Tik Tok
Attitude	Tik Tok	11	Attitude Tik Tok
Behavior	User	11	Behavior User
Belief	Ccp	11	Belief Ccp
Belief	Data Privacy	11	Belief Data Privacy
Belief	Government Priorities	11	Belief Government Priorities
Belief	They	11	Belief They
Belief	Ukraine Aid	11	Belief Ukraine Aid
Emotion	Government	11	Emotion Government
Emotion	Joe Biden	11	Emotion Joe Biden
Emotion	People	11	Emotion People
Intention of future Behavior	Ban Tik Tok	11	Intention of future Behavior Ban Tik Tok
Belief	Foreign Aid Package	10	Belief Foreign Aid Package
Belief	Truth	10	Belief Truth
Belief	Us Congress	10	Belief Us Congress

Step 9: We reorganized the data so that the main unit of analysis becomes the author of the "expression type by object" combinations. The 76 "expression type by object" combinations from 2081 separate authors were then sorted to determine how many times an author expressed themselves about the same combination. The frequencies ranged from 1 to 8. It is important to note here again how many combinations were found under the same original search of "tik tok ban" and how problematic it would have been to consider all information found under this search to be about the same topic. Given that our goal is to carry out analyses requiring more than a single in-

stance of "expression type by object" combination by author, we decided to keep only the authors that had expressed combinations with frequencies of two or more.

We found 239 authors who expressed themselves two or more times about the same "expression type by object" combination. When we focused only on these 239 authors, we found there were 55 unique combinations of "expression type by object." See Table 10.3 for the frequency distribution of the 55 unique combinations.

Table 10.3: Unique combinations of "expression type by object" for authors who expressed themselves 2 or more times about a same combination.

Expression Type by Object	Frequency
Belief Tik Tok Ban	285
Belief Tik Tok	51
Belief Biden	30
Belief Government	28
Belief Trump	24
Belief Congress	23
Belief China	17
Belief America	16
Emotion Speaker	14
Belief Israel	14
Belief Senate	12
Belief X	10
Belief Joe Biden	10
Belief Republicans	10
Belief Us	10
Belief Democrats	9
Emotion Tik Tok Ban	9
Belief Us Government	8
Belief Ukraine Aid	6
Belief Meta	6
Intention of future Behavior Tik Tok Ban	6
Belief Foreign Aid Package	5
Belief Bill	5
Belief Facebook	5
Behavior Tik Tok Ban	5
Belief Tik Tok Ban Bill	4
Belief They	4
Belief Ban	4
Belief U.S.	4
Belief Bytedance	4
Belief President	4
Belief Social Media	4
Belief People	4
Behavior Speaker	4
Emotion User	4

Table 10.3 (continued)

Expression Type by Object	Frequency
Attitude Tik Tok Ban	4
Belief Instagram	2
Emotion Tik Tok	2
Belief Foreign Aid Bill	2
Belief Free Speech	2
Emotion Ban	2
Belief Speaker	2
Belief Ccp	2
Belief Politicians	2
Belief Foreign Aid	2
Belief Youtube	2
Belief Tik Tok Bill	2
Belief USA	2
Belief Ukraine	2
Belief House	2
Intention of future Behavior Speaker	2
Emotion Joe Biden	2
Belief Taiwan	2
Belief National Security	2
Belief Americans	2

Tools used for Step 9: Excel and R

Step 10: We organized the data file by author so that each author is followed by 55*2 columns. The 2 count is based on the minimum number of indicators for the same construct within the context of psychometrics. We knew most authors had probably not expressed themselves more than twice about each of the 55 combinations and that some authors had probably expressed themselves more than two times about a specific combination (there were 239 such authors). When examining the combinations of "expression type by object" present in the data, we found the following combinations had the highest frequencies:

  Belief about Tik Tok Ban: 285
  Belief about Tik Tok: 51
  Emotion about Tik Tok Ban: 9

Given that "Belief about Tik Tok Ban" has the highest frequency, we decided to exclusively focus on this specific "expression type by object" for the rest of the analysis. There were 97 authors who expressed themselves twice about the topic of "Belief about Tik Tok Ban" and 25 authors who expressed themselves more than twice about this same combination.

Tools used for Step 10: R for frequency calculations and Excel for the pivot table.

Step 11: For authors who only expressed themselves two times (n=97), we visually examined the semantic contents of their "Beliefs about TikTok" to verify they shared a common meaning. Out of a total of 123 pairs of "Belief about TikTok ban" expressions that ChatGPT identified as sharing a common meaning, we found 78 to not share a common semantic meaning, 6 to be almost sharing a common semantic meaning, 10 to be exact replicas but not retweets, and 29 to be sharing a common semantic meaning without being exact replicas. We removed from the data the 78 that did not share a common semantic meaning.

For authors who expressed themselves more than 2 times about "Belief about TikTok Ban," we visually inspected the semantic contents of all expressions provided by each author and picked the two closest semantically. Out of a total of 25 authors who expressed themselves more than twice about their "Belief about Tik Tok Ban," we found 12 pairs of expressions that overlapped in meaning and 12 pairs that did not overlap in meaning. We removed from the data the 12 pairs across which we could not find an overlap in meaning.

Examples:

Below are three sets of expressions among those who expressed themselves more than twice. We needed to ensure that the expressions generated by the same individual and that we consider belonging to the same construct are very similar. This similarity also needed to be found across pairs of expressions authored by other individuals. We understood that it would be almost impossible for pairs of expressions about Tik Tok bans to be the same across authors. However, we needed to ensure they shared many attributes and reflected a belief about Tik Tok Ban. Here are pairs of expressions that illustrate this idea of similarity:

Azhanpakistan (A)	Tik Tok ban is more important for government.
Azhanpakistan (A)	Government focusing on Tik Tok ban because it's election season.
gamblerlost53 (Filiberto Cavazos)	Extorted Congress to include Ban with Ukraine aid.
gamblerlost53 (Filiberto Cavazos)	Republican Congress trying to extort democratic Senate to ban Tik Tok or no Ukraine aid.
malcolmshabazz6 (Malcolm Shabazz)	It's official – -Democrat Joe Biden just signed the bill to ban Tik Tok
malcolmshabazz6 (Malcolm Shabazz)	The Senate – just passed a bill to BAN Tik Tok

All three pairs of expressions, though not identical, share three attributes: belief, tik tok ban, and government.

Below is an example of expressions made by the same individual that are similar but not exact replicas are:

TALK1370 (Talk 1370)	Bill that could ban TikTok has been attached to the House foreign aid package.
TALK1370 (Talk 1370)	Legislation that could force a TikTok ban revived as part of House foreign aid package.

Below is an example of pairs of expressions by the same individual that did not share considerable attributes in common and had to be removed from the analysis.

Brazil201 (Alex)	The real question is when the Tik Tok ban goes into effect in January (the courts won't strike it down it was passed under national security concerns) we know it will be removed from the App Store the question is will IOS and android comply in just bricking the app.
Brazil201 (Alex)	Tik Tok ban means the fly over state people go back to the fly over states.

Here is another example of no overlap in meaning between two expressions made by the same individual:

marshawn_k79599 (Marshawn Kramer)	Hahhahah NO wonder they want to ban tik tok god forbid we talk and KNOW the truth!!!
marshawn_k79599 (Marshawn Kramer)	Now since we are able to communicate did you see they are hiding tik tok ban in with the Ukraine.

Tool used for Step 11: Visual inspection

Step 12: When combining all expression sets that were two or more that we had verified for overlap in meaning, we ended up with a total of 48 pairs of expression by object about "Belief about Tik Tok Ban."
Tool used for Step 12: Excel

Step 13: By following the road map of the Red Flags Approach provided in chapter 9, we computed the zero-order correlation between the 48 pairs and obtained $r=.62$, $n=48$, $p<.001$. That's a sizeable positive association indicating the sentiments in each pair of indicators were generally pointed in the same direction. That is exactly what we expect to find when looking at two indicators of the same construct. Given that we had checked the semantic content of each pair of indicators, and that the correlation was positive and sizeable, we then explored whether the data can be tested for validity and reliability. Given that we only had two indicators of the same construct, and no indicators for any additional construct, our testing of content validity through factor analysis was limited. Nevertheless, the single factor that we could test accounted for 81% of the variance in the data, indicating that it is reasonable to hypothesize that both indicators could belong to a single invisible construct. The size of each factor loading was .91. Since it was now reasonable to propose that both indicators belong to the same invisible construct, we then tested the indicators for reliability by using Cronbach's Alpha and obtained an Alpha= .77, which is excellent. By first subjecting the two indicators of "belief about Tik Tok Ban" to factor analysis we found that the results support the notion that both indicators underly a common latent variable. And then next, when testing these two indicators for reliability, we found a large Cronbach's Alpha. Both outcomes are quantifications of the errors due to measurement (EDM) in social media text. To the best of my knowledge, this is the first demonstration that it is possible to quantify systematic and random measurement error associated with information extracted from social media text.

Tool used for Step 13: SPSS

Step 14: At this point of the analysis, we computed an estimate of the construct score for each of the authors in our data set by averaging the sentiment scores across each pair of indicators. By doing so, we arrived at the sentiment of each author's belief about Tik Tok Ban. These scores represent quantifying an invisible thought-process building block: belief about Tik Tok ban. What do we do with these scores once we compute them? The answer to this question falls under the statistical analyses and hypothesis testing tasks listed as Step 10 of Table 2.1 of Chapter 2 and they exceed the scope of this book. The objective of these statistical analyses is to test relationships among variables and learn about how a thought-process's building blocks are interrelated. Normally, we would do such testing guided by some pre-existing theoretical framework (for example the Theory of Planned Behavior (TPB) see https://people.umass.edu/aizen/tpb.html).

To give the reader an idea of what is possible, if the gender of the authors were available, we could simply compare males to females in terms of the sentiment imbedded in their belief about Tik Tok Ban to see if there are gender differences. We could correlate the belief about Tik Tok ban with the volume of Tweets authors have sent in the past month to see if more active authors tend to have a more positive or less positive belief about the Tik Tok Ban. When we have evidence that we captured an invisible building block of a thought-process pertaining to a specific topic, we can determine its relationship to other building blocks. By doing so, we would be shedding light on the thought-process relating to specific topics.

An assessment of what worked and what still needs to be improved for this methodology to become fully usable

Step 1: The searching for Tweets on the "TikTok ban topic" from January through May 2024

Improvement: The limitation has to do with the database we're using and how much coverage it provides us with the corpus relevant to the topic we set out to analyze.

Steps 2, 3, 4, and 5: All involved the automated removal of retweets and the focus on individuals and not organizations.
Improvement: Automation cannot be relied on without checking for errors, locating errors, and removing errors.

Step 6: Use ChatGPT to analyze the Tweets and split them into expression types by objects.
Improvement: In the summer of 2024, ChatGPT could only process 200 Tweets at a time to do our analysis per our specification.

Step 7: The ability of ChatGPT to identify an expression type by a single object and scoring a sentiment for each combination.
Improvements: As of summer 2024, ChatGPT was pretty good at identifying expression types and scoring sentiments but had a high rate of not limiting itself to a single object for each expression combination despite our instructions. This means we still needed to manually check for errors and split "expression type by object" combinations to arrive at single objects.

Step 8: The ability of ChatGPT to notice minor variation in spelling errors and automatically combine these under a same category.
Improvement: As of summer 2024, ChatGPT could not deal with objects spelled slightly differently and considered them separate despite our instructions to count them as the same. We attempted to have ChatGPT resolve spelling differences, but the results were unsatisfactory. As such, we had to do this task manually.

Step 9, Step 10: Reorganizing the data so that the main unit of analysis becomes the author of the expression type by object combinations.
Improvements: No issues.

Step 11: ChatGPT's ability to correctly point out two expression types by objects that overlap in meaning.
Improvements: There were frequent discrepancies between the ChatGPT reading of semantics within two expression-by-object combinations deemed to be the same and our reading of these semantics. Had we not manually checked on these, then pairs of "expression type by object" would have been combined even though they didn't share enough semantic similarity. Examples of semantic similarity and overlap in the content of text-based expressions were provided in the earlier explanation of what was done in Step 11.

Step 12: The ability of the method we followed to quantify measurement errors.
Improvement: Even though we began with a sample size of 53806 Tweets, we ended up with only 48 pairs of "expression type by object" combinations that were

indicators of the same invisible construct. The limitation of obtaining the 48 pairs is that our sample size is small and limited to a single construct. In addition, a reader might wonder whether the 48 pairs of expression types by objects represent the information conveyed by the original 53806 Tweets. And that is a worthy concern. However, it is important to note that the 53806 Tweets dropped to 3,404 after removing retweets and organization senders. It is also important to note, despite searching for Tweets about TikTok Bans, when we broke the contents up of these Tweets by "expression type by object," we found 4589 unique combinations, and only a few of these were specific to the topic of TikTok Ban. After looking at how often people expressed themselves about these various combinations, we found only 76 combinations about which people expressed themselves 10 or more times. And not all of these were specific to TikTok Ban. And out of those specific to TikTok Ban, there were 55 unique combinations about which the same individual had expressed themselves twice or more. And when looking at the frequencies of these combinations, the three that had the most frequencies were: Belief about Tik Tok Ban: 285, Belief about Tik Tok: 51, and Emotion about the Tik Tok Ban: 9

Based on these frequencies, the only combination with enough data to analyze was Belief about Tik Tok Ban with 48 authors, each with a pair of expressions about their belief about it.

Limitations of the proposed methodology

1. This methodology works only if individual identifiers are available to match two or more social media expressions to the same individual. But, even if an identifier is not available and the entire methodology is not feasible, it would still be incredibly beneficial for researchers analyzing social media text to break the whole text up by the distinct "expression type by object" present within it. This would make the data analyses more valuable and meaningful and provide better insight into what has been posted online.
2. The sample of "expression type by object" needs to be enormous for the methodology to yield indicators for more than one construct. With more than a single construct, we can use confirmatory factor analysis to test that the measures of one construct are not capturing another construct, which isn't possible to do when all you have is a single construct. The size of the final sample will be a function of the initial corpus of social media expressions about the topic being researched, the span of time this topic was discussed, and the number of regular authors about this topic over time. The larger the corpus, the longer the span, the more regular the authors, and the greater the likelihood that this methodology will yield more than a single construct with multiple indicators. With more than

a single construct, each of which has multiple indicators, a researcher can fully use the analytic tools to test whether invisible factors exist among the indicators.
3. The AI assistant we used couldn't handle analyzing many cases at a time. We had to provide it with small chunks of Tweets (<201), which made the analysis period tedious and lenghty. Given these AI assistants' rapid evolution, I strongly believe this limitation will soon be overcome.
4. As seen from the steps we followed and provided earlier, there is still a high level of error in the AI Assistant's ability to execute our instructions, with the exceptions being its abilities to identify expression types and score sentiment. This means humans still need to thoroughly check errors at various stages of the process. However, as I stated above, given the rapid evolution of these AI assistants, these errors will become fewer over time, and I expect that human checking and intervention will become minimal.
5. Concerning the indicators or "expression type by object" resulting from the process detailed above, we can expect less homogeneity in the contents of "expression type by object" within and across individuals. This is unlike the case of solicited expressions, where the researcher can, by design, get respondents to react to an identical set of statements. A reader might find that if expressions made by individuals are non-identical, this would directly violate the notion of validity in measurement discussed in earlier chapters of this book. It is helpful to remember that, even when using solicited self-report measures, while a researcher can expose participants to an identical statement and ask for a reaction, they cannot control how the respondent interprets it. And there will always be variation in how statements are interpreted across individuals. A researcher's only way to check on how much variation in interpretation occurred is by quantifying the errors due to measurement (EDM) via validity and reliability techniques applied to the measures designed to capture the same construct. The same is true for unsolicited self-reporting in social media text. We cannot expect to find many unsolicited expressions, either by the same individual or across individuals, that are identical to one another (unless they are retweets, and those should be removed from the data set). We can expect that there will be variation in the expressions across individuals even if these statements are pointing at the same "expression type by object" combination. However, we should ensure these expressions across individuals have more in common with one another than they are unique, and what they share should be the same "expression type by object" combination.
6. Studies using social media text cannot set out to investigate relationships among specific thought-process building blocks since there is no guarantee the desired building blocks will be found in the data. Determining which building blocks are available is through a process of derivation after the data has been collected. One might wonder if this makes this approach to text analysis exploratory. It is partially exploratory in the sense that a researcher cannot know ahead of time which building blocks are present in a data set. But it is also confirmatory if a researcher sets

out to find building blocks of a thought-process (e.g., beliefs, attitudes, etc.) rather than let either AI or some other tools tell the researcher what random variables exist in a data set. Suppose the search for thought-process building blocks is the approach taken. In that case, testing the relationships between/among the building blocks uncovered should be guided by existing theories that specify relationships among these building blocks (e.g., Ajzen, TPB, or relevant others). In this manner, the testing will also be confirmatory.

7. One major limitation of this methodology is that a sentiment score is the only quantification of a thought-process building block currently possible. Why is this a limitation? The reason is that sentiment is not the only quantification needed. This is the case since, for many beliefs, the strength with which a person holds a belief, regardless of sentiment, will vary across people. For example, if two people say: "The islands of the Bahamas have sunny beaches." This would be a neutral or slightly positive statement from a sentiment viewpoint. From a strength of belief viewpoint, Dave might hold this belief strongly, while Annie might hold this same belief lightly. The sentiment score will not differentiate between Annie and Dave's strength of belief. A way of scoring strength of belief is currently absent in social media text analysis. Our current inability to quantify the strength of belief is a significant limitation for another reason: when breaking up social media text into building blocks of a thought-process, the most commonly occurring building block, by far, is "belief." While the object of the beliefs might vary widely (e.g., belief about Biden's policy on oil production or belief about Biden's age affecting his decisions), many building blocks found in social media text are beliefs. This has been a consistent pattern from when I started coding social media text in 2014 with the help of graduate student coders to my coding of social media text with an AI assistant in 2024.

Each text analysis project should aim to uncover the building blocks of a thought-process. The flow chart below adapts the one provided in Chapter 3 to illustrate the mindset that needs to be adopted in the context of text analysis after scraping social media content pertaining to a specific topic.

Figure 10.6 shows the mindset that needs to be adopted by a researcher when extracting thought-process building blocks from social media text. Every task included in the mindset needs to be followed by a quality control check done by the research team.

Figure 10.7 represents a slight modification to the Red Flags Approach (RFA) roadmap provided in Chapter 9. Here, we start by looking in Phase 1 at expression types by object combinations obtained after asking the AI assistant to dissect social media text expressions into building blocks of a thought-process and scoring each for sentiment on a -9 to +9 scale. We only focus on those combinations for which we had more than one indicator per author. We then compute inter-item correlations for each set to confirm quantitatively that we have reason to believe the sets overlap in meaning. Once this is done, we can confirm their content validity. Once validity is confirmed,

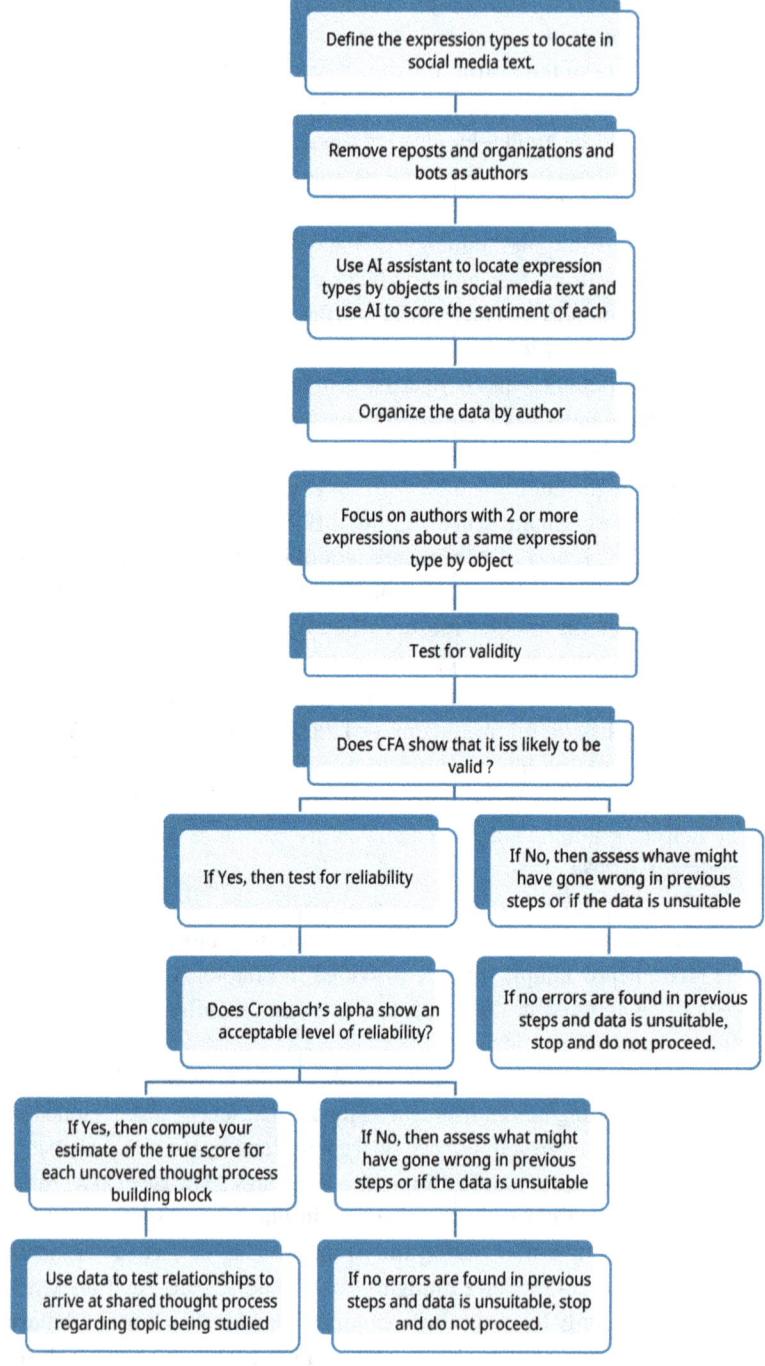

Figure 10.6: A mindset for analyzing unsolicited self-report expressions made by individuals on social media. Source: Author.

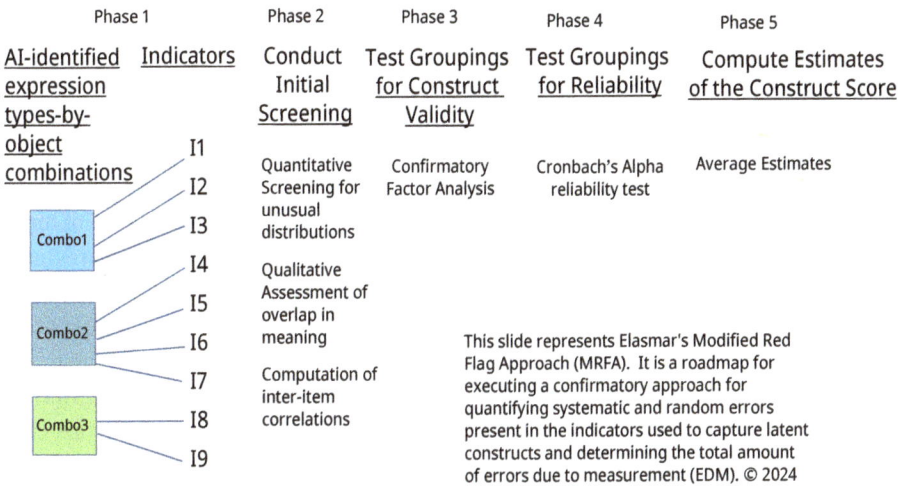

Figure 10.7: A modified Red Flags Approach (RFA) for analyzing unsolicited self-reports found on social media.

we can test the indicators for reliability. If these indicators survive the preceding phases, then estimates of true scores can be computed for each of the constructs that these indicators were found to reflect. And, of course, these would be the scores used when testing theory-driven thought-process models.

A researcher interested in applying the modified Red Flags Approach (RFA) phases will use a partially exploratory approach at the start of Phase 1 but a fully confirmatory approach in subsequent phases. The first phase involves exploratory processes, which come from the fact that a researcher cannot know ahead of time what specific thought-process building blocks they will find in social media text. However, it is partially exploratory if a researcher sets out to find building blocks that have been confirmed to exist in thought-processes by existing theoretical frameworks within the context of cognitive psychology and related areas (e.g., Theory of Planned Behavior (TPB); beliefs, attitudes, emotions, intentions, etc.). Phase 2 of the modified Red Flags and subsequent phases use solely confirmatory procedures. In Phase 3, a confirmatory approach should be used when using factor analysis procedures to test whether it is reasonable to consider multiple indicators belonging to the same latent (invisible) construct. In Phase 4, the reliability coefficient should only be computed for indicators that passed Phase 3. Overall, the modified Red Flags Approach is still mostly confirmatory in its approach. When it comes to testing thought-process models, which is beyond the scope of this book, while a researcher's testing is limited to the building-blocks they were able to extract, they should still use an established theory to guide the testing of relationships among the building blocks they found.

Conclusions and takeaways

This chapter aimed to build a bridge between the established science of self-report measurement traditionally applied in the context of surveys and experiments and the emerging science of opinion-extraction focused on social media text content. It started by proposing that text expressed on social media should be considered a form of self-report. This chapter then proposed five shifts that would advance the science of opinion-extraction from social media text: (1) A shift to using unsolicited text expressions to arrive at the invisible; (2) A shift from analyzing a social media post as a whole to analyzing its parts; 3) A shift from considering social media text to be the unit of analysis to making the humans producing it be the unit of analysis; (4) A shift in the precision of quantifying the sentiment embedded in each expression; and (5) A shift to quantifying errors associated with extracting the invisible from social media text content. This chapter demonstrated that these shifts are not abstract contentions but realistically achieved with the assistance of an AI Assistant. This chapter then presented the foundations of a methodology for analyzing unsolicited text expressions made on social media, followed by a new mindset that opinion-extraction researchers are recommended to follow (see Figure 10.6) and a related roadmap in the form of a modified Red Flags Approach (RFA) (Figure 10.7). This roadmap is currently the only way to quantify systematic and random errors in information extracted from social media text. The materials presented in this chapter are not only relevant to academics involved in opinion-extraction across multiple fields of study. The materials also apply to industry practitioners trying hard to find productive ways of using AI applications to better understand consumers. Using AI assistants to quantitatively transform text expressed by individuals on social media into building blocks of a shared thought-process is at the core of the theory-building pursuit of academics and the practical needs of industry professionals.

References

Ajzen, I. (1985). From Intentions to Actions: A Theory of Planned Behavior. In: Kuhl, J., Beckmann, J. (eds) *Action Control*. SSSP Springer Series in Social Psychology. Springer, Berlin, Heidelberg.

Amangeldi, D., Usmanova, A. and Shamoi, P. (2024). Understanding environmental posts: Sentiment and emotion analysis of social media data. *IEEE Access (12)*, 33504–33523.

Bosnjak M, Ajzen I, Schmidt P. (2020) The Theory of Planned Behavior: Selected Recent Advances and Applications. *Europen Journal of Psychology*, 16(3):352–356. doi: 10.5964/ejop.v16i3.3107. PMID: 33680187; PMCID: PMC7909498.

Cai, H., Xia, R., & Yu, J. (2021, August). Aspect-category-opinion-sentiment quadruple extraction with implicit aspects and opinions. In *Proceedings of the 59th Annual Meeting of the Association for Computational Linguistics and the 11th International Joint Conference on Natural Language Processing (Volume 1: Long Papers)* (pp. 340–350).

Çeliktuğ, M. F. (2018). Twitter Sentiment Analysis, 3-Way Classification: Positive, Negative or Neutral?. *2018 IEEE International Conference on Big Data (Big Data)*, Seattle, WA, USA, 2098–2103, doi: 10.1109/BigData.2018.8621970.

Elasmar, M. G. (2007). *Through Their Eyes: Factors Affecting Muslim Support of the U.S.-led War on Terror*. United States: Marquette Books.

Elasmar, M. (2019). *Validity and Reliability Challenges when Extracting Public Opinion Trends from Social Media Expressions*. In World Association for Public Opinion Research (WAPOR) Conference. Ontario, Canada.

Fishbein, M., & Ajzen, I. (1972). Attitudes and opinions. *Annual Review of Psychology*, 487–544.

Fishbein, M., & Ajzen, I. (1975). *Belief, Attitude, Intention and Behavior: An Introduction to Theory and Research*. Reading, MA: Addison Wesley Publishers.

Fiske, S.T., & Taylor, S.E. (1984). *Social Cognition*. New York, N.Y.: Random House.

Gao, L., Wang, Y., Liu, T., Wang, J., Zhang, L., & Liao, J. (2021, May). Question-driven span labeling model for aspect–opinion pair extraction. In *Proceedings of the AAAI conference on artificial intelligence 35*(14), 12875–12883.

Qi, Y., Shabrina, Z. (2023). Sentiment analysis using Twitter data: a comparative application of lexicon- and machine-learning-based approach. *Social Network Analysis and Mining 13 (1)*, 31–45. https://doi.org/10.1007/s13278-023-01030-x.

Rosenthal, S., Farra, N., & Nakov, P. (2019). SemEval-2017 task 4: Sentiment analysis in Twitter. *arXiv preprint arXiv:1912.00741*.

Strapparava, C. (2004). WordNet-Affect: an affective extension of WordNet. In *Proceedings of the 4th International Conference on Language Resources and Evaluation (LREC 2004)*.

Valarmathi, B., Gupta, N. S., Karthick, V., Chellatamilan, T., Santhi, K., & Chalicheemala, D. (2024). Sentiment Analysis of Covid-19 Twitter Data using Deep Learning Algorithm. *Procedia Computer Science, 235*, 3397–3407.

Xu, Q.A., Chang, V. & Jayne, C. (2022). A systematic review of social media-based sentiment analysis: Emerging trends and challenges. *Decision Analytics Journal, 3*, 100073.

Chapter 11
A recap and some notes on the relevance of self-report measurement in the age of Artificial Intelligence (AI)

I began this book by discussing the intuitive need for humans to see the invisible aspects of other humans through their behaviors. Chapter 1 introduced the idea of behavioral indicators through which we attempt to see invisible aspects of other humans. These indicators allow us to make important building blocks of human thought-processes visible. At the end of Chapter 1, I asked whether we could use self-report indicators to see invisible building blocks of a thought-process instead of using behaviors. I then contextualized self-report measurement in Chapter 2 and showed its location among the typical stages of the method of science.

In Chapter 3, I started with how researchers can think of self-report measures as indicators of the invisible and ended with the diagram of the self-report measurement mindset (see Chapter 3, Figure 3.6). This self-report measurement mindset is beneficial to both academic and industry researchers. The idea is simple: shared human thought-processes consist of building blocks that include knowledge, beliefs, attitudes, intentions, and behaviors, which are, for the most part, invisible. Self-report measures, whether unsolicited or solicited, can help make these building blocks visible. Once the building blocks are visible, data analysts can model the interrelationships present among these building blocks and arrive at shared thought-processes held by groups of individuals about specific topic areas. The mindsets presented in Chapter 3, Figure 3.7 and Chapter 10, Figure 10.6 embody these ideas. These mindsets are applicable no matter what technological developments come our way or what types of self-report data becomes available.

However, errors due to measurement (EDM) are a significant obstacle between our desire to see the invisible building blocks and the data we gather through self-report measurement. In Chapter 4, I shared the methodology that led to distilling the literature to produce Chapters 5 through 8. Those chapters, while not comprehensive, guide researchers on how to preempt aspects known to introduce large amounts of errors into self-report measures. Others can certainly adopt the methodology described in Chapter 4 to expand the guidance provided in this book.

Even with the best intentions and good planning, self-report measures always have errors. Chapter 9 presented a roadmap researchers can use to quantify the amounts of errors due to measurement (EDM) present in their studies. Knowing how much EDM exists will determine whether a researcher can use the building blocks they attempted to measure to uncover relationships among them and illustrate shared thought-processes of specific groups of individuals about particular topics. Chapter 10 proposed and demonstrated a methodology for extracting thought-process building blocks from social media posts, and quantifying the errors due to measurement (EDM) associated with the extraction of these building blocks.

The question undoubtedly on everyone's mind is whether the arrival of AI will nullify all knowledge about self-report measurement we have acquired through science over a period that exceeds 100 years.

Undoubtedly, AI's emergence is an exciting development in the evolution of self-report measurement science (see Chapter 10). AI is well suited for aiding researchers in coding and quantifying unsolicited self-report measures, such as those revealed in Tweets and other social media posts. Will AI ever totally replace traditional solicited self-report measures? As I demonstrated in Chapter 10, the science of unsolicited self-reports for extracting thought-process building blocks from social media posts is still evolving.

My prediction is that, for the foreseeable future, AI will not replace traditional self-report measurement, where a researcher carefully develops measures and administers them to study participants. Within this area of expertise, AI will be an extender of existing science rather than its replacement. There are two main reasons for my prediction. The first relates to a researcher's ability to hypothesize relationships among specific variables and then proceed to test these relationships. This is a basic tenet of the method of science. However, when extracting thought-process building blocks from social media, as described in Chapter 10, you cannot know ahead of time which building blocks you will be able to extract. You will be limited to the variables you have at hand after you extract these variables. So, hypothesizing relationships ahead of time about a wide array of variables is simply not realistic in this context. The second reason has to do with a researcher's ability to quantify the strength of the beliefs they were able to extract from social media. I cannot foresee a way to quantify, through AI or other forms of content-coding, the strength of human beliefs by analyzing their freestyle expressions made through social media text. Beliefs are, by far, the most common form of expression made through social media text, and beliefs are a key building block of all thought-processes corresponding to many topics. While AI can certainly quantify the valence present in the extracted beliefs, it cannot quantify the strength of these beliefs. For the foreseeable future, the only way to do this is through traditional (solicited) self-report measurement.

I began this book by saying that when readers finish it, they will know what I mean by self-report measurement. With these final paragraphs, I hope this book has helped you understand the goals and mechanics of self-report measurement and realize its possibilities for seeing the invisible building blocks of human thought-processes.

List of figures

Figure 1.1 A formal representation of an intuitive measurement process. Source: Author —— 11
Figure 3.1 A vivid illustration of behavior versus thoughts. Source: Elasmar, 2024 —— 30
Figure 3.2 A vivid illustration of behavior versus thoughts. Source: Elasmar, 2024 —— 31
Figure 3.3 A continuum of concept complexity and invisibility. Source: Author —— 32
Figure 3.4 An Invisible to Visible Framework (ITVF) for conceptualizing self-report measurement. Source: Author —— 34
Figure 3.5 The Invisible to Visible Framework used for impulse buying. Source: Author —— 38
Figure 3.6 The location of validity and reliability in the Visible to Invisible Framework. Source: Author —— 47
Figure 3.7 A self-report measurement mindset (SRMM). Source: Author —— 52
Figure 9.1 Adopting the TPB as a theoretical framework for understanding students' intention to continue using Facebook in the future – selected variables. Source: Author —— 155
Figure 9.2 The Red Flags Approach (RFA) —— 158
Figure 9.3 A sample frequency distribution of a measure. Source: Author —— 167
Figure 9.4 Inter-item correlations for the measures in the case study —— 169
Figure 9.5 Rotated factor (component) matrix for the measures in the case study. Source: Author —— 170
Figure 9.6 Rotated factor (component) matrix when testing three factors for the measures in the case study. Source: Author —— 172
Figure 9.7 Reliability analysis for the measures of "social trust" —— 173
Figure 9.8 Reliability analysis for the measures of "perceived encouragement" —— 173
Figure 9.9 Reliability analysis for the measures of "escapism motivation" —— 174
Figure 9.10 Validity and reliability results for "Escapism Motivation" within the ITVF. Source: Author —— 175
Figure 10.1 Visible behavior regarding a tree —— 180
Figure 10.2 Visible behavior versus invisible thoughts regarding a tree —— 181
Figure 10.3 Social Cognition as a Conceptual Framework for Understanding Human Expressions. Source: Elasmar, 2007 "Basic Process of Social Cognition Highlighting Opinion as an Outcome" (p. 48) —— 182
Figure 10.4 Hypothetical schema components related to evaluating an item of clothing —— 182
Figure 10.5 An Overall Model of International Public Opinion about the U.S.-Led War on Terror in 7 countries. Source: Elasmar (2007) —— 183
Figure 10.6 A mindset for analyzing unsolicited self-report expressions made by individuals on social media. Source: Author —— 204
Figure 10.7 A modified Red Flags Approach (RFA) for analyzing unsolicited self-reports found on social media —— 205

List of tables

Table 1.1	Yes and No answers on the four selfishness indicators that you observed —— 12	
Table 1.2	Numerically coding the four indicators for four individuals that you dated —— 13	
Table 1.3	Universals of Intuitive Measurement for Less Visible Human-related Concepts —— 14	
Table 1.4	Numerically coding the four indicators for four individuals you dated with five indicators —— 15	
Table 2.1	Typical 12 Steps of a Research Process following the Method of Science —— 19	
Table 3.1	A comparison of solicited and unsolicited self-report along key characteristics —— 29	
Table 3.2	Universals of intuitive measurement for more invisible human-related concepts —— 37	
Table 3.3	Assumptions made about respondents for self-report measures to achieve their purpose —— 39	
Table 3.4	Assumptions made about the measures for self-report measures to achieve their intended purpose —— 40	
Table 3.5	Facets of validity in self-report measurement —— 44	
Table 3.6	The Four Levels of Measurement —— 48	
Table 4.1	Assumptions made about respondents for self-report measures to achieve their intended purpose —— 58	
Table 4.2	Assumptions made about the measures so that they can achieve their intended purpose —— 59	
Table 5.1	Assumptions made about respondents for self-report measures to achieve their intended purpose —— 60	
Table 5.2	Assumptions made about the measures for self-report measures to achieve their intended purpose —— 61	
Table 6.1	Assumptions made about respondents for self-report measures to achieve their intended purpose —— 77	
Table 6.2	Assumptions made about the measures for self-report measures to achieve their intended purpose —— 78	
Table 7.1	Assumptions made about respondents for self-report measures to achieve their intended purpose —— 96	
Table 7.2	Assumptions made about the measures so that they can achieve their intended purpose —— 97	
Table 8.1	Assumptions made about respondents for self-report measures to achieve their intended purpose —— 128	
Table 8.2	Assumptions made about the measures so that they can achieve their intended purpose —— 129	
Table 9.1	Constructs used in this case study and their corresponding measures —— 157	
Table 10.1	ChatGPT's Analysis of Thought Building Blocks —— 188	
Table 10.2	Frequency of "Expression Type by Object" Combinations —— 193	
Table 10.3	Unique combinations of "expression type by object" for authors who expressed themselves 2 or more times about a same combination —— 195	

Index

19-point scale 93, 186
3-point scale 186
5- to 7-point scale 186

academic projects 22
academic researchers 22
accuracy of recall 142
acquiescence 132
advance contact 97–99
altruistic appeals 105
analyze the data 22
analyzing social media text 178
appeal 104–106
appeal to social norms 106
applied statistics 22
artificial intelligence 28, 73
assumed knowledge 129
attribute 7

background search 20
Balanced Inventory of Desirable Responding 136
balanced scales 134
behavioral indicators 9
behavioral measurement 14
behaviors 5, 7–10, 12, 14, 16, 18, 25, 29, 31, 33, 48, 72, 74, 136, 147–149, 180, 186, 188, 191, 208
bias 62
big data 28–31, 178
BrandWatch 187

capture the variation 25
charitable incentives 115
ChatGPT 191
choice modeling 66
Classical Test Theory 10, 34
closed-ended questions 72
coding 15, 73
cognitive burden 66, 84
cognitive demands 62
cognitive effort 79, 84, 146, 149
cognitive processes 147
collect the data 22
combined appeal 105
completion time 147
comprehension 33
comprehension 147
computer coding 73

concept 32
confidentiality 100, 122–123
confirmatory factor analysis 162, 168, 171
construct 32
construct validity 43–44
contacting respondents 97
content 60
content validity 44
continuum 32
convergent validity 44
correlation matrix 161, 163, 167
cronbach's alpha 153, 165, 173–174, 199

data analytics 30
data privacy 123
decision-making 26
Decomposition Strategy 142
deliberately lying 39
dependent variable 154
direct appeal 106
discriminant validity 44
don't know 77
double-barreled measure 61

egoistic appeal 105
errors 9
errors due to measurement 35
estimates of a construct's score 166
experiments 21
expression type by object 192
externalization 13

face validity 44
fact-based knowledge 131
factor analysis 43, 153
factor loading 163–164, 170–171, 175
feelings 5–7, 25, 28, 32–33, 90, 179, 186, 191
floaters 79
follow-up contact 98
forced-choice measures 134
formal measurement 7, 17
formal observations 6
formalization 13
Frame of Reference Bias 143
free-form 72–73
freestyle text 60

Golden Assumption 33
gradation of reactions 90

help-the-sponsor appeal 105
human characteristics 18
human thoughts 7

implicitly double-barreled 63
incentives 113, 115
indicators 5–7, 9–10, 12–16, 18, 36–38, 42–43, 45–47, 51, 53, 69, 149, 153, 162, 178–179, 184–186, 192, 196, 198–199, 201–202, 208
industry projects 22
industry researchers 22
informal observation 6
information retrieval 147
Information Theory Hypothesis 91–92
Instructional Manipulation Check 147
insufficient effort responding 146
intentions 5–7, 25, 29–30, 33, 48, 59, 152, 159, 180, 186, 188, 191, 208
inter-item correlations 169
interval 48
intuitive measurement 7, 11
invisible 5–10, 12–16, 18, 23, 25, 31–39, 43–44, 47, 51, 53, 60, 77, 153, 159, 163, 171, 174–175, 179–181, 184–186, 199, 201–202, 206, 208–209
invisible concept 10
Invisible to Visible Framework 34, 38, 47, 163, 165, 168, 174
item non-differentiation 147
item-specific 133–134

judgement 33

knowledge 7

landmarks 142
length of a measure 64, 66
levels of measurement 48
life event history calendars 144
literature review 20
loss framing tactic 106
lotteries 113
lottery incentives 115

mandatory appeal 106
Marlowe-Crowne Social Desirability Scale 136
measurement error 3, 25, 35, 61, 152, 165, 187, 202

measurement modeling 34
measurement of the invisible 13, 18
measures 21, 134
mental processing 33
method of science 19
middle response category 82
mindset 3, 5–7, 25, 31, 50–52, 158, 184–185, 203–204, 206, 208
monetary incentives 113–116
motivation 99, 123
motivational text 73
multiple indicators 9
Muslim 183

natural zero 48
neutral 77
nominal 48
non-floaters 79
number of categories 91–92
number of contacts 98
number of points 77
numerals 13, 21–22, 42, 48, 160, 163, 165, 175

open-ended measure 72
opinion-extraction 28, 178
opt-out responses 83
order effect 68
ordinal 48
outliers 160
overlap in meaning 198

participants 21
pattern of behavior 10
Pearson's correlations 153
personal interest 125
personalization 109
placement 60
poll 28
population 21
precision 47
primacy effect 87
principle components factor analysis 162
privacy 20, 96, 100, 122–123, 185
promise to give feedback 106
promised 113
prompted intervention 147–149

qualitative assessment 37–38, 160–161
quantifying errors 134, 157, 186–187, 206

quantitative 21
quantitative meaning 21
questionnaire 26

random error 9
ratio levels 48
ratio of information 23
recall 39
recall accuracy 143
recency effect 87
red flag 158, 161, 164, 167–168,
　　171–172
Red Flags Approach 152
reliability 25, 45
reliability coefficient 46, 152, 165–166, 175
research design 21
research question 20
research report 22
respondent abilities 128
respondent familiarity 79
respondent motivation 123
response 33
response categories 1, 60, 74–75, 77–78, 82–84,
　　86, 88–89, 91–92, 147
response choices 61–62, 64, 86, 88
response latency 62
response order 86
response process 33
response scale 42, 64–65, 82–84,
　　89–90, 159
retrieval 33
reverse coding 160, 162, 167
rewards 113
robust 160
Rotated Component Matrix 163
rule of thumb 165

saliency 142
sample 21
sampling 21
satisficing 146–149
Satisficing 146
scaling 13
scarcity appeal 106–107
schema 181
second-order factor 163
Self Report Measurement Mindset 50

self-awareness 32
self-disclosed expression 28
self-disclosed expressions 28
self-report measurement 14, 25
self-report measurement principles 152
semantic differential 91
semantic meaning 197
sensitive information 122
sensitive questions 137
sentiment 93, 179, 185–186, 188–191, 199–200,
　　203, 206
simple concepts 32
Simplify 149
single indicator 9
skewed distributions 160
social cognition 182
social desirability 136
social media 28
social media post 181
social media text 2, 28, 93, 178–179, 184, 186–187,
　　190, 202–203, 206, 209
solicited expressions 181
solicited self-report 28
sources of variables 20
speeding 147
statistical analysis 36
storytelling 22
straight-lining 160
subjective knowledge 130
surveys 21
systematic error 9

taxonomy 180
theoretical framework 50, 153–155, 168, 199
theoretical frameworks 20
theoretical models 22
theories 19
Theory of Planned Behavior 18
theory-building 22
thought-process 14, 29, 36, 50, 54, 75, 153, 155,
　　166, 176, 178–181, 183–185, 187, 190, 199,
　　202–203, 206, 208–209
timing of contact 98
topic knowledge 130
true reflection 36
truthful 39
type of dependent variable 154

unidimensionality 162
universals of intuitive measurement 14, 37
unsolicited expressions 181
unsolicited self-report 28, 204, 209

validity 25, 43
variable 1, 7, 20, 36, 44, 48–49, 144, 154–156, 166, 175, 199

variables 7, 32
variation 22
varimax rotation 162
visible 32

willing to disclose 39

www.ingramcontent.com/pod-product-compliance
Lightning Source LLC
Chambersburg PA
CBHW080358030426
42334CB00024B/2916